# EAT ALBERTA FIRST

# Eat Alberta First

A YEAR OF LOCAL RECIPES FROM
WHERE THE PRAIRIES MEET THE MOUNTAINS

KAREN ANDERSON

TOUCHWOOD

TouchWood Editions
touchwoodeditions.com



Edited by Lesley Cameron
Cover and interior design by Jazmin Welch
Photography credits listed on page 371

Cataloguing data available from Library and Archives Canada
ISBN 9781771514026 (softcover)
ISBN 9781771514033 (electronic)

TouchWood Editions acknowledges that the land on which we live and work is within the traditional territories of the Lkwungen (Esquimalt and Songhees), Malahat, Pacheedaht, Scia'new, T'Sou-ke, and W̱SÁNEĆ (Pauquachin, Tsartlip, Tsawout, Tseycum) peoples.

We acknowledge the financial support of the Government of Canada through the Canada Book Fund and of the Province of British Columbia through the Book Publishing Tax Credit.

Canada
BRITISH COLUMBIA

This book was produced using FSC®-certified, acid-free papers, processed chlorine free, and printed with soya-based inks.

Printed in China

27 26 25 24 3 4 5

For those who take tender loving care
of the life force that is this earth's soil.
In doing so, you take care of every living thing.

“Knowledge is useless unless it is shared.”

—YVONNE JOBIN, CREE ELDER

# CONTENTS

# INTRODUCTION

*Eat Alberta First* is both a cookbook and a manifesto. While the region of Alberta is specific, the aim of the book—to encourage people to source, cook, and eat locally and to keep that top of mind—can be adopted by anyone, anywhere.

Since 2006, I've joyfully promoted the health of soil, food, and people as a writer, cooking instructor, and founder of Alberta Food Tours Inc. I am constantly impressed by the quality and abundance of food Alberta produces. A great example of our dedication to food is how seriously outnumbered we are by cattle in this province. We have 4 million people and 5 million cattle. However, cattle have only been in Alberta since the late 1800s. Compare this with bison, which have been here for over 120,000 years and have survived against the odds. In fact, the bison's survival is a great conservation story. At one point there were more than 40 million bison on the Great Plains of North America. The colonizing governments of the United States and Canada both had policies of assimilation or annihilation toward Indigenous people. They killed almost all the bison to take away their key food source while they forced them onto reservations and made them purchase beef rations. In 1909, the government of Alberta bought the last herd in North America, about 400 animals, from a rancher in Montana. Through continuous conservation efforts since that time, the population has now recovered from the point of extinction to a half million across North America. It still thrills me when I see them roaming the ranchlands and plains of Alberta.

Of course, that land has changed too. Where grasslands once sustained millions of bison, grains and pulses flourish now. Alberta's rich black soil and long summer days also produce a great variety of vegetables and Prairie-hardy fruits, many of which are pollinated by the work of over 1,500 beekeepers tending 300,000 colonies. Alberta bees produce about 40 million pounds of honey a year. Some of it is used at meaderies, which, along with distilleries and breweries, are booming thanks to legislation that removed the minimum production amounts that were formerly barriers to entry for these craft industries. Access to glacier-fed water sources and the world's best quality grains—which are often found literally just out the back door of many of these enterprises—are other factors helping these businesses win awards the world over.

I feel so privileged to live, cook, and eat in this amazing province—and I've had many adventures along the way. Riding shotgun in the cab of a million-dollar combine near Airdrie, I've marvelled at the abundance, the technology, and the grain growers' stamina. I've trudged into the swampy bush in Athabasca to photograph a wild rice harvest. Foraging nature's bounty in the foothills of the Rockies, I've felt pure and genuine awe as I spotted and picked wild mushrooms. Chilling out in the back of a pickup, I've found great peace among a herd of massive but quietly grazing bison. I've photographed a barn full of turkeys on a minus-30 day and followed a long-legged farmer up a hill only to come face to face with his herd of water buffalo trotting straight toward us. I've bottle-fed calves, eaten strawberries still warm from the sun, kept backyard bees, and learned to make sausage and cheese. I've cooked roving community hall feasts for over a dozen Mad Hatter daylong farm tours long before there was a wonderful thing called Open Farm Days.

My work as a food journalist and food tour operator, researching and writing about all Alberta has to offer, led me to co-author a book called *Food Artisans of Alberta*. In writing that book, I searched for young farmers and innovators as well as elder farmers who've spent their whole lives on the land. I learned equally from both. Along the way I fell in love with farmers' and ranchers' stories and with the art and tradition of storytelling. My passion landed me columns on the radio and in print. I've taught cooking lessons, travelled the world, and written a Taste Canada award-winning Indian cookbook called *A Spicy Touch*. I found a second calling in life that feels as important and rewarding as my first.

Confession time: I'm not a professionally trained chef and I wasn't always a food entrepreneur. I was a nurse for over two decades. I left that career because all too often I was looking after people whose illnesses were essentially caused by a lack of knowledge about food and the skills required to cook it. That created a deep longing in me to break the cycle by developing people's knowledge and choices around food. Those dreams came true to a

**TOP:** BISON HERD IN LACOMBE COUNTY; **BOTTOM:** LEONA STAPLES OF THE JUNGLE FARM GIVES A WAGON RIDE

certain extent. But deep down, I wanted more. I wanted to share my love of Alberta's food and connect it to good old-fashioned home-cooking techniques, to help people make the most of the bounty on their doorsteps. And then came the COVID-19 pandemic.

# Pandemic Possibilities

Since the pandemic hit in 2020, people who are dependent on food from far away have experienced supply chain disruptions. Many people have spent LOTS more time at home and have eaten out less. That means they've had to rely on their own cooking skills—or lack thereof.

My company, Alberta Food Tours, has helped to grow a strong grassroots community of people who love to support small local businesses. They are Alberta locals and international travellers; Gen Zers, Millennials, and Boomers; stay-at-home parents and professionals from a plethora of sectors; chefs and home cooks; and even influencers and bloggers. Though they have many differences, they share a passion for food, and we love staying in touch with them through our social media accounts and monthly newsletter. As the reality of pandemic life hit home in month three of lockdown in the spring of 2020, we noticed a lot of our community reaching out for help with sourcing local ingredients. They also wanted fun, healthy recipes that were tried, true, and easy. We learned that although our community loved to eat, they didn't all know how to cook. Why? There are several plausible reasons for this.

After the Second World War, it became increasingly standard for both parents to work outside the home. Consumer marketing also

TRAIL'S END RANCH,
PARKLAND

played a role in the decline of home cooking. Major marketing campaigns promoted processed and ready-made food items as offering freedom from "the chains" of the kitchen. The marketers were feeding into the developing women's liberation movement where traditionally unpaid "women's work" like cooking became less valued than going out to work and bringing home an income. Little did people know they'd risk losing food sourcing and growing knowledge as well as cooking skills in exchange for that convenience. The result is that many families have now gone three generations without a competent cook in the home. I was one of the lucky ones in that respect. I grew up cooking at the side of my mother, two grandmothers, AND a great-grandmother. I was constantly absorbing their wisdom, tips, and tricks via some magical apron string osmosis and quiet encouragement. Now that I'm sixty, the yearning to share what I've learned from all the great people I've had the privilege to cook with is almost overwhelming.

So, through Alberta Food Tours, I channelled this yearning into action, and my team and I began publishing pantry lists, sourcing notes, and a collection of recipes celebrating Alberta's signature foods in our monthly newsletter. Our community loved it. The whole thing warmed my local-loving heart.

The pandemic has been cruel on many levels. But in my case it brought me an opportunity to raise local consciousness about the fundamental importance of sourcing and cooking healthy food, and to continue work I'd previously started and loved. In 2018, I co-authored *Food Artisans of Alberta: Your Trail Guide to the Best of Our Locally Crafted Fare* with my friend Tilly Sanchez. In that book we wrote about 200 farmers, ranchers, and food artisans and the diverse food they produced. I always thought a recipe collection that showcased the bounty of Alberta-grown or Alberta-made foods would be a great follow-up. Thankfully, my publisher, TouchWood Editions, agreed.

And that brings me to *Eat Alberta First.* I've written it to guide you through a year of life in an Alberta kitchen and to connect you with food producers through recipes that use their produce, no matter what level of cook you are. From the pantry lists to the recipe collection and appendix, you'll find ingredients that truly reflect Alberta's geography, climate, and signature foods: bison, beef, canola, honey, Red Fife wheat, root vegetables, and saskatoon berries. Whether you're a novice, a competent cook, or a highly proficient gourmand, you'll find plenty of coaching and challenges throughout.

But first, let's talk a bit about the peculiarities of Alberta's seasons, the recipes, the ingredients, and the impact I hope this book will have.

THE HERBERT FAMILY AT TRAIL'S END RANCH, PORCUPINE HILLS

# Alberta's Seasons

I haven't always lived in Alberta. I arrived in Calgary in September 1984 as a twenty-three-year-old nurse to find the city covered in a blanket of white. The leaves froze on the poplar trees. Then they turned brown and promptly fell to the ground. The next week, a second summer arrived. It was 30 degrees Celsius. Larches turned golden and cotoneasters crimson, and my initial fears that I'd moved to a colourless, inhospitable place faded with every warm smile that greeted me.

I learned right off the bat that the weather and seasons in Alberta are different from the neat seasonal quarters I'd grown up with in the Maritimes. In my first week here, I experienced the two great Alberta weather axioms:

- There are really only two seasons: winter and not-winter.
- We never know when we get up each morning which of those seasons we'll be enjoying.

Other maxims I've learned include:

- Forget planting an annual garden until after June 1.
- Feel free to wear shorts when it's 10 degrees Celsius.
- While you're at it, ask to be seated on the patio where people will be donning their Wayfarers and sipping brews like it's the first of July.
- Keep a stash of emergency blankets . . . for your garden.
- Never let a few feet of snow and minus 40 stand between you and the chance to go to a gathering with great grub.

I especially love the last one. Turns out our weather has a lot to do with what we do in our kitchens, the rhythm of our days, and what foods we eat. And after nearly forty years in this place, I reckon that under our umbrella of two seasons, there are at least six subtle seasons we need to account for and flow with.

I've essentially structured *Eat Alberta First* around this idea of six seasons, each with its own set of food requirements and eating habits.

**THE LONG, DARK, AND DEEP WINTER:** This chapter is based on the premise that to prepare for the depth and breadth of our winters, you need to concentrate on filling your larder so that you always have something to cook no matter what's going on outside. I begin with "Provisioning 101: How to Stock a Pantry to #EatAlbertaFirst All Year Long." If you're going to stock your larder, you might as well support the local economy as you do it. The essential pantry items are separated out according to cooking ability. As you develop your skills in the kitchen, you can slowly add to your pantry and experiment with new ingredients.

TRAIL'S END SUMMER RANCH HOUSE IN THE PORCUPINE HILLS NEAR NANTON

**CABIN FEVER SEASON:** As our days get longer but temperatures stay well below zero, I prescribe "Keep Calm and Bake On" as an antidote to cabin fever. In this chapter, I share an old family recipe for Sweet Sourdough Starter (page 71) that you can use for recipes like cinnamon rolls, strudel, and a quintessential chocolate cake. You'll be reaching time and again for that magical sourdough container at the back of your refrigerator.

**NEITHER HERE NOR THERE:** This season is also known as spring in some places. In this chapter I share basic guidelines on foraging and recipes that use foraged foods because eventually greens and fungi do shoot from the soil of our meadows and forests. It's a great feeling to know that they're there and great fun to know what to do with them. Presenting a Morel Mushroom Cheese Spread (page 107) followed by Bison Meatloaf with Cranberry Barbecue Glaze (page 113) to friends you've invited round or pouring Chokecherry Syrup (page 101) over your pancakes on a weekend will go a long way to increasing your pride in and connection to this land.

**FULL-ON SUMMER:** This is when nature cranks up the heat. The recipes in this chapter are all about savouring every ounce of summer and cooking food for the great outdoors. Along with casual things you can throw together in an instant like Broek Pork Acres' Pulled Pork (page 155), you can also present jaw-droppers like Cedar-Planked Prime Rib Roast of Alberta Beef (page 159). Get in the summer mood with Lip-Smacking, Finger-Licking, Messy, Good Ribs (page 157), Bing Cherry Butter Tarts (page 171), Prairie Berry Squares (page 177), and Summer's Every Fruit Cake (page 173).

COMBINING CANOLA NEAR AIRDRIE

**HARVEST HURRY-UP:** This chapter will prepare you for the brief time when the bounty of summer is overflowing in gardens and markets and we want to preserve as much of the season as possible. "Canning and Preserving Basics" will introduce you to the principles of canning, which you can put to good use by practising the eight preserve and pickle recipes I've provided. Once you've learned how easy it is to put up your own Classic Canned Tomatoes (page 191) or Lady Ashburnham Mustard Pickles (page 205), you'll have a tough time living without them.

**FALL BACK:** Maybe it's the potential for a freak September blizzard, the days getting shorter again, or children returning to school, but fall brings busyness. This chapter's theme is batch-cooking, which not only teaches planning and life skills but can also foster community. When you learn to make extra for your freezer, you not only pay yourself forward but also have the bandwidth to help others. Big-batch recipes like Refrigerator Bran Muffins (page 247) are a great gift for new parents up at night for feedings. Containers of Triple "S" Soup (page 221) or Chunky Pasta Sauce with Hot Italian Sausage (page 235) along with Sheet Pan Chocolate Chippity-Chunk Cookie Bars (page 255) left in a basket for friends in crisis express your love in so many ways. These actions are the quickest way I know how to build community. And, if you're in a farming community, Chipotle Bison Chili (page 227) or Trail's End Classic Beef Stew (page 231) make great meals for branding or combining crews.

The last chapter of this book is called "Celebrations, Feasting, and Entertaining through the Year." Its contents reflect the diverse cultures that are part of both the history and the future of this place. There are festivals throughout the year in Alberta where we can learn about and taste the food of all the cultures that make up this province. It's a chance to be neighbourly and make new friends. Growing up in a small town in New Brunswick, I never dreamed I'd have such opportunities. Alberta is the place where this happened for me. Maybe you won't go on to find a loving mentor and write an Indian cookbook like I did, but you might have the chance to learn how to pinch pirohy, roll sushi, or wrap samosas. So, whether it's making lucky dishes for Lunar New Year, preparing a harvest feast for Thanksgiving, or celebrating the sweetness of friendship at Diwali, I hope the recipes in this chapter help you not only appreciate our diversity but actively celebrate it.

Of course, all the fabulous produce and other ingredients don't just appear by magic. In the appendix, I share a list of Alberta food artisans. They're organized by six geographical regions and then subdivided by the food categories you're most likely to be searching for. You'll find artisan products; baked goods, tea, and coffee; bees and honey; charcuterie and sausages; cheese and dairy; chocolate makers and confectioners; cooking schools and specialty foods; craft beer, cider, fruit wine, mead, and distilleries; foragers, foraging classes, and foraged foods; fruits, fungi, and vegetables; grains, seeds, and pulses; meat, poultry, and pork; and sustainable fish and seafood.

Isn't that a fantastic assortment? Turns out our province is the ultimate cook's pantry. If you ask me, there's nothing better than living close to people who dedicate their lives to growing and making beautiful ingredients for us to enjoy. I hope you will support them with all your heart and hard-earned dollars too.

**LEFT:** DYLAN AND DAUGHTER JOCELYN BIGGS AT TK RANCH NEAR HANNA; **RIGHT:** PICKING PEAS AT EDGAR FARMS, INNISFAIL

# About the Recipes

I've talked a lot about food and cooking but at this point you might be wondering if I have recipes you'll actually want to cook. As I confessed earlier, I'm not a professional chef, so let me tell you why I think you'll love the recipes you'll find in this book.

I started cooking when I was ten years old. My mom worked part-time and my three siblings and I were assigned nights to cook supper or wash up. There were lots of fights about whose turn it was to do what but ultimately, it was all right there on the calendar and we learned to be responsible for feeding and cleaning up after others. We mastered the basics by making all the mistakes a cook can make. I won't tell you how many times I burnt the potatoes because I was trying to watch *The Flintstones* in the TV room while I was cooking.

Somewhere in my teens, I started to like cooking. Probably because of how much I like eating, but beyond that, it became a way to relax and unwind. It became my creative outlet, and I started to play and experiment. I loved to leaf through the *Canadian Living* and *Chatelaine* magazines in my mom's beauty salon and pick out things to make. At college and as a young nurse I cooked for my roommates. When I had a little extra money, I took cooking lessons. When I became a food journalist, I often interviewed chefs and asked for their recipes. Chefs in professional kitchens use ratios and make huge volumes of food, so I learned to recipe test and translate their work so home cooks could enjoy their recipes.

I eventually had the opportunity to become the recipe tester and writer for Taste Canada Hall of Fame cookbook author Noorbanu Nimji of the *A Spicy Touch* cookbook series. I spent nine years at her side and learned to test, test, test and taste, taste, taste until a recipe was truly tried and tested. Noorbanu had a very refined palate and was completely dedicated to getting it right for her fans. She has sold over a quarter million cookbooks, so it's safe to say she succeeded.

Since 2011, I've had my own blog called *Savour It All*, where many of the recipes in this book were tested and refined before being posted. There's also a great mixture of recipes that were handed down to me by my family and some from friends who are home cooks or professional chefs. Because I love people, am not shy about asking for recipes, and have travelled to many places, there are lots of cross-cultural tastes I've adapted for this recipe collection.

The recipes are presented in a slightly unusual format. My team at Alberta Food Tours are younger than me. They didn't grow up with cooking mentors. They asked me to include equipment lists. They are busy people and don't want to read through the whole recipe to figure out what equipment they need to use. They also wanted the recipes to feel like I'm there with them so I opted for a conversational tone with headings like "Makes," "Takes," "What You Need to Gather," and "What You Need to Do," instead of the more formal "Yield," "Time," "Ingredients," and "Method." To inject some of that magical apron string osmosis that I benefited from as a child, there are lots of tips and guidance. The time listed for each recipe includes the active and total times you'll need to make the dish. It includes a generous amount of prep time to account for varying levels of ability. I explain when you need to allow time for marinating or proofing and separate that timing for clarity. I also highlight what you can do ahead. You'll find lots of sidebars throughout the book to explain things a novice cook might not understand and lots of variation ideas for proficient cooks who want to take flight and wing it. The underpinning theme for all the recipes, though, is that they all showcase Alberta's ingredients no matter what the flavour spin is.

**LEFT:** RHONDA ZUK HEADON OF THE CHEESIRY, KITSCOTY; **RIGHT:** FREE-RANGE CHICKENS

# About the Ingredients

As I noted earlier, I've arranged the recipes by season not only because many dishes turn out best when the ingredients are in season locally but also because our bodies crave certain foods at certain times of the year. Local food doesn't have to travel thousands of miles to get to us, which means it's also fresher when it arrives—and fresher always tastes better. So, guideline number one when making the recipes in this book is to use the freshest local, seasonal products you can find. Of course, depending on the season, that might be a bit of frozen summer garden surplus or batch-cooking from your own freezer—or some of the pantry items you preserved in harvest season.

Here are a few notes on some of the standard ingredients I use in the recipes in this book. (Check out pages 37–61 for more detailed information on ingredients.)

## MEAT

It's always good to keep a selection of meat in your freezer if you can. Many meat producers sell quarter, half, or whole butchered animals at very reasonable prices. Buying in bulk is unarguably quite a financial commitment but it usually works out to be less expensive per pound. And within a few years, your savings will offset the cost of an extra freezer. Bonus: When you buy local, you have the peace of mind that comes from having a relationship with the producer who has raised their animals from their birth to your plate. You can often visit their ranch or farm and see for yourself how the animals live. I'd rather spend a little more on meat and eat it a little less often to have that kind of quality.

## FLOURS

Here in Alberta we are blessed with a wide range of freshly milled flours. I occasionally list whole wheat, Red Fife, or other heritage wheats for certain recipes but for the most part, if a recipe calls for flour, I use unbleached all-purpose flour. I avoid bleached flour for a few reasons. The purpose of aging flour is to let flavour develop with time. Time, however, is money. So some processors bleach flour to speed up the aging process to save time and money. To my palate, flour bleached with chemicals like benzoyl peroxide, potassium bromate, or chlorine have a bitter taste rather than a rich, developed taste. There are also health implications. Bleached flour is refined to the point where the vitamin- and mineral-rich bran and germ of the wheat kernel have been removed. Unbleached flour is slightly denser, but its flavour is obtained naturally through aging. **TIP:** Unless a recipe calls for a heaping cup or Tablespoon of flour, measure it as a level cup or Tablespoon for best results.

## EGGS

I used large organic free-range eggs when testing the recipes for this book. If you can't afford organic or free-range, just use large.

## SUGAR

I love the taste and texture of organic cane sugar but because granulated sugar is more widely available, that's what I used in testing all the recipes in this book (unless otherwise specified). While cane sugar crystals are slightly larger and light gold in colour, they can be substituted in equal measure for white granulated sugar.

## MILK

The fat content of milk is specified for each recipe.

## LEMONS AND LEMON JUICE

In some recipes I list fresh lemon zest or juice but in others I specify store-bought bottled lemon juice because the recipe needs the acid to be a particular pH and I know the pH of store-bought lemon juice is consistent.

WHOLE GRAIN BREADS

# Organic Label versus Organic Matter

I'm often asked if I use exclusively organic ingredients in recipes. I'm not hung up on that label. I think it's far more important to find out how producers raise their plants and animals. Start having conversations about soil practices. If you don't know the link between soil and food, you're not alone but here's the current situation.

According to the United Nations Food and Agriculture Organization, 52 percent of agricultural lands on earth are degraded to the point of desertification. Years of intensive farming, use of chemical inputs, plowing, real estate development, and other non-regenerative practices have led to the change from living soil to dead sandy desert. In desertified soils, the biomass of microorganisms has fallen to below 0.5 percent. Living productive soil has a biomass of between 3 and 6 percent.

Ideally, plants use photosynthesis to capture gaseous carbon and turn it into liquid carbon that leaks into the soil biomass through their roots through something called the plant-microbial bridge. The microorganisms "pay" the plants for the carbon they need to live with the vitamins and minerals they metabolize from the soil. When plants have access to vitamins and minerals they are strong and healthy and so is everything that eats them. Back in the soil, the microbes turn the liquid carbon into sequestered solid carbon, which helps hold water. Cover crops, animal manure, and other forms of compost or humus all keep soil healthy. Soil is heading to extinction as I write this. Fortunately, you can join a movement called #SaveSoil at savesoil.org to help turn this around. One day, I hope we see food labelled by its percentage of soil organic matter. The higher the soil organic matter, the more nutrients provided to food, to us, and to all of life.

# Wild Foods

One more thing. Alberta has an abundance of wild foods. I share some principles for foraging responsibly and hope you come to include wild foods in your diet. They are beyond organic. They come from the richest soil on earth. I hope you will treasure them as I do and fall in love with the recipes in the book where their flavours have a chance to shine through. When you eat them, you are truly eating Alberta first.

# The Impact of Eating Alberta First

Regenerating soil and putting the idea to #EatAlbertaFirst into action could have a profound effect, not only on your own health but also on the health of the local economy. According to Alberta Agriculture and Forestry, food grown or made in the province and sold through farmers' markets and farm (gate) retail is valued at $753.7 million and $279.3 million respectively. There are over 40,000 farms in Alberta. Most grow commodity grains or livestock to feed the world. Only 1,925 of those farms—less than 5 percent—are greenhouses, fruit and vegetable, and "miscellaneous" crop farms. These smaller farms are the ones that stand to gain the most when we shift to #EatAlbertaFirst. And it's a realistic goal. There are about 1 million households in Alberta, so if we all spend $10 a week more on local food, made or grown in Alberta, we could contribute another $520 million to the local economy. A mere $20 a week would push this figure over $1 billion annually.

When I was researching this book I called Donovan Kitt from The Homestead, a farm in Peace Country, to catch up on developments in his area. Donovan and his wife, Lisa Lundgard, are the only market garden vegetable growers left in that area. He told me that the other four market gardeners at the Grande Prairie Farmers' Market retired after Christmas

A FORAGED MOREL MUSHROOM NEAR MILLARVILLE

2021 and would not be returning. With the average age of a farmer in Alberta around fifty-six, we'll be seeing more retire very soon. Canada has lost 70 percent of the farmers in its under-thirty-five category in just twenty-five years. What will become of the land without the next generation? Who will grow our food?

By shifting how we spend money on food to increase our local purchases, we can have a huge impact on the future of food and health in our province. We can support young agrarians who would like to farm and we can increase the security of food availability in our system. It takes great knowledge and business savvy to succeed in farming.

Farmers need—and deserve—to be paid what doctors and lawyers are paid. If food could be labelled by how much organic content is in the soil, with 3 percent being the minimum, the whole system of farming would change. With that much organic biomass in the soil, the vital nutrients in food will be there to keep people healthy. And bonus: scientists have estimated that soils could sequester over a billion additional tons of carbon each year, and the higher the organic mass, the more carbon that is stored. In other words, we could realistically reverse climate change. An agricultural system that pays credits to farmers by how much carbon they store and a premium for how much nutrition is in their food would ensure the future of food and the health of all living beings and the planet.

While we are reimagining the future, forget what you thought you knew about Alberta and its food. It's time to go beyond the stereotypes. I love the look of pride I see when Albertans first hear about the list of what's considered Alberta's signature foods. These foods aren't widely talked about, and because they're right in front of us we tend to take them for granted. Ask a local about what to eat in Alberta and they'll most likely recommend Alberta beef. Pressed beyond this, they are often stumped about what else is special to this place. When I share that bison has been here for 120,000 years and is a keystone conservation species, they nod their head. "Ah, yes," they say, "bison is wonderful." When they learn canola was developed here and we are Canada's largest honey producer, they stand a little taller. When we discuss all the grains and pulses Alberta and our Prairie province siblings grow for the world, they are amazed. When we add in the sweetness of our root vegetables and that saskatoon berries are indigenous to this land, their chests puff up like a farmyard rooster's. When you really take stock of what's here, it makes you want to dive into the bounty and make the absolute most of it.

May I suggest that you do that by cooking the nostalgic yet timely recipes that celebrate our signature foods in this book? Reclaim the joy of nourishing yourself and your family by cooking from scratch. And let me know how you make out. Join our community on:

**INSTAGRAM** @albertafoodtours
**FACEBOOK** @Alberta Food Tours Inc.
**OR FOLLOW AND DM ME PERSONALLY:** @savouritall or @eatalbertafirst

I welcome your questions, comments, and suggestions. When it comes to food and life, good things happen when we savour it all.

ME AT HOME IN MY KITCHEN

CHAPTER 1

# THE LONG, DARK, AND DEEP WINTER

We end each year and start a new one in the long, dark, and deep winter. If the sun shows up at all, it's mighty shy about it. The temptation to become a hibernating mammal is strong. But that's not what Albertans do. Instead, we get our cool on.

We ski champagne-quality snow on world-renowned front-country ski hills. We quench the human desire to explore with backcountry sojourns on skis and snowmobiles. We soak up breathtaking natural settings while skating on wild lakes, ponds, and sloughs. We ice-fish, snowshoe, and toboggan. When we have to be inside, we trundle children to arenas for hockey or skating. Some of us curl. Some line dance. Many of us are up to our eyeballs in seed catalogues, literally plotting the next growing season. Getting together for good food and good company is a must during the winter months.

Because we can't store fat on our bodies and sleep it off over the winter like our hump-shouldered cinnamon bear friends, provisioning and preparing for winter make life a lot more enjoyable. The First Nations of Alberta believed they were twin spirits with the bison. They used every part of the bison. Hides were used for clothing and shelter, and bones for tools and utensils; meat was dried as jerky or combined with fat and saskatoon berries to make pemmican cakes for winter survival. We can learn from their wise ways and stock our pantries, refrigerators, and freezers not only to over-winter well but also to thrive all year.

Grocery stores give us the illusion of plenty but the reality is they are really just distribution centres with about three days' worth of supplies. If the pandemic has taught us anything it's that it's good to have some depth to our pantry. A pantry is a good place to go for inspiration for your cooking year-round but we tend to do so more in the winter when we spend more time inside, there's no fresh food from our gardens, and farmers' markets have a greatly reduced choice of local produce. Time spent stocking our pantries to #EatAlbertaFirst in winter will reward us all year round.

# Provisioning 101: How to Stock a Pantry to #EatAlbertaFirst All Year Long

The local grocery store has evolved into the modern-day pantry. My mother used to shop once a week. These days, most of us simply pop to a shop whenever we need a few things. And if we don't feel like cooking, delicious ready-made meals are only a call away. But then COVID-19 happened and we learned there's nothing like a crisis to banish convenience.

I'm sure most of us are acutely aware of the pluses of stockpiling staples (and not just toilet paper). With an inventory of staple ingredients on hand you're always prepared to cook. Certainly, one of the key take-aways of this pandemic is the need for preparedness.

I have a large pantry in my home. My husband says it's like living with a happily hoarding hobbit. If my Alberta Food Tours team needs an obscure spice or food item, I tell them to check with me first. I've been happily married (to the same person even) for over thirty years and cooking for over fifty. And I've travelled and shopped at markets all over the world.

My pantry contents reflect ten trips to India, a half-dozen trips to Mexico, multiple culinary escapes and cooking lessons in France and Italy, three weeks exploring the cuisine and culture of Thailand, and countless coast-to-coast-to-coast travels in Canada and the US. I also have an extra refrigerator and freezer in my basement and an herb garden by my kitchen door, and I sell local food Alberta Cares Packages as part of my company to boot. But it wasn't always this way. I can remember slowly setting up kitchens and pantries each time I moved in my twenties and early thirties. I didn't develop my knowledge about Indian food until I encountered Noorbanu Nimji when I was in my early forties. I've been fortunate to travel extensively and have (legally) brought fascinating things through Canadian customs. So, take heart. The journey of one thousand ingredients begins with a single purchase.

WELCOME TO MY PANTRY!

The same can be said for equipping your kitchen. Good equipment, especially sharp knives, makes cooking easier. It took me a long time and a fair chunk of cash to fully equip my kitchen. When my son moved out I was impressed with how he toured thrift shops and scoured online marketplaces until he found everything he needed. He thought he'd paid too much for a particular kettle until he saw it new for $100—he paid $10. Along with recycling and upcycling, I also see young people sharing and borrowing what they need. So clever. Read through the list of equipment, get creative, and before you know it you'll have what you need.

## TIPS FOR GETTING STARTED

Before you can stock your pantry, it's a great idea to take inventory and get organized. This is also a great opportunity to declutter.

- Donate unopened, unexpired goods you know you'll never use to your local food bank.
- Get rid of those expired salad dressings at the back of the refrigerator.
- Organize what you're going to keep according to a logic that makes sense to you. (See below for more on this.)
- Keep things in clear containers and label the containers with what they contain and the date you filled them.

Store things so they're as visible as possible—you'll use what you can see.

To me, pastas, grains, dried legumes, and cereals go together. I'm full of beans, and so one whole cupboard in my pantry is also full of beans—dried and canned. Canned goods, condiments, and saucy things bunch together on another level. Breakfast items, coffee, and teas are stored near the toaster. I have one huge drawer with all my baking flours, sugars, fruity bits, coconut, and CHOCOLATE. Nuts and seeds are in the door of my upright freezer. Oils and vinegars take up a cupboard close to my stove. My spices are in two pull-out cabinets on either side of the stove.

## COOKING ABILITY

Another important aspect of stocking a pantry is to think about your cooking ability. My pantry expanded naturally with my cooking ability and yours will too. This book is meant to help novice cooks to make food, competent cooks to make progress, and proficient cooks to enjoy new challenges. So the pantry items listed are organized according to those three levels.

Professional chefs are the experts. The rest of us are on a continuum somewhere between novice and proficient—or in cooking terms, we're somewhere between learning to boil an egg and whipping up a soufflé. (These terms come from the groundbreaking work of a nurse-philosopher named Patricia Benner and her *From Novice to Expert* [Addison-Wesley, 1984] model of skills acquisition.)

Wondering what level of cook you are? Let's take a look.

Read through the three descriptions of cooking levels—novice, competent, and proficient—and decide which one best describes your ability. Use your corresponding pantry list, and the ones preceding it if you like, to stock up as you can afford and as space in your home allows.

### Novice cooks

Novices, in general, have little experience of the situations in which they're expected to perform, and the activities involved in such situations can look mysterious. Novices depend on rules for guidance, so if you're at this level, you seldom deviate from a recipe. You may be missing a mentor in your life to demystify cooking. Your refrigerator and cupboards might look like those of Bridget Jones with not much more than moldy cheese and chocolate sauce.

If some or all of this sounds like you, you're a novice. Relax. It's all good. This just means you have the greatest opportunity to learn. With staples like pasta, grains, canned tomatoes, and frozen vegetables and proteins on hand, there are lots of yummy dishes you can make.

To give your culinary literacy a boost, in the next section I'll explain why the ingredients in your list are important. And I'll share some ideas for easy things you can make with them as we go along.

## Competent cooks

Competent cooks have enough experience to see how their actions fit into a plan. They lack the speed and flexibility of a proficient but can deal with many of the contingencies cooking throws at them. Conscious, deliberate planning helps them be efficient and organized. Competents will take on multi-course meals and complex recipes. If you're a competent cook, you're looking to be stretched. Sundays might be your fun day when you try out something new. You like to go to farmers' markets and specialty shops for inspiration. You subscribe to food blogs, follow cool Instagram accounts (@dinnerwithjulie, anyone?), and watch Food Network shows.

If this sounds like you, you likely already have the novice-level essentials in your pantry. The ingredients you'll be adding will help you spread your wings and fly to proficiency.

## Proficient cooks

Proficient cooks perceive situations as a whole. Their performance is guided by maxims and their perception is broad. They take in nuances and know when something's about to go—or has already gone—off track and how to get it back on track. If you have all the ingredients in the novice's and competent's pantry lists plus some fancy-schmancy international cuisine ingredients to boot, we'll say you're proficient. But you might also relate to the description below.

You take bread-/sausage-/cheese-making workshops, travel to learn about cooking and food, and like to try the latest gadgets. People LOVE to come to dinner at your home and you love to entertain and eat out too. You likely have most of the pantry ingredients I've listed but will enjoy scanning the list in case, God forbid, you don't.

Hopefully, some of the special occasion recipes and the variations throughout the book will give you some small challenges. I hope you'll enjoy adding them to your repertoire.

## LISTS OF PANTRY ESSENTIALS BY COOKING LEVEL

Each pantry staple category is organized by cooking level. Start stocking your pantry at the novice level and move on to the competent and proficient levels as you feel ready. Buy a few items each week as you can afford them.

Throughout this pantry list, you'll find suggestions for recipes for each level of cook. They're all achievable and delicious. I rate the recipes by levels as well.

Of course, the primary goal of this book is that you source as many ingredients from Alberta as is humanly possible. I've always maintained that we can grow Alberta's economy from within. When we do, we might even bring back diversified, regenerative family farms at the same time. So, to move us toward this goal, you'll find #EatAlbertaFirst tips throughout the book. These tips share how to source Alberta versions of key ingredients. Though the ideal approach might be to use fresh herbs as much as possible, it's often more practical to use dried herbs and spices. You'll know your pantry is power-packed when you usually only need to add a few fresh ingredients to cook many recipes from scratch.

Cooking is meant to be a fun, joyful, and nourishing activity. People who cook their own food usually eat better and weigh less. They save money. Cooking is a great creative outlet. It also promotes optimal brain function. You use executive skills for planning, timing, and sequencing. Tasting, touching, smelling, and observing stimulate your senses. You gain manual dexterity and you use many facets of memory as well. Cooking has been shown to increase longevity and reduce the risk of developing Alzheimer's disease—but if that's not enough, the tastes you create are their own reward.

Here are the categories of things in a well-provisioned pantry:

- salt
- spices
- oils
- vinegars
- condiments and sauces
- preserves and pickles
- canned goods
- baking supplies
- pasta, grains, dried legumes, and cereals
- refrigerator items (dairy and produce)
- freezer items (frozen fruit, vegetables, seeds, nuts, and proteins)

Let's go through each category, gain some background understanding, and take a look at the lists by levels of cook. (I've listed the ingredients by how likely it is that a novice cook will own them. If you find ingredients that aren't used in this book, it's because they're things I love. I hope you'll have fun exploring and experimenting with them.)



GREAT PLAINS BISON AT ELK ISLAND NATIONAL PARK

## Salt

Today, salt is inexpensive and widely available because of its importance in food preservation and the fact that the human body needs it for the regulation of fluid balance. The saying "worth one's salt" stems from a time when Roman soldiers were partially paid in salt rations. Salt comes either from salt mines or from the sea. There are many variations in the products that end up in our kitchens. As with all the lists, I'll order them by priority for purchasing and from basic necessity to fancy and fun to have.

- Table salt is processed and refined with additives to help it flow freely.
- Iodized salt has iodine added, which is important in parts of the world where natural iodine isn't available as it helps prevent goitre (hypothyroidism).
- Kosher salt is an additive-free coarse-grain salt. It's used by Jewish people who keep kosher and by cooks who like the taste and texture and don't want additives in their cooking. Most professional bakeries use kosher salt to add precision to their baking.
- Sea salt results when sea water is evaporated. It comes in fine and coarse flakes.
- Maldon salt is sliced crystals of salt. It makes a lovely finish on a bed of tomatoes.
- Fleur de sel is from France and has flower-shaped crystals that form when winds blow across the top of salt beds. It's very expensive—but bursting with flavour.
- Rock salt is greyish because it's not as refined as other salts and it has more minerals. It's used as a bed for serving mussels or oysters or added with ice when making ice cream in an old-fashioned crank machine. Thai cooks also use it in many dishes.

**NOVICE:**

- **IODIZED SALT:** Everyday household salt.
- **KOSHER SALT:** Use it for baking.
- **SEA SALT:** It's just a bit saltier than kosher and will be called for in some dishes where the taste of the sea brings a dish alive. For example, I'd use sea salt if I was making a seafood chowder or boiling water to cook a lobster or steaming clams.

**COMPETENT:**

- **FLEUR DE SEL:** Sprinkle it on greens with hazelnut or walnut oil and the flavour will burst forth.
- **MALDON SALT:** Use it to finish vegetable dishes or sprinkle it over brownies or sliced tomatoes with a drizzle of olive oil and balsamic vinegar.

SIGN FOUND AT EAGLE CREEK FARMS IN BOWDEN

**PROFICIENT:**

- **HIMALAYAN PINK, HAWAIIAN RED, HICKORY SMOKE:** You can have a lot of fun with these beautiful finishing salts. When I make edamame beans for an appetizer, I always present them with Hawaiian red salt. Himalayan pink looks and tastes great on top of a batch of brownies.

## Spices

If a spice is more than six to twelve months old, it's likely missing a full flavour profile. Think of a spice's flavour like musical notes on a scale. You can still make music without all the notes but it won't be as rich or enjoyable. So, forget about buying those huge containers that are so cheap at the big-box stores. Buy small quantities more often and store them away from light and direct heat.

**NOVICE:**

- **PARSLEY, SAGE, ROSEMARY, THYME, DILL, OREGANO, BASIL, SUMMER SAVORY:** I can't imagine living without these stalwart spices. They're great for flavouring grilled meats, soups, turkey stuffing, and Italian sauces.
- **BAY LEAVES:** They enhance slow-cooked stocks, stews, and tomato sauces.
- **CELERY SALT:** It's great for the rim of a Caesar or to add depth to a potato salad.

- **GARLIC SALT:** If you can't get fresh garlic, this will add a powerful flavour to grilled meats and you'll use it when you make Broek Pork Acres' Pulled Pork (page 155).
- **ONION SALT:** Same as above.
- **RED CHILI FLAKES:** They add a mellow heat as an ingredient or a little zip when sprinkled on a finished dish. You'll use them when you make Homemade Ricotta (page 277).
- **TEX-MEX CHILI POWDER:** Also known as just chili powder, this lends a Tex-Mex flavour to chili, fajitas, and tacos. You'll need some for Chipotle Bison Chili (page 227).
- **CURRY POWDER:** Until you master the art of Indian spice blending, this generic mix, a convenience food invented by the British, will help give any dish an Indian twist.
- **WHOLE BLACK PEPPERCORNS:** Always grind your own for the brightness of flavour this King of Spices can deliver.
- **VIETNAMESE CINNAMON:** This is the strong bold taste we associate with apple pie and cinnamon buns. You'll use it to make Sweet Sourdough Cinnamon Rolls (page 81).
- **SWEET HUNGARIAN PAPRIKA:** This is a must-have for barbecue rubs, potato salad, and devilled eggs.
- **STEAK SPICE:** Montreal, Chicago, or Hy's (which was founded in Calgary), I like them all. This is an absolute essential in Alberta where beef cattle outnumber humans. I like to sprinkle it over Roasted Potato and Root Vegetable Fries (page 147) too.
- **TURMERIC:** This is a quintessential Indian spice. I love to add just a pinch to my Chicken and Wild Rice Soup (page 219) to give it a golden glow.

**COMPETENT:**

- **CAYENNE POWDER:** Use this for clean, sharp heat.
- **CUMIN:** Stock both ground and cumin seeds. It's a signature flavour in both Mexican and Indian cooking.
- **GREEN CARDAMOM:** Keep whole pods, crack them, and grind the seeds as needed. The flavour is sweet and peppery with a bit of eucalyptus. It's very useful for Indian curries, chai, puddings, and fruit desserts.
- **GROUND GINGER:** Use it for baking and some Indian and Chinese dishes.
- **CORIANDER:** Keep whole seeds and roast and grind them as you need them. They add a lemony pop of flavour to rubs, marinades, pickles, potato salad, and curries.
- **MARJORAM:** This adds depth of flavour to stews and meat dishes.
- **MUSTARD POWDER:** This is essential in potato salad and many savoury dishes. I use Keen's.
- **MUSTARD SEEDS:** Keep both black and yellow mustard seeds. The yellow seeds are for pickling and some Bengali dishes, and the black are usually tempered in oil as the base flavour in most of the Indian dishes I cook.
- **WHOLE NUTMEG:** Use a microplane grater to release the flavour from the whole spice each time a recipe calls for it instead of a powdered version that's lost its flavour.
- **CLOVES:** Keep the whole buds and roast and grind them as needed. Cloves are sweet and peppery; great with the smoky taste of ham, hearty stews, and sweet apple and pear desserts.

- **TRUE CINNAMON:** This is also known as Sri Lankan cinnamon. It's a mild, amalgamating spice used in Indian and Mexican cooking.
- **STAR ANISE:** Add this when poaching pears in wine or making sweet puddings or savoury stews.
- **FENNEL SEEDS:** These deliver a lovely licorice taste. I put them in a holiday biscotti with cranberries, white chocolate, and lemon. You'll also note this flavour in Italian sausages and rubs for seafood, pork, lamb, and beef.
- **SAFFRON:** This is expensive, but a little goes a long way. If you can't smell a hay-like fragrance it's too old. Use it for flavour and for the golden hue it gives dishes.
- **POPPY SEEDS:** These are fun for everything from muffins to breads to crackers.
- **SESAME SEEDS:** Add these to baking and to salads. They're also an essential ingredient in Korean and Japanese cuisines.
- **WHITE, GREEN, AND PINK PEPPERCORNS:** Use white pepper when you want to add a barnyard-y fermented flavour. Green and pink just up your pepper game.

## #EATALBERTAFIRST TIPS:

- **THE SILK ROAD SPICE MERCHANT** is an Alberta-based company with a quick turnover in their spices so you can be assured you're getting the freshest quality.
- **CHICKADEE FARM ORGANIC HERBS** in Flatbush grows and sells their own sweet basil, celery leaves, thyme, marjoram, summer savory, dill, tarragon, sage, oregano, an Italian blend, parsley, and lovage along with medicinal herbs and herbal teas.

**PROFICIENT:**

- **ANCHO CHILI POWDER:** Use this because by now you like to make your own chili powder blends and this is a great base.
- **CHINESE FIVE-SPICE POWDER:** This is great on ribs, especially lamb ribs.
- **HERBES DE PROVENCE:** Sprinkle it on oil-rubbed lamb chops for the grill, on oven fries, or on chicken before you roast it.
- **JUNIPER BERRIES:** Use them in accordance with the axiom "What grows together, goes together." In Alberta, that means adding them to elk and bison stews.
- **ZA'ATAR:** This is a Middle Eastern spice mix that's great with olive oil spread on a warm pita or in Greek yogurt as a dip.
- **PIMENTÓN DE LA VERA:** This Spanish paprika adds a smoky flavour to any dish without you firing up the grill.
- **DRIED CHILIES:** Keep a variety of whole chilies for Indian, Mexican, and Thai cooking especially.
- **SUMAC:** Use it to add colour to any plate and frequently in Middle Eastern dishes.
- **SICHUAN PEPPERCORNS:** Add this to marinades for a sweet licorice-y bit of heat.
- **LOOMI (DRIED BLACK LIMES):** These are called for in many Middle Eastern dishes. They add a tart flavour whole or ground.
- **GALANGAL:** This is great to have on hand if you like to make your own tom yam Thai soup.
- **GARAM MASALA:** This is a warming spice blend used to finish Indian dishes and to bring all the flavours together. See page 346 for a recipe.
- **TURKISH BAHARAT:** This blend of Middle Eastern spices usually includes black pepper, cardamom, cloves, cumin, nutmeg, coriander, and paprika. The warm flavours are used to add depth to soups and rice, meat, fish, and chicken dishes.

FRESH GREENS AT
MITCHELL BROS. RANCH
NEAR PINCHER CREEK

### SESAME SALMON WITH ALBERTA HONEY:

Mix together 1 Tablespoon Alberta honey, 2 teaspoons toasted sesame oil, and 1 teaspoon sambal oelek. Spread over a salmon fillet on foil and grill to candied perfection—about 10 minutes at 400°F.

## Oils

There are many culinary oils on the market, and I'll expand on some of them in the lists below, but with so many kinds of olives (about 2,000), I'm going to share a bit more information about olive oils here to help you shop with savvy. They can be divided into four main taste categories:

1. **DELICATE AND BUTTERY:** Use these in mild vegetable and fish dishes.
2. **FRUITY AND FRESH:** These are good for seafood, cooked greens, warm pasta, and vegetable salads.
3. **GREEN AND HERBACEOUS:** These hold up well in bruschetta, warm pastas, spicy greens, and garlicky bean dishes, and on grilled meats.
4. **PEPPERY AND RIPE:** These are good for grilled breads, rich cheeses, fish, and pasta dishes.

In each of the categories above you'll find olive oils that are mass-produced blends for everyday use, high-end blends for dressings or drizzling, and estate-grown oils used for finishing food.

**NOVICE:**

- **EXTRA VIRGIN OLIVE OIL (EVOO):** Look for a well-priced EVOO with low acidity (less than 1 percent).
- **ORGANIC COLD-PRESSED CANOLA OIL:** This Alberta signature food will be bright gold like the flowers it comes from when you buy organic. The taste will be mustard-y because canola comes from the *Brassica* or mustard family of vegetables. Use it in salad dressings and some baking. Or, for a splurge, use it to deep-fry potatoes.
- **SUNFLOWER OIL:** Use this when you need a neutral-tasting oil for baking or frying.

**COMPETENT:**

- **COCONUT OIL:** Use it extensively for vegan, South Indian, and Thai recipes.
- **TOASTED SESAME OIL:** This is a star ingredient in Asian cooking and salad dressings.

**PROFICIENT:**

- **FLAX OIL:** Use it in smoothies or in dressings for savoury grain-based salads.
- **HAZELNUT AND AVOCADO OILS:** With a little sprinkle of fleur de sel, just a teaspoon of any of these oils is a lovely way to dress baby greens.
- **CHILI-INFUSED OIL:** This is a great pizza topper. You can also use it for finishing a vegetable dish or steak off the grill.
- **TRUFFLE OIL:** Keep this in the refrigerator and drizzle it on fresh Alberta asparagus in season, hot off the grill.

### #EATALBERTAFIRST TIP:

Try Highwood Crossing organic canola and flax oil (page 365).

## Vinegars

Most vinegars are straightforward. We use them to add acid and balance the flavours in recipes, especially fatty ones like salad dressings. Balsamic vinegars are different. Depending on how long they've aged, they're used differently in cooking, so I'll review them in more detail here. There are four distinctions to note when it comes to balsamic vinegars. I want to thank my friend Lina Castle, the founder of Lina's Italian Market in Calgary, for teaching me about these and for making them available long before they were cool.

**BASIC SALAD DRESSING:** 1 part sweet, 1 part acid, and 2 parts oil.

1 **TRADITIONAL BALSAMIC VINEGARS:** These are usually made from the must of Trebbiano grapes. They are aged in casks of different woods descending in size as the vinegar evaporates and are quite thick and syrupy. The original and authentic aged balsamics are made by families who pass down their recipe from generation to generation. They can cost $50 for an ounce and should be labelled Aceto Balsamico Tradizionale with a DOP (Denominazione di Origine Protetta) stamp. This is a European Union certification that guarantees an ingredient's quality, production, and place of origin. Use them sparingly. Drizzle them over parmesan as an appetizer, over grilled fish or veal as a main, or over ice cream or fresh strawberries for dessert. Add freshly ground black pepper to those balsamic strawberries for a taste-gasm.

2 **ARTISANAL BALSAMICS:** These are aged for less time than traditional balsamics and are available at moderate prices. They should carry an IGP (Indicazione Geografica Protetta) stamp as they're usually made by consortiums with protected geographical indication.

3 **IGP MODENA:** When you find this on a label it guarantees the contents are made from grape varietals typical of—but not necessarily from—Modena (Albana, Ancellotta, Fortana, Lambrusco, Montuni, Sangiovese, and Trebbiano). The grapes can be from anywhere and only need to be processed in Modena. This is the only way balsamic vinegar of Modena can be produced in enough volume to meet current demands.

4 **INSTANT BALSAMIC:** This is really just red wine vinegar with artificial flavour and colours added. Read the label.

**NOVICE:**

- **WHITE WINE, RED WINE, APPLE CIDER:** These are great basics because they are inexpensive and frequently listed in recipes.
- **BALSAMIC GLAZE:** This is a reduction of the fancy balsamic vinegars. Drizzle this and a little good olive oil with just a sprinkle of salt and pepper and people will think you've power-dressed your salad.

CANOLA IN FULL BLOOM NEAR FALHER IN PEACE COUNTRY

### #EATALBERTAFIRST TIPS:

- **ALCHEMIST VINEGARS** from Tippa Distillery makes four Alberta vinegars (page 363).
- Najm Al-Tameemi, a beekeeper in Iraq, arrived in Edmonton as a refugee in 2015 and missed **MARAM HONEY VINEGAR** so much he decided to start making it and other organic honey specialty foods (page 356).

**COMPETENT:**

- **RASPBERRY, SHERRY, CHAMPAGNE, AND RICE WINE:** Use these in salad dressings, marinades, and sauces galore.

**PROFICIENT:**

- **MIRIN:** This is similar to sake but with less alcohol and more sugar. I use it to balance salty soy sauce in Asian-inspired salad dressings.
- **AGED BALSAMICS:** Read those labels carefully and find the level you love in both taste and price.

## Condiments and sauces

Condiments and sauces add pizzazz to everything from sandwiches to soups and casseroles. It's easy to accumulate more than you need, so check expiry dates and plan menus that will help you use up those nearing their best-before dates. Once you start looking, you'll be delighted with how many Alberta-made treats you can find in this category.

**NOVICE:**

- **MUSTARDS:** Keep both an Alberta grainy and a Dijon on hand. They're useful for glazes, sandwiches, and sauces. In salad dressings, mustard acts as a natural emulsifier to help the oil and vinegar stay together.
- **ROASTED RED PEPPERS:** Add these to Green Beans with Herbs (page 335), and use in sandwiches and on pizza.
- **PESTO:** Add this to pasta with grilled chicken and steamed broccoli for a super-quick meal or use it to garnish Easy-to-Multiply Tomato Soup (page 223).
- **MAYONNAISE:** Use it as a sandwich spread or as the base for dressings like Never-the-Same-Way-Twice Coleslaw (page 139).

- **KETCHUP:** From hot dogs and hamburgers to eggs and meatloaf, ketchup is a favourite with many people, and many Alberta condiment makers now offer their own versions.
- **BARBECUE SAUCE:** Use this to finish burgers and steaks, to top meatloaf, or as a sauce or dip for your favourite smoked meats.
- **WORCESTERSHIRE SAUCE:** This is an important addition to gravies and sauces for both colour and flavour.
- **TABASCO SAUCE:** This adds a tame zip to dishes.
- **SOY SAUCE:** Soy is filled with umami and adds saltiness and colour to dishes.
- **STORE-BOUGHT BROTH AND/OR BOUILLON CUBES:** Chicken, beef, and vegetable are great to have on hand for when you run out of your own Homemade Stock (page 215).
- **HONEY:** Another Alberta signature food; source local and use it in salad dressings, baking, and, of course, on toast with tea.
- **MAPLE SYRUP:** This is great for pancakes and waffles but also for salad dressings. So many of the salad dressings I make are enhanced by maple syrup as a sweetener (when I'm not using Alberta honey, that is). Because maple tree roots draw the sap from deep underground, scientists are now realizing the incredible number of minerals and vitamins it contains.

**COMPETENT:**

- **TASTE #5 UMAMI PASTE:** Use it in your next meatloaf. Trust me.
- **HARISSA PASTE:** Add it wherever you need zing.
- **ALMOND AND CASHEW BUTTERS:** These are useful when making energy balls and in vegan cooking.
- **SAMBAL OELEK:** I use this mild chili paste as a substitute for fresh green chili paste (you can substitute 1:1) in my Indian cooking.
- **HOISIN:** Use this as a great base flavour for stir-fry dishes.
- **OYSTER SAUCE:** Ditto, but choose a premium one like Lee Kum Kee's.
- **FISH SAUCE:** This is a key ingredient in Thai cooking. I use the Red Boat brand.
- **THAI CURRY PASTE:** Remember, red is the mildest and green the hottest.
- **SRIRACHA OR TABASCO:** I prefer Tabasco. It's a bit milder. Add a few drops to gravies and stews to give them depth of flavour.

**PROFICIENT:**

- **GOCHUJANG:** This is a Korean sweet-with-heat chili paste that's quite addictive. Use it to coat a grilled chicken or meatloaf. Add it to salad dressings or peanut sauce.
- **MANGO CHUTNEY:** Add this for depth of flavour to curries, pour it over cheese, and serve it with lamb dishes.
- **TAMARIND PASTE OR CHUTNEY:** This is an essential for Indian and Persian dishes.
- **MISO:** Put a Tablespoon of this in boiling water with some chopped scallions and diced tofu and you've got a meal.
- **WASABI:** I like hot and spicy wasabi and usually need more than what my favourite sushi place sends.
- **CHILI BEAN PASTE:** This is a great part of a flavour base along with aromatics like garlic, ginger, and soy sauce for Asian stir-fry dishes.
- **ROSE HARISSA PASTE:** This is called for in Middle Eastern and Persian dishes where sultry heat retains floral elegance.

RAINBOW CARROTS

## #EATALBERTAFIRST TIPS:

- Two of my favourite Alberta-made ketchups are Bodacious Tomato Ketchup made by the Wolfe family in Peace Country and Preserved Ketchup made by chef Vanessa Rundell in Strathmore.
- MEAT restaurant in Edmonton makes their own Bourbon, Cherry, Spicy, and Mustard barbecue sauces to enjoy with the meats served fresh from their smokers. They also sell them for our at-home enjoyment. Canmore's Bow Valley BBQ Sauce company has a fun lineup of barbecue sauces available throughout the province. Another favourite is Amazing Dad's BBQ Sauce made with organic honey in Peace Country.
- Read honey labels carefully to make sure you know what you're buying, and look for local. Pure, raw, unpasteurized honey never goes bad. Five-thousand-year-old honey from the pyramids was still edible. The only reason honey is pasteurized is to extend its ability to stay liquid. If honey becomes crystallized, just place the container in a bowl of hot water and repeat until it is liquid again. Be wary of honey from other countries. Some use brown rice syrup to save money. Alberta honey has a lush, creamy white texture; I've taken it as gifts all over the world and, where customs allows honey into a country, it's always gratefully received.
- The Canadian Prairies grow most of the world's mustard. Much is shipped to Dijon, made into a paste and shipped back as a premium product. Several Alberta companies make their own mustard. Look for Brassica, Tubby Dog, Luco's, Cian's, and Bustard's mustard for a true taste of Alberta.

## Preserves and pickles

I grew up in a small town without much access to fresh fruits and vegetables in the winter, and my family came to think of preserves and pickles as the bright spot of our meals. In chapter 5, you can learn to make your own. Or stock up on Alberta-made favourites at farmers' markets around the province.

> Make an easy puttanesca sauce by cooking 1 Tablespoon of capers along with some black olives, anchovy paste, and garlic in olive oil before adding your favourite tomato sauce. Spoon it over pasta and you've got an instant dinner.

**NOVICE:**

- **CAPERS:** Intensely salty with a bite, these are a great addition to Mediterranean dishes and on top of bagels with lox.
- **ANCHOVY PASTE:** Use it in puttanesca sauce, make a Caesar salad dressing, or add it to seafood pasta dishes.
- **SALSA:** Look for a fresh local one or make your own (page 197).
- **PESTO:** Make your own by processing 2 packed cups of basil, ½ cup parmesan, ½ cup pine nuts, and enough olive oil to make a smooth paste.
- **SUN-DRIED TOMATOES IN OIL:** These are great for making dips like Red Lentil and Sun-Dried Tomato Hummus (page 275) and for adding depth to sauces and soups.
- **FRUIT JAMS AND JELLIES:** Raspberry, apricot, marmalade, crabapple. Use these on toast and as cake filling, or combine apricot jam with mustard, shallots, and herbs to coat pork tenderloin or ham.
- **PICKLES:** Asparagus, carrots, green beans, beets, bread and butter, corn. The world is better with pickles in it. Use pickled asparagus as a deluxe topping for a Bloody Caesar.

**COMPETENT:**

- **DRIED MUSHROOMS:** Porcini and morels are great reconstituted with hot water and added to sauces. Save and use the mushroom water to thin the sauces.
- **OLIVES IN BRINE:** Use these for charcuterie boards, pasta sauces, and tagines.

**PROFICIENT:**

- **ROSE WATER:** This lasts for a very long time and is used in Middle Eastern and Persian recipes to add the delicate floral notes of roses.
- **ORANGE WATER:** This adds a subtle citrus component to desserts.
- **KIMCHI:** This spicy Korean fermented cabbage is traditionally a side but is also fabulous in pancakes with scallions and shrimp with sesame oil and soy as a dip.
- **PRESERVED LEMONS:** These are used extensively in Moroccan cuisine because the time involved in preservation increases the intensity of the lemon flavour while decreasing the bitterness.

### #EATALBERTAFIRST TIP:

Whenever you're at a farmers' market in Alberta, seek out the pickle and preserve makers to amplify your pantry's power.

- **HORSERADISH:** This is always welcome wherever Alberta beef is served because the acid and heat of the horseradish balance the richness of the meat.
- **DRIED CHILIES:** Kashmiri, hot Indian, Mexican poblanos, cascabels . . . keep an assortment to spice things up when required.
- **CRISPY FRIED SHALLOTS:** With their rich caramelization, they add depth of flavour to Indian cooking, especially for Festive Vegetable Biryani (page 347).

SIGN AT THE SASKATOON FARM IN DE WINTON

## Canned goods

With their long shelf-life, a supply of canned goods is an important part of an emergency kit for any home. Soups, beans, tomatoes, and tins of fish could keep you going for a long time and because they are already cooked, they can even be consumed at room temperature if necessary. Just be careful to choose low-sodium options when you can as they are always healthier.

NOVICE:

- **EVAPORATED MILK:** This is useful for baking and soups because the evaporation process creates a creaminess that otherwise takes a long time to achieve.
- **SWEETENED CONDENSED MILK:** So many squares, a truly Canadian dessert category, contain this ingredient that it's very useful to have around.
- **TOMATOES:** I always have cans of cherry, peeled whole, and crushed. Avoid diced tomatoes as most of their flavour is lost in the processing. Try canned fire-roasted tomatoes. They're yummy.
- **TOMATO SAUCE:** Look for organic brands with no salt added. I like the (4-cup/1-litre) bottles of Rega brand strained tomato sauce.
- **TOMATO PASTE:** I usually buy a case of twelve cans at a time to save money. I also keep a squeezable tube in my refrigerator for times when a recipe calls for only a teaspoon or two.
- **OLIVES:** I keep cans of sliced and whole black olives.
- **ORGANIC LOW-SODIUM CHICKEN AND BEEF BROTH:** The broth in Tetra Pak boxes tastes better than the canned types.
- **TUNA (PACKED IN WATER AND SUSTAINABLE):** Great for sandwiches or tuna casserole.
- **CREAMED CORN:** You'll need this for Hot Pepper Cornbread (page 135) and it's handy for making corn chowder too.
- **KIDNEY BEANS:** Red and white are staples for chilies and soups.
- **WHITE CANNELLINI BEANS:** Use as a side dish, eat them on toast, or add to soups and stews. Make an appetizer by caramelizing sliced onion in olive oil and then adding garlic, the beans, and a bit of fresh rosemary.
- **CHICKPEAS:** Make your own hummus or use them in chilies, stews, and soups.
- **CHERRY PIE FILLING:** Great in pies but also on top of cheesecake or to make Sweet Sourdough Fruit Strudel (page 87).
- **APPLESAUCE:** Combine with cottage cheese, bran buds, cinnamon, and a chopped apple for a power brekkie on the run or serve with pork chops or a pork roast.

**COMPETENT:**

- **BABY CLAMS AND CLAM JUICE:** Make chowder or linguini with clam sauce, or add this to puttanesca sauce (page 49) for clam puttanesca.
- **COCONUT MILK AND COCONUT CREAM:** These are used extensively in the cuisines of both South India and Thailand, where coconut trees are plentiful, for a smooth texture and to balance the heat of chili-based curries with the sweetness of coconut.

**PROFICIENT:**

- **WATER CHESTNUTS:** These are useful for appetizers and Asian dishes.
- **CHIPOTLES IN ADOBO:** I love how these add a smoky southwestern zip to Mexican and Tex-Mex dishes. Plus, you need them for Chipotle Bison Chili (page 227).

## Baking supplies

If you've got the room, devote one drawer in your kitchen cupboards to baking supplies. I keep my stand mixer on the counter right above mine and measuring spoons and baking utensils nearby. It's amazing how quickly a recipe comes together when you know where everything is. When it comes to the most important baking supply—flour—we are blessed in Alberta to still have farmers growing both variety and heritage breeds like Red Fife, Park, einkorn, rye, barley, spelt, and buckwheat. The heritage breeds spawned modern-day varieties and then fell out of favour because they were more challenging to grow or harvest. Because of their great flavours, though, they have re-emerged and are all available from Alberta flour millers. Most of them are organic too. Give them a try. The flavours will wow you.

**NOVICE:**

- **CHOCOLATE:** Keep chips, chunks, flakes, and bars of white, milk, semi-sweet, and dark on hand at all times.
- **COCOA POWDER:** Use Dutch processed cocoa for the colour it brings and the fact that the cocoa's natural acids have been removed in the processing. Brands like Hershey's still contain those acids, so the flavour may not be as smooth.
- **VANILLA:** Use only pure vanilla extract. Avoid anything that says artificial vanilla.
- **UNBLEACHED ALL-PURPOSE FLOUR:** Bleached flour is treated with several chemical agents that can affect the flavour of your baking. Need I say more?
- **QUICK-COOKING OATS:** Enjoy them for breakfast and in cookies and breads.
- **UNSWEETENED SHREDDED COCONUT:** This is great for baking and some South Indian dishes.



ACADIA VALLEY GRANARY MUSEUM

ALBERTA
WHEAT POOL
ACADIA VALLEY
ALBERTA
POOL
ACADIA VALLEY
CN
COCKSHUTT

### #EATALBERTAFIRST TIP:

Red Fife wheat is an Alberta signature food. Highwood Crossing Foods, Gold Forest Grains, and Heritage Harvest all grow and sell it.

- **BAKING SODA:** Also known as sodium bicarbonate, this is a BASE that needs an ACID (buttermilk, lemon juice, yogurt, cream of tartar, molasses, and others) in the recipe to react and create carbon dioxide. Carbon dioxide bubbles allow your baked goods to leaven.
- **BAKING POWDER:** This is a mixture of baking soda, cream of tartar (a dry acid), and sometimes cornstarch. It can leaven during mixing and also when exposed to heat.
- **CORNSTARCH:** This is a thickening agent for marinades, sauces, gravies, glazes, soups, casseroles, and pies and other desserts.
- **GRANULATED OR CANE SUGAR:** A mainstay for baking and preserving.
- **ICING SUGAR:** Use it for making icing and desserts.
- **BROWN SUGAR:** This is used for both sweet and savoury dishes like Dynamite Dick's Five Bean Beans (page 149).
- **MOLASSES:** Use this as a syrup, as a sweetener, in glazes, and, of course, in all things gingerbread.

**COMPETENT:**

- **DRIED FRUITS:** You'll use raisins and dried cranberries, dates, apricots, and cherries in various baking recipes in this book. They're also a great addition to charcuterie boards.
- **WHOLE WHEAT FLOUR:** Add fibre and increase the vitamins in your baking with this.
- **OAT FLOUR:** This is a great alternative to wheat flour. It's easy to make by pulsing oats in your food processor until they become a fine flour.
- **STEEL-CUT OATS:** Beyond being a healthy breakfast cereal and baking ingredient, these are used in Mrs. Beaton's Oatcakes (page 279).
- **GELATIN:** Use this in no-bake cheesecakes and molded salads.
- **LIGHT CORN SYRUP:** Use this in quick treats like Puffed Wheat Squares (page 253).
- **YEAST:** You'll need this for various baking projects, especially for the Sweet Sourdough Starter (page 71).
- **SKIM MILK POWDER:** Lots of bread and baking recipes call for this, as does Colton's Bannock (page 103).
- **GRAHAM AND CHOCOLATE COOKIE CRUMBS:** Use these as a base for squares and pies.

**PROFICIENT:**

- **BREAD AND PASTRY FLOUR:** None of the recipes in this book call for this but it's still handy to keep in the freezer if space allows.
- **VANILLA BEANS:** Use them to make vanilla sugar or add the seeds to homemade ice cream, chocolate chip cookies (to die for), and other baking triumphs.
- **ALMOND, RICE, AND COCONUT FLOURS:** A member of our family has celiac disease, so for me, these are important substitutes for wheat and gluten products.
- **HERITAGE FLOURS:** Look for Red Fife, Park, einkorn, rye, barley, spelt, and buckwheat.

## Pasta, grains, dried legumes, and cereals

Variety is the name of the game with these ingredients. They are packed with energy and add interesting tastes and textures to our diets. Quinoa's rise to popularity got people thinking about what other grains we might have been overlooking. Check out the list below and see what you might like to try.

NOVICE:

- **POLENTA IN A TUBE:** You can cut this in rounds and use it instead of pasta noodles for lasagna.
- **RICE:** Stock long-grain white basmati and you'll be ready for countless meals.
- **QUINOA:** Use red for Alberta Energy Bites (page 251) and regular for pilafs and salads.
- **DRIED PASTA:** Macaroni, spaghetti, fettuccine, shells—so many shapes and so little cupboard space.
- **BREAD CRUMBS:** I like both Italian seasoning and panko.
- **CRACKERS:** Keep rice, water, seed, and wheat crackers on hand for soups and snacks.
- **LENTILS:** Red, green, and brown are all quick-cooking for soups and sides.
- **BREAKFAST CEREALS:** Choose the ones you love, but also keep a supply of bran flakes for Hit the Trail Cookies (page 249) and Original All-Bran for Refrigerator Bran Muffins (page 247).

COMPETENT:

- **RICE:** Jasmine and brown basmati up your rice game considerably.
- **RICE NOODLES:** I love vermicelli and pad Thai shapes.
- **WHOLE GRAINS:** Couscous, large-flake oats, cracked wheat, natural bran, wheat berries, kasha, wehani, cornmeal, and polenta are all staples.
- **MORE LEGUMES:** I cook lots of legumes and always have dried mung beans, split peas, chickpeas, black beans, du Puy lentils, and navy and cannellini beans on hand.

PROFICIENT:

- **WILD RICE:** With a nutty flavour and chewy texture, this Canadian grass seed is an interesting addition to pilafs, pancakes, soups, and stews. Use it to make Chicken and Wild Rice Soup (page 219).
- **ARBORIO RICE:** Essential for risotto.
- **BOMBA RICE:** Perfect for paella.
- **ARROWROOT AND TAPIOCA STARCHES:** These are alternatives to cornstarch as thickening agents.
- **CHICKPEA FLOUR (BESAN):** Use this to make Indian breads and appetizers.
- **FARRO:** This is great for Italian soups and stews.

## Refrigerator items (dairy and produce)

Every great chef manages their refrigerator to avoid waste and we home cooks should do the same. Fortunately, refrigerators have see-through drawers and helpful organizing functions to help us do this. Keep categories like drinks, snacks, and condiments together. Wet a paper towel and wrap it around the stems of fresh herbs, then place them in a plastic bag to keep them fresh as long as possible. Avoid storing ethylene-producing onions and apples with other fruits and vegetables as they may cause them to ripen too quickly. Check expiration dates regularly and use things up before they need to be discarded.

NOVICE:

- **CHEESES:** Parmesan will keep for a very long time. Goat cheese, Gouda, Swiss, cheddar, and cream cheese are great additions to many dishes.
- **MILK:** Cow, almond, soy, oat, cashew—there are lots of choices for milk now.
- **PLAIN GREEK OR REGULAR YOGURT:** Enjoy yogurt on its own, or in salad dressings, smoothies, and baking.
- **BUTTER:** I generally use unsalted for baking and salted for the table.

### #EATALBERTAFIRST TIP:

Some of my favourite organic egg producers in Alberta include Four Whistle Farm, Mans Eggs, and Happiness by the Acre.

- **NUT BUTTERS:** I rotate between almond, cashew, and peanut butter.
- **LARGE BROWN ORGANIC EGGS:** Look for small farm producers of organic eggs from chickens raised with care.
- **CARROTS, ONIONS, AND CELERY:** Known as *mirepoix*, this flavour-enhancing combo was popularized in the eighteenth century by the Duc de Lévis-Mirepoix's cook. When cooked together, these crown jewels of flavour serve as the base for many sauces, stocks, soups, and stews.
- **GARLIC:** The hardneck varieties grow very well in Alberta and are a cosmic flavour bomb compared with their imported cousins.

COMPETENT:

- **GREENS, GREENS, GREENS:** Stock living lettuces whenever you can. Alberta greenhouses grow fantastic ones.
- **APPLES:** Look for BC Tree Fruits for the most local apples available.
- **GINGER:** Fresh shiny knobs keep well in the refrigerator.
- **FRESH HERBS:** Basil, cilantro, dill, mint, parsley, sage, rosemary, and thyme are the most common.
- **JALAPEÑOS:** Use these to add zip to salads and dressings.
- **SCALLIONS (GREEN ONIONS) AND SHALLOTS:** These are little flavour bombs that add great texture as well.
- **BACON:** With so many Alberta bacon makers, why choose something from far away? Often those brands need to use more chemicals in their bacon for transport and shelf-life stability.

**PROFICIENT:**

- **GHEE:** This clarified butter, used in Indian cooking, has a long shelf-life when stored in the refrigerator.
- **AGED CHEESES:** Cave-aged Gruyère and real Parmigiano-Reggiano are worth every penny. And because they bring so much flavour to a dish, you can use them sparingly.
- **LIMES AND LIME JUICE:** Use them to balance fatty sauces with the acid this citrus supplies. Avoid wasting the zest or rind by saving it in a plastic bag in the freezer.
- **LEMONS AND LEMON JUICE:** Lemon juice adds citrus zip to sauces, salad dressings, and desserts.
- **TAHINI:** Use it when you make your own hummus or in baking and salad dressings.
- **BEETS, TURNIPS, KOHLRABI, CELERIAC, PARSNIPS:** Root vegetables are Alberta signature foods. Our cold nights cause sugars to concentrate in the roots of these plants, making them sweeter than in other climates. You'll taste the difference whether eating them raw, in slaws, or when roasting them in the oven.
- **POTATOES:** Buy red and white waxy potatoes for potato salad. Yellow-fleshed, Yukon Gold, russets, and Agrias are for mashing. Yams and sweet potatoes are for mashing, baking, or oven fries. Roast or grill fingerlings and baby potatoes and make extra for hash browns to go along with a weekend breakfast.

DO NOT put potatoes in the refrigerator. Store them in a cool, dark place, ideally between 7 and 10 degrees Celsius. Use them up quickly and discard any that have turned green. They contain a toxin called solanine.

## #EATALBERTAFIRST TIPS:

- Aged Grizzly Gouda from Sylvan Star in Sylvan Lake is a great local substitute for imported parmesan cheese. Sylvan Star is Canada's most award-winning cheesemaker.
- Alberta Pike from Innisfail started making Gouda in 2020.
- Lakeside Farmstead from Sturgeon County makes cloth-bound and aged cheddars, curds, and cultured butter.
- Fairwinds Farm and Noble Meadows make great goat cheeses.
- Bles-Wold Dairy near Lethbridge specializes in premium yogurt products.
- Alberta has two independent organic dairies, Vital Green Farms and Rock Ridge Dairy, for milk, yogurt, butter, and basic cheeses.

## Freezer items (frozen fruit, vegetables, seeds, nuts, and proteins)

Depending on the size of your family, an extra freezer can pay for itself very quickly. Its biggest benefit is that you can take full advantage of sales and bulk-buying—and remember, frozen fruits and vegetables have nearly the same nutrient content as fresh. For example, you can freeze fruits in season easily to enjoy all year round: spread them out on a baking sheet, put them in the freezer until frozen, and then bag them and remove the air. If that's not enough to convince you, wait until you get to all the batch-cooking recipes in chapter 6. Trust me, you're going to want a freezer.

**NOVICE:**

- **FROZEN BUTTERNUT SQUASH:** Add to stews, boil and mash as a side, or use it to make Triple "S" Soup (page 221).
- **FROZEN CHOPPED SPINACH:** This is inexpensive, loaded with vitamins, and so versatile. Use it to make Chunky Pasta Sauce with Hot Italian Sausage (page 235).
- **FROZEN PEAS AND CORN:** These are workhorses that can brighten any dish. Use the corn to make Alberta Sunshine Eggs (page 315).
- **PROTEINS:** It's great to have some ground beef, hot Italian sausages, chicken breasts, fish fillets, and shrimp ready to thaw so you can always pull a meal together.
- **BERRIES:** Frozen raspberries, blueberries, haskaps, and saskatoons are especially handy for baking.

**COMPETENT:**

- **BISON AND BEEF:** Keep stewing meat and roasts on hand.
- **STRAWBERRIES AND RHUBARB:** With these in the freezer you can make jams and Overnight Rhubarb Sauce (page 169) whenever the notion strikes.

**PROFICIENT:**

- **BAGS OF BONES AND VEGETABLE BITS:** See the recipe for Homemade Stock (page 215) to understand why you need these.
- **NUTS AND SEEDS:** These stay fresher in the freezer. Keep chia, sunflower, flax, hemp, and pepita seeds and almonds, cashews, walnuts, pecans, peanuts, pine nuts, pistachios, and hazelnuts on hand.
- **MAKRUT (FORMERLY KNOWN AS KAFFIR) LIME LEAVES:** You'll find these in the freezer at Asian grocers and they're lovely to have handy for Thai curries and soups.

- **CURRY LEAVES:** Whatever I don't use fresh, I rub with a little oil and freeze.
- **CRANBERRIES AND SEA BUCKTHORN BERRIES:** These add tartness to baking.
- **EDAMAME BEANS:** These are a great appetizer and an excellent way to add protein to salads.
- **SCALLOPS, SALMON, LING COD, LOX:** Each year, I buy a skipperotto.com Community Supported Fishery share and get frozen sustainable seafood direct from coastal BC fisher families.
- **LAMB SHANKS:** You can treat lamb shanks in the same way you would treat a leg of lamb. Think of it as individual portions. Also, use them for Lamb Shanks in a Saskatoon and Pinot Noir Sauce (page 317).

FRESHLY PICKED STRAWBERRIES AT THE JUNGLE FARM

# The Well-Equipped Kitchen

Well-designed and practical tools make cooking more enjoyable. It may take a few years to fully equip your kitchen but if you're just getting started in the kitchen, here are the items I use for the recipes in this book.

## BAKEWARE

- baking sheets (two or three 12 × 14-inch unrimmed for ease of sliding cookies off)
- cooling racks (two large)
- jelly roll pan, also known as a rimmed baking sheet (two large [12 × 16-inch])
- large flame-proof roasting pan with a V-rack
- metal loaf pan (9 × 5-inch)
- muffin tins (regular and mini non-stick)
- parchment and wax paper plus aluminum foil
- pie plates (glass, metal, or ceramic)
- Pyrex baking pan set in three sizes (7 × 11-, 9 × 13-, and 11 × 15-inch)
- round metal cake pans (two 9 × 2-inch)
- round soufflé or casserole dish (1½-to-2-quart)
- springform pans (9-, 10-, and 12-inch)
- square metal baking pan (9 × 9-inch)

## BOWLS AND STORAGE CONTAINERS

- glass canning jars and assorted-size containers with lids
- metal, glass, and/or ceramic mixing bowls
- small bowls for prep
- wooden salad bowl
- zipper-locking bags in assorted sizes



ANTIQUE BUTTER SPREADERS
AT HIGHWOOD CROSSING FARM

## COOKWARE

- carbon steel flat-bottomed wok
- cast-iron frying pan
- crêpe pan
- deep-sided frying pan
- double boiler
- Dutch oven (6-to-8-quart)
- non-stick frying pan (12-inch)
- saucepans (1-, 2-, and 4-quart)
- stockpot (8-quart)
- water bath canner (canning bath) with jar and lid lifters

## GRATERS, GRINDERS, AND ZESTERS

- box cheese grater
- electric spice (coffee) grinder
- microplane grater
- pepper mill
- zester

## KNIVES AND CUTTING SURFACES

- bread knife
- carving knife and fork set
- chef's knife (8-inch)
- kitchen shears
- mandoline
- paring knife
- sharpening steel
- wooden cutting board with rim for catching juices

## LINENS

- dishcloths
- napkins, placemats, and tablecloths as you can afford them
- oven mitts
- pot holders
- tea towels

## MEASURING EQUIPMENT

- electronic kitchen scale (I'd be lost without mine)
- instant-read thermometer
- measuring cup set
- measuring spoon set
- oven thermometer
- ruler

## SMALL APPLIANCES

- blender (I use a Vitamix for best results)
- coffee maker
- food processor
- hand-held immersion blender
- rice cooker (5½-cup)
- slow cooker
- stand mixer
- tea kettle

## SMALL GENERAL-USE TOOLS

- can opener
- cheesecloth
- cherry pitter
- citrus juicer
- citrus reamer
- corkscrew
- funnels (regular and wide-mouth)
- hand-held potato masher and/or potato ricer
- kitchen twine
- measuring tape and/or ruler
- metal skewers
- salad spinner
- spring-release ice cream/cookie dough scoops in various sizes
- tea ball
- thick rubber gloves
- trivets
- vegetable peeler

## SMALL PASTRY TOOLS

- bench knife/scraper
- biscuit/cookie cutters
- offset icing knife
- pastry blender
- pastry brush
- pie server
- rolling pin

## SPOONS, SPATULAS, WHISKS, AND TONGS

- balloon whisk
- flat whisk
- ladle
- metal, wooden, and slotted spoons
- spatulas of various sizes (silicone and metal)
- spoon rest
- tongs

## STRAINERS

- fine mesh sieve
- metal colander
- skimmer
- wire sieve

### #EATALBERTAFIRST TIP:

Knifewear opened in Calgary in 2008 and has been selling Japanese kitchen knives across the world ever since. The knives are carbon steel, hand-forged masterpieces. They make chopping feel as effortless as slicing a hot knife through butter. I love mine so much I often travel with them.

CHAPTER 2

CABIN
FEVER
SEASON

Once your pantry is stocked you might as well bake, because it's only February and winter is a long way from over. It's time to get cozy and employ the "Keep Calm and Bake On" cure to get you through cabin fever season.

Cabin fever, a certain level of irritability and restlessness resulting from an extended confinement indoors during winter, usually peaks when the days start getting noticeably longer. Flirtatious chinook winds escalate the feverish hope of an end to winter. They melt the snow and *occasionally* bask us in 20 degree Celsius days. Outdoor patios fill as fast as skating rinks melt. Then, wham! We slam into another snowbank of reality. Winter's deep freeze returns. Though we itch for more time outside, we retreat to our shelters and embrace coziness to get us through.

And what is cozier than the smell of freshly baked bread? The pandemic revived the great Canadian tradition of keeping a sourdough starter. Flour and yeast sales skyrocketed. But I am skeptical about how many of those ambitious sourdough start-ups of 2020 are still alive and kicking today.

In this chapter, I share a sweet sourdough that's much easier to maintain than its wild yeast cousin. When you aren't using it, you just pop it in the freezer. This is the secret to how my mother and I have kept our family's going since the 1970s.

Of course, once you've made your starter you'll be looking for ways to use it, so I'm also including several scrumptious recipes that make the most of its unique texture and taste. These recipes will get you through to March and the spring solstice.

# A Sweet Sourdough Primer

Commercial yeast wasn't available until the late 1800s. Before then, all bread was either unleavened or made with a pre-ferment of wild yeast sourdough starter. Wild yeast sourdoughs can take weeks to start. This sweet sourdough, however, uses some commercial yeast and will be up and running in just five days. And here's the best part: when you want a break from caring for it, you simply freeze it. Feel free to name your sourdough starter. Mine is Hermione because, just like Harry Potter's friend Hermione Granger, it lets me pull a lot of goodies from my enchanted container.

Be sure to read through the following tips before you start creating your own magic.

**SWEET SOURDOUGH STARTER TIPS:**

- Keep the initial starter in a glass or pottery container for best results.
- Never use a metal container and never leave a metal spoon in the starter.
- The initial starter should have a clean sour milk odour.
- The liquid will separate from the batter when it stands for several days but this doesn't matter.
- If you feed it after each use, it will thrive.
- If it turns moldy or develops an off-odour, throw it away and start over.
- If you'll be leaving the starter for longer than 14 days between uses, freeze it until you're ready to use it again. Before using, let it stand at room temperature for several hours so that it's completely thawed and a bit bubbly.

**SWEET SOURDOUGH FEEDING TIPS:**

- Always feed your starter after each use.
- Wait at least 24 hours after feeding before using again.
- Always keep at least 1 cup of the sourdough from the previous batch

# Sweet Sourdough Starter

**MAKES** 1½ to 2 cups.
The texture and quantity varies because of humidity and the age of the starter.
**TAKES** A few minutes on the first 3 days to start. Then you feed it on day 4 and use it on day 5.
**RATING** All levels

**WHAT YOU NEED TO GATHER**

Measuring cups and spoons
Large glass bowl
Whisk
Tea towel
Storage container
Wooden spoon

2 cups flour
3 Tablespoons sugar
1 package (2¼ teaspoons) active dry granular yeast
1 teaspoon salt
2 cups lukewarm water

**WHAT YOU NEED TO DO**

1. Mix the flour, sugar, yeast, and salt together in a large glass bowl and gradually whisk in the water until smooth.
2. Cover the bowl with a tea towel and sit it in a warm (25°C to 30°C), draft-free place for the first 3 days. Your oven with just the oven light on works well.
3. Stir the starter 2 to 3 times a day for the first 3 days or until it is bubbly and producing a yeasty aroma.
4. Transfer the starter to a larger bowl, jar, or plastic container on day 4 and feed it according to the directions on page 72. Now cover partially (just tilt the lid, don't seal it) and refrigerate.
5. Use the starter on day 5.
6. Feed it again after using it, then place it back in the refrigerator until next use.

Active dry, instant (quick-rise, rapid-rise, or bread machine), or fresh (cake, compressed or commercial): which yeast should you use? Fresh yeast has a short shelf-life, must be refrigerated, and is most commonly used by baking professionals who are producing a commercial scale of baking. Active dry yeast has large granules of dried yeast that require proofing (briefly combining the granules with sugar and warm water to reactivate the microorganisms). The microorganisms feed on the sugars in flour and release the carbon dioxide that gives your bread its lift and flavour. Instant yeast granules are much smaller and are easily incorporated into the recipe along with other dry ingredients without proofing.

## HOW TO FEED YOUR SWEET SOURDOUGH STARTER

**MAKES** 2 additional cups of sourdough starter
**TAKES** 5 minutes
**RATING** All levels

**WHAT YOU NEED TO GATHER**

Measuring cups
Bowl
Whisk
Wooden spoon

1 cup flour
1 cup skim, 2%, or whole milk
½ cup granulated sugar

**WHAT YOU NEED TO DO**

1. Whisk the flour, milk, and sugar in a large bowl until there are no lumps. Then, stir this feed into the existing sourdough starter and store it in the refrigerator until you're ready to use it.

## HOW TO SHARE YOUR SWEET SOURDOUGH STARTER

**#EATALBERTAFIRST TIP:**

Check out realbreadalberta.com for rates on bulk flour purchases.

**WHAT YOU NEED TO DO**

1. Give a friend 1 cup of your starter (and all your recipes, of course). Then feed your starter.
2. Tell your friend to feed their starter once and leave it in the refrigerator for a day. They can then use up to 1 cup of it in a recipe, feed their sourdough again, and carry on baking.
3. Pass on all the guidelines listed above. (Better still, give them a copy of this book!)

HERMIONE

# Sweet Sourdough No-Knead Bread

**MAKES** 1 large round loaf
**TAKES** 10 minutes' active time + 8 to 18 hours' resting + 2 (or up to 4) hours' proofing + 30 minutes' baking
**RATING** Competent to proficient

There's nothing like the smell or taste of buttered bread fresh from the oven. Try this with butter hot from the oven, with soup, for sandwiches, or with Trail's End Classic Beef Stew (page 231). I make it fairly often because of how good it tastes and how little actual hands-on time there is.

**WHAT YOU NEED TO GATHER**

Large glass or pottery bowl
Measuring cups and spoons
Whisk
Wooden spoon
Tea towel
Parchment paper
Ovenproof 10-inch frying pan
Plastic wrap
6-to-8-quart cast-iron enamelled Dutch oven
Sharp knife or razor blade
Tongs or a spatula
Wire rack

3 cups flour
¼ teaspoon active dry or instant yeast
1½ teaspoons kosher salt
1½ cups warm water (105°F to 115°F)
1 cup Sweet Sourdough Starter (page 71)
Cooking spray
Soft butter as needed

**WHAT YOU NEED TO DO**

1. Whisk the flour, yeast, and salt together in the bowl and then use a sturdy wooden spoon to fold in the water and sourdough until a loose shaggy ball forms (depending on your climate, you may or may not need a little extra water).
2. Cover the bowl with a tea towel and place it in the oven for 8 to 18 hours. If your oven has a proof setting (85°F to 90°F), use that. Otherwise, just leave the oven light on.
3. Place a piece of parchment paper inside a 10-inch frying pan and spray it lightly with cooking spray. Transfer the dough to a flat surface, knead it 10 to 15 times, and then shape it into a ball by pulling the edges into the middle on the bottom side. Place the dough on the parchment in the frying pan, seam side down, and rub the exposed exterior with a light coating of soft butter.
4. Cover the dough ball loosely with plastic wrap and let it rise at room temperature until it has doubled in size and does not spring back when you poke it with a finger, about 2 hours. When you cover the dough ball, also set a timer for 90 minutes. When it goes off, preheat your oven to 500°F and place the Dutch oven, complete with its lid, on the middle rack while the oven comes to temperature.
5. Meanwhile, reset the timer for 30 minutes. When it buzzes, and the dough is ready, use a sharp knife or razor to score the top with a long slit (or use your own design) about ½-inch deep.
6. Remove the Dutch oven from your regular oven and use the parchment paper as a sling to carefully transfer and lower the bread into it. Cover with the lid and return it to the middle rack.

7 Reduce the oven temperature to 425°F, bake the dough for 30 minutes, then remove the lid. If your bread is golden brown, it's done (mine usually is at this point). If it isn't, continue baking until it is golden brown. If you have an instant-read thermometer, you can also check the internal temperature. It will read 200°F when the bread is done.

8 Remove the Dutch oven from the oven, take off the lid, and let the bread cool in the Dutch oven for a few moments. Use tongs or a spatula to transfer your loaf to a wire rack to finish cooling.

## #EATALBERTAFIRST TIP:

- Are you keen to learn more about bread making? Consider taking an online or in-person class through Awn Kitchen in Edmonton, BreadLove in St. Albert, or the Cookbook Co. Cooks in Calgary.
- In 2006, the *New York Times* writer Mark Bittman created no-knead bread to help home bakers achieve the same crispy crust, light and airy crumb, and full flavour in sourdough baking that previously only professional bakers with specialty ovens could achieve. The wet dough and slow fermentation are the keys to success. Bittman's testing showed you can leave the bread to proof for as little as 8 hours but leaving it for up to 18 will more fully develop the flavour. Just don't leave it longer, or you'll risk a flat, overproofed loaf. Using my sweet sourdough starter takes the flavour profile up a notch or three.

# Sweet Sourdough Chocolate Cake with the Buttercream-iest Chocolate Icing

## SWEET SOURDOUGH CHOCOLATE CAKE

**MAKES** 10 to 12 servings
**TAKES** 20 minutes' active time + 50 minutes' baking time + cooling time
**RATING** Competent to proficient

My mom got her sweet sourdough starter and recipes from her dear friends Gerry Van Tassel and Alice Groom in the early 1970s. Mom made about twenty of these chocolate layered cakes every August for the annual church sale in my hometown of St. Andrews, New Brunswick. You should've seen our kitchen table. She charged a whopping $20 per cake in the early days. They were legendary—and they've since become my husband's favourite birthday cake.

### WHAT YOU NEED TO GATHER

Two 8-inch round cake pans
Measuring cups and spoons
Whisk
Glass bowl
Stand mixer
Spatula
Cake tester or toothpick
2 wire racks

¾ cup boiling hot water
⅔ cup cocoa
1¾ cups flour
1½ teaspoons baking soda
1 teaspoon salt
½ teaspoon baking powder
1⅔ cups sugar
⅔ cup sunflower or other neutral-tasting vegetable oil
3 large eggs
1 cup Sweet Sourdough Starter (page 71)
1 teaspoon vanilla extract

### WHAT YOU NEED TO DO

1. Preheat the oven to 350°F and grease and flour the cake pans.
2. Pour the boiling water into a bowl or large measuring cup and whisk in the cocoa. Set aside.
3. Whisk the flour, baking soda, salt, and baking powder together in a bowl and set aside.
4. Place the sugar and oil in the bowl of a stand mixer fitted with the paddle attachment and beat until fluffy. Beat in the eggs one at a time, scraping down the sides of the bowl after each addition. Add the sourdough and vanilla and beat until smooth.
5. Beat in half the flour mixture followed by half the cocoa mixture until smooth. Repeat with the remaining flour and cocoa mixtures.
6. Divide the batter between the 2 cake pans and place on the middle rack in the oven. Bake until a cake tester inserted in the centre comes out clean, 40 to 50 minutes.
7. Invert the cakes from the pans onto wire racks and let cool completely before icing the layers.

## THE BUTTERCREAM-IEST CHOCOLATE ICING

**MAKES** Generous icing for 1 cake or 24 cupcakes
**TAKES** 20 minutes' active time
**RATING** Competent to proficient

This icing is the stuff of cake dreams. My friends Carolyne McIntyre-Jackson and Jodi Willoughby, the founders of Crave, taught me that beating the butter for 8 to 10 minutes is what produces the smoothness that qualifies this as the buttercream-iest icing you've ever tasted. It's great to have friends who are baking pros.

### WHAT YOU NEED TO GATHER

Measuring cups and spoons
Stand mixer
Spatula
Offset icing knife
Cake stand or plate

1 cup unsalted butter, at room temperature
½ cup salted butter, at room temperature
¾ cup cocoa powder, sifted
4 cups icing sugar, sifted
3 Tablespoons whipping cream
1½ teaspoons vanilla extract

### WHAT YOU NEED TO DO

1. Place both butters in the bowl of a stand mixer fitted with the paddle attachment and beat on high speed until pale yellow and fluffy, about 8 minutes. Stop occasionally to scrape down the sides of the bowl.
2. Add the cocoa and beat on medium speed until smooth, about 1 to 2 minutes.
3. Add the icing sugar, whipping cream, and vanilla and beat on low speed until well combined, stopping to scrape down the sides of the bowl as needed. Continue to beat the mixture on low to medium speed until you have your desired fluffiness, then ice the cake.

### PRO TIP:

If you set the butter out on the counter before you start to make the cake, it should be at room temperature by the time you need to make the icing.

MEDALTA
POTTERIES LTD

# Sweet Sourdough Cinnamon Rolls

**MAKES** 8 to 12 rolls
**TAKES** 25 minutes' active time + 15 to 20 minutes' baking time
**RATING** Competent to proficient

These are my favourite cinnamon rolls. Their texture is a cross between bread and cake, and the dough soaks up the cinnamon and brown sugar and rises beautifully. Enjoy them for a special breakfast treat or coffee time visit.

### WHAT YOU NEED TO GATHER

8 × 8-inch baking pan
Measuring cups and spoons
Large bowl
Whisk
Wooden spoon
Rolling pin
Pastry brush
Knife
Wire rack

Butter, to grease the baking pan
1 cup Sweet Sourdough Starter (page 71)
1 egg, beaten
⅓ cup sunflower or other neutral-tasting vegetable oil, plus more for the pan
1 cup flour, plus more for kneading
2 teaspoons baking powder
½ teaspoon baking soda
½ teaspoon salt
2 Tablespoons butter, melted
¼ heaping cup brown sugar
1 teaspoon Vietnamese cinnamon

### WHAT YOU NEED TO DO

1. Preheat the oven to 425°F and grease the baking pan with butter.
2. Whisk the sourdough with the egg and oil in a large bowl until smooth.
3. Stir in the flour, baking powder, baking soda, and salt until everything comes together.
4. Sprinkle a flat surface with a bit of flour and empty the dough onto the counter. Knead it for just a few turns, until it's smooth, then roll it out to a rectangle about 8 × 12 inches.
5. Brush the dough with the melted butter and sprinkle the sugar and cinnamon evenly over top.
6. Roll the dough, starting from a short side. Cut the log into 8 to 12 evenly sized rolls. Place the rolls in the baking pan.
7. Bake on the middle rack for 15 to 20 minutes or until golden brown.
8. Remove from the oven and serve warm or cool completely in the pan on a wire rack.
9. Store in an airtight container and freeze any you don't eat within 24 hours.

### PRO TIP:

If you wait a few days and feed your Sweet Sourdough Starter (page 71) a few times, you can double this recipe and bake 12 large rolls in muffin tins. They're showstoppers.

# Sweet Sourdough Pancakes and Waffles

**MAKES** 4 servings
**TAKES** 20 to 30 minutes' active time
**RATING** All levels

These pancakes and waffles are a weekend staple in our home. Try them with Chokecherry Syrup (page 101) and a side of Billionaire's Bacon (page 315).

**WHAT YOU NEED TO GATHER**

Griddle or waffle maker
Large bowl
Measuring cups and spoons
Whisk
Spatula

Melted butter or cooking spray, to coat the griddle or waffle maker
1 cup Sweet Sourdough Starter (page 71)
2 eggs
1 teaspoon vanilla extract
½ cup milk
⅓ cup (for pancakes) or ½ cup (for waffles) sunflower or other neutral-tasting vegetable oil
1 cup flour
2 teaspoons baking powder
¼ teaspoon baking soda

**WHAT YOU NEED TO DO**

1. Heat a griddle or waffle maker and grease it with melted butter or cooking spray.
2. Whisk the sourdough starter, eggs, vanilla, milk, and oil in a large bowl until smooth. Gradually whisk in the flour, baking powder, and baking soda.
3. Pour the batter according to the size of pancakes or waffles you'd like. A ½ cup of batter per pancake or waffle works well.
4. If you're making pancakes, leave them on the griddle until bubbles form and the bottom is brown. Flip them and cook until golden on the underside as well. If you're making waffles, follow the cooking directions for your waffle maker.

### VARIATIONS:

Add 1 cup of chopped apples, bananas, berries, pecans, or bacon, or a mixture of these, to the batter for fun flavour changes.

# Sweet Sourdough Biscuits

**MAKES** 2 dozen
**TAKES** 15 minutes' active time + 10 to 15 minutes' baking time
**RATING** All levels

My younger sister Laurie reminded me that our family called these biscuits "Monster Muffins." We loved the fact that Mom had a "monstrous" blob of starter that she had to feed in the back of our refrigerator. She also reminded me that although this recipe calls for rolling out the biscuits, Mom just grated some cheese into the dough and dropped it by the Tablespoon onto a baking sheet. I love them rolled and cut, but they're pretty fantastic as "Monster Droppings" too. Enjoy these with Chicken and Wild Rice Soup (page 219) or Trail's End Classic Beef Stew (page 231).

**WHAT YOU NEED TO GATHER**

Measuring cups and spoons
Large bowl
Whisk
Wooden spoon
3-inch cookie cutter
Parchment paper
Baking sheet
Wire rack

2 cups flour, plus more for kneading
4 teaspoons baking powder
1 teaspoon baking soda
½ teaspoon salt
1 cup Sweet Sourdough Starter (page 71)
½ cup sunflower or other neutral-tasting vegetable oil

**WHAT YOU NEED TO DO**

1. Preheat the oven to 375°F.
2. Whisk the flour, baking powder, baking soda, and salt together in a bowl, then use a wooden spoon to stir in the sourdough and oil until the mix comes away from the side of the bowl.
3. Turn the batter out on a floured surface and knead it about 10 times.
4. Pat the dough into a flat disc about 1 inch thick.
5. Cut the dough into biscuits and transfer them to a parchment-lined baking sheet.
6. Bake on the middle rack of the oven until golden, 10 to 15 minutes.
7. Serve warm or remove to a wire rack to cool completely before storing in an airtight container for up to 24 hours or freezing for up to 2 weeks.

## VARIATIONS:

Add ½ cup of grated cheddar or parmesan and a few teaspoons of chopped fresh herbs to the batter for another savoury rendition. Or spread the tops with butter and sugar before baking, split them when they're done, and use them to make strawberry shortcakes with piles of berries and freshly whipped cream.

# Sweet Sourdough Fruit Strudel

**MAKES** 12 large or 24 dainty squares
**TAKES** 15 minutes' active time + 30 minutes' baking time
**RATING** All levels

Keep cherry pie filling, apple sauce, or Overnight Rhubarb Sauce (page 169) in your pantry, refrigerator, or freezer and use them in this recipe for the fastest dessert in the West.

**WHAT YOU NEED TO GATHER**

9 × 13-inch glass baking pan
Measuring cups and spoons
Stand mixer
Bowl

*For the cake*

Butter, to grease the baking pan
1 cup flour
2 Tablespoons sugar
½ teaspoon baking soda
½ teaspoon salt
1 cup Sweet Sourdough Starter (page 71)
¼ cup sunflower or other neutral-tasting vegetable oil

*For the fruit filling*

1 can cherry or apple pie filling or Overnight Rhubarb Sauce (page 169)

*For the topping*

1 cup flour
½ rounded cup brown sugar
½ cup butter, melted
½ teaspoon ground cinnamon

**WHAT YOU NEED TO DO**

*For the cake*

1. Preheat the oven to 350°F and grease the baking pan with butter.
2. Place the flour, sugar, baking soda, and salt in the bowl of a stand mixer fitted with the paddle attachment and add the sourdough and oil. Beat on slow speed until thoroughly mixed.
3. Press the mixture into the baking pan.

*For the fruit filling*

1. Spread the fruit filling of your choice over the dough base.

*For the topping*

1. Using your fingers, combine the flour, sugar, butter, and cinnamon in a bowl and sprinkle evenly over the fruit filling.

*To bake*

1. Bake on the middle rack until golden on top and cooked through on the bottom, about 30 minutes. A glass baking dish lets you see this clearly.
2. Serve with whipped cream or ice cream.

# Sweet Sourdough Banana Bread

**MAKES** 1 large loaf
**TAKES** 30 minutes' active time + 60 minutes' baking time
**RATING** All levels

Make this as one very large loaf or two to three smaller loaves. The bread is light and moist and the pecans crisp up during baking to add lots of flavour.

**WHAT YOU NEED TO GATHER**

Loaf pan
Parchment paper
Measuring cups and spoons
Stand mixer
Sifter
Large bowl
Spatula
Cake tester or toothpick
Wire rack

Butter, to grease the loaf pan
1 cup sugar
⅓ cup butter
1 egg
1 cup mashed banana (about 2 medium)
1 cup Sweet Sourdough Starter (page 71)
2 cups flour
1 teaspoon salt
1 teaspoon baking powder
½ teaspoon baking soda
¾ cup chopped pecans

**WHAT YOU NEED TO DO**

1. Preheat the oven to 350°F. Grease a loaf pan with butter and line it with parchment paper.
2. Place the sugar and butter in the bowl of a stand mixer fitted with the paddle attachment and beat on medium-high until creamy and fluffy. Add the egg and beat again until smooth.
3. Mix in the banana and sourdough starter on low speed.
4. Sift the flour with the salt, baking powder, and baking soda into a bowl and then add it and the pecans to the mixture in the stand mixer. Beat on low speed just until blended, then use a spatula to transfer the batter to the prepared loaf pan.
5. Bake on the middle rack until a cake tester or toothpick inserted in the centre comes out clean, 60 to 65 minutes.
6. Use the parchment paper to lift the loaf from the pan and let it cool on a wire rack.
7. Enjoy with butter and tea or coffee.

CHAPTER 3

# NEITHER HERE NOR THERE

This is when we have one foot in winter and one in not-winter. We're trying to move ahead in the year but we're stuck doing the splits. This neither here nor there time is also known as Alberta's spring.

Unlike other places, in Alberta the move into spring is no easy progression. In fact, Alberta singer-songwriter Ian Tyson has a song called "Springtime in Alberta" where he captures the mood of his lover and our spring weather perfectly. To paraphrase what he sings, seemingly endless skies of blue are chased away without a warning by another winter storm coming raging through. That's springtime in Alberta all right.

What can we do when our weather is akin to a temperamental lover who has us walking on eggshells? Slowly but surely the sun rises higher in the sky. It works its magic, the land begins to thaw, and spring blossoms. First Peoples and foragers know to walk softly on the land during this season, to be patient and observant, and to revel in the glory as nature reveals her generous bounty once again. Depending on the year and the part of the province, new life, manifesting as edible greens, delicate blossoms, and hard-to-find fungi, starts shooting up from the earth between April and June. In this chapter, I share foraging tips and recipes from Indigenous and forager friends that will help you make the most of these gifts.

### #EATALBERTAFIRST TIP:

Two of the great harbingers of spring from local farms and gardens are asparagus and rhubarb. The Alberta asparagus season is short but incredibly sweet (it tastes like fresh green peas). Look for it from mid-May until the end of June.

# Foraging 101: Exploring First Peoples' and Foraged Foods

Foraging is the act of acquiring food by hunting, fishing, or gathering edible plant matter. If you're going to head into Alberta's fields and forests in search of food, it's good to be clear about your motivation and to have a plan. There are a few (sometimes very physically) thorny issues you might want to think through before you venture out. You need a safe and legal place to forage and you need enough knowledge of plants that you won't eat something that will harm you. When you're starting out, it's a great help to have a mentor to help you develop knowledge of what's edible in your locale. But mostly, there's the possibility of free and delicious food.

Agriculture allowed our species to settle in one place. Cities evolved during the industrial age. We then gradually lost direct contact with the source of our food and came to expect an abundance of cheap and convenient food choices regardless of our geography or the season.

Compare this with the traditional lives of Indigenous people, who not only survived but also thrived thanks to their keen senses and knowledge of every local plant and animal species. Brenda Holder, owner of Mahikan Trails, which operates out of Sundre, Canmore, and Banff, is following in her family's footsteps as Cree guides of the Kwarakwante of Jasper, where she grew up. She offers guided walks and workshops where she not only identifies plants and shrubs but also shares the ways Indigenous people used them to survive for millennia. I have great respect for Holder's knowledge-keeping. Most of us are far removed from the connection between nature and our survival.

Today's massive food distribution systems mean that most of us "forage" at a modern grocery store, armed with cash or credit cards. You might wonder if foraging is a postmodern reaction to this. Or perhaps it's a Luddite-type statement or an extreme form of a 100-mile diet. Perhaps you see it as merely an elitist fad reserved for the wealthiest of palates in search of novel flavours. It could be a bit of all these or something entirely more practical.



JULIE WALKER OF FULL CIRCLE ADVENTURES

CRAFT

Time in nature is good for our mental and physical health. Time spent learning about edible plants also continues the transfer of local knowledge that would otherwise be lost.

I was fortunate to grow up fishing and picking wild strawberries, blueberries, raspberries, and fiddleheads with my family in New Brunswick. My brain has always liked to know the names of things in nature, and as I've matured I've made it a point to learn about Alberta's particular habitat. I've lived here for almost 40 years now. Slowly, I've grown as a home cook, gardener, and outdoors person.

Some of my favourite Alberta foraged food finds include wild rose petals, dandelion greens, broadleaf plantain, common blue violet flowers and leaves, tender young fireweed shoots, meadow rue leaves, horseradish root, spruce tips, wild strawberries, raspberries, huckleberries, juniper berries, stinging nettle, and puffball and morel mushrooms.

If you don't feel confident about foraging alone, you can enlist the help of experts. Joseph Brennan of Canadian FunGuy (page 362) offers backcountry foraging expeditions in Southern Alberta and BC. Kevin Kossowan of From the Wild (page 358) and Julie Walker of Full Circle Adventures (page 364) offer seasonal foraging walks near Edmonton and Turner Valley respectively. Walker advises would-be foragers to come prepared.

If you decide to embark on your own foraging expedition, here are a few things you might find useful to pop in your backpack:

- field guides for plant identification
- garden trowel for digging
- pocket knife
- garden scissors
- collapsible bag
- various sizes of resealable plastic bags for sorting and storage of different plants
- heavy gardening or latex gloves (it's wonderful to find stinging nettles but they're called *stinging* nettles for a reason)
- high waterproof boots
- wide-brimmed hat

- brightly coloured clothing in hunting season
- camera
- water bottle
- at least two guidebooks to help you identify which plants are edible (Walker also uses the following rhyme to help her remember the generalities of berry edibility: If it's white, don't bite; if it's red, use your head; if it's blue, it's good for you)

Foraging is not always about limits. If you get to know plants that are considered invasive, you can pick all you like because they are generally species that were accidentally (or thoughtlessly) introduced to North America. They have no natural predators here and replicate in a "noxious" way. Dandelions, garlic mustard, chicory, broadleaf plantain, and chickweed are great examples of these noxious but edible "weeds." When asked about the sustainability of foraging, Walker suggests the following guidelines: take only 5 percent of a healthy population of more than fifty plants that you see in any area and never pick in provincial or national parks. It's illegal.

QUINTON CROW SHOE, MEMBER OF THE PIIKANI FIRST NATION

In 2011, I was a scout and guide for a PBS TV documentary about Alberta's culture and cuisine. That story starts with the First Nations and their relationship with bison so I arranged a visit to Head-Smashed-In Buffalo Jump, a UNESCO World Heritage Site dating back over 6,000 years. There, we met with Quinton Crow Shoe, a cultural interpreter and member of the Piikani First Nation. Crow Shoe shared how First Peoples used every part of the animal. He also shared a Piikani prophesy that both the bison and First Peoples would nearly die out but that both would come back to prosper once again. The bison have returned. Now, it is time for the people to thrive again.

Walker urges caution when picking in areas where plants may have been sprayed with pesticides or herbicides such as along roadsides. You also need permission before you pick on private property. She's expanded her access to the plants she loves—such as horseradish, lamb's quarters, and saskatoon berry bushes—by cultivating a "wild garden" in her backyard.

Mushrooms are perhaps the pièce de résistance of foraging but only a tiny fraction are actually edible; the rest can kill you. Untamed Feast and Canadian FunGuy are two Alberta companies that have turned foraging for mushrooms (and other wild edible plants) into viable commercial enterprises providing employment in communities where opportunities were previously lacking. These experts forage sustainably in places so remote there is no fear of exhausting nature's bounty. The success of these Alberta companies is surely a sign that foraging has become such a rare skill that people will pay a premium for these products. But, again, when it comes to mushrooms, the good-tasting edible ones are rare.

Eric Whitehead of Untamed Feast knows about 100 edible mushrooms of the 4,500 to 5,000 that grow in North America. But, he says, "Just because it's edible doesn't mean it's incredible!" According to Whitehead, "There are really only about 10 or 12 mushrooms that are worth harvesting for the flavour they deliver—especially if you are harvesting them commercially."

I've experienced the thrill of finding morels, but more than that, I've learned to forage with integrity and the time I've spent on this land has yielded much more than delicious, nutritious food. It's brought me a deeper appreciation of nature itself.

**OPPOSITE:** CHOKECHERRIES; **LEFT:** SPRUCE TIPS FOR TEA; **RIGHT:** FORAGED MEADOW RUE, NETTLE, AND VIOLETS

# Chokecherry Syrup

**MAKES** 15 cups
**TAKES** 6 hours total (with fairly constant attention)
**RATING** Proficient

Two days before her unexpected death in 2020, I asked my friend Amy Willier if she'd contribute a recipe to this book. Amy and her mother, Yvonne Jobin, were partners of Alberta Food Tours' Canadian Signature Experience tour in Calgary's Inglewood through their business, Moonstone Creation. Cree Elders, they shared what bison and saskatoon berries meant to Indigenous people with guests from around the world. Amy knew exactly what recipe she wanted to share: Chokecherry Syrup. She'd spotted some chokecherries near her home the previous summer and made a makeshift sack from her shirt to transport them home for this favourite treat. Amy enjoyed it drizzled over pancakes. You can also pour it on ice cream or cheesecake, use it as a basting glaze for poultry or pork, or use it as a tart ingredient in a salad dressing. I love to add a Tablespoonful to soda water for a refreshing fruit cordial with ice and mint.

**WHAT YOU NEED TO GATHER**

Jars
Baking sheet
Lids and rings
Small saucepan
Measuring cups and spoons
Large bowl
Colander
Large pot
Fine mesh sieve
Small bowl
Wide-mouth funnel
Dishcloth
Lid lifter
Canning bath
Jar lifter
Terry cloth towel

12 cups cleaned chokecherries
12 cups sugar
½ cup store-bought orange juice
1 Tablespoon bottled lemon juice

**WHAT YOU NEED TO DO**

1. Put your canning jars through the dishwasher to sanitize them and place them on a baking sheet in a 200°F oven until needed. Place the rings and lids in a small saucepan of boiled water.
2. Dump the chokecherries into a large bowl and cover with water. The bad fruit and any loose stems or other debris will float to the surface. Skim those off, strain the chokecherries through a colander and return them to the bowl, refill the pot with water, clear off any remaining debris, and repeat the process a few times until there is no more debris. Drain the fruit a final time and remove any large stems from the fruit clusters but don't worry about the smaller ones.
3. Place the cleaned chokecherries in a large pot and add just enough water to cover them. Bring to a boil on high heat, then reduce to a simmer and stir occasionally until the juice turns a dark mauve, about 30 minutes.
4. Strain the juice through a fine mesh sieve over a large bowl. Gently press on the chokecherry pulp in the sieve to get all the liquid, but be careful not to mash it, as you want the juice to be clear. Clean the pot, as you'll need it again.
5. Measure the juice after it has been strained. You should have about 12 cups. If you have less, you can halve this recipe. Or you can put the chokecherry pulp back in the pot, add enough water to cover the pulp, boil it for another 30 minutes, and press it again to get the right amount of juice.

6 Place the still warm juice in the clean pot. If it's not warm, heat it up until just warm. Don't let it boil. Stir in the sugar and the orange and lemon juices and cook over medium heat until the sugar dissolves. Now increase the heat to medium-high and stir while bringing it to a boil. Reduce the heat to low and then simmer for about 3 to 4 hours with just an occasional stir to check the consistency. Test to see if the juice has reached a syrup consistency at the 3-hour point by pouring a little into a small bowl, placing it in the refrigerator, and allowing it to cool completely. It's easier to judge how syrupy it is once it's cooled. Once the syrup has reached the desired consistency, it's time to preserve it.
7 Use a funnel to pour the hot syrup into the prepared jars, leaving about ½ inch of headspace. Wipe the lip of each jar with a clean, damp dishcloth and use the lid lifter to lift the lid. Wipe it dry and place it on top of the jar. Apply the ring loosely and set aside until you have completed all of the jars.
8 Fill a canner or large pot about a third full with warm water. Gently place the jars inside the rack, and lower it into the water. Make sure the jars are covered by about 1 inch of water, but not much more than that (you may need to add more water or take some out). Raise the heat on the stove to high and let the water come to a boil, then reduce the heat to medium-high to let it gently boil for 10 minutes. Carefully remove the jars from the canner with a jar lifter. Wrap them in the towel so they cool slowly. You should hear gentle pops as the jars seal. Keep any jars that don't seal in your refrigerator and eat them up over the next few weeks.

# Colton's Bannock

**MAKES** 12 bannock biscuits
**TAKES** 10 to 13 minutes' active time + 17 minutes' baking time
**RATING** All levels

The word "bannock" comes from the Gaelic word meaning morsels. The Scottish brought their bannock recipe to Canada and made it with oats and wheat. But long before they arrived, Indigenous people made a bannock-like bread with flours of ground maize, roots, or bulbs. As colonization progressed, white flour and sugar took the place of the previously healthy ingredients. My friend Yvonne Jobin, a Cree Elder from Northern Alberta, says, "Our Native people tend to forget how we've accepted some aspects of colonization and adapted things as our own, like bannock." While many aspects of colonization have been traumatic, bannock not only is popular but also is both a celebratory and a comfort food for many reasons. It's tasty. And it's versatile: it can be baked, fried, or wrapped around a stick and toasted over a campfire. Yvonne halved her usual recipe to teach it to her grandson, Colton Willier. Hence the name. Double it, if you like.

**WHAT YOU NEED TO GATHER**

Measuring cups and spoons
Large bowl
3-inch cookie cutter
Baking sheet

2½ cups unbleached all-purpose flour
½ cup whole wheat flour
½ cup skim milk powder
3 Tablespoons baking powder
2 Tablespoons organic cane or brown sugar
½ teaspoon salt
½ cup softened salted butter, cubed
1 cup lukewarm water

**WHAT YOU NEED TO DO**

1. Preheat the oven to 425°F.
2. Mix both flours, the milk powder, baking powder, sugar, and salt together in a large bowl. Use your hands to rub the softened butter into the flour mixture until it is well distributed and the mixture has clumps the size of small peas or lentils.
3. Add ¾ cup of the water and bring the mixture together using the fingers of one hand. Slowly add the remaining water until all the flour at the bottom of the bowl joins the rest to form a soft and smooth dough ball.
4. Flatten the dough on a floured surface until it's ½ inch thick.
5. Use a cookie cutter to cut the dough into pieces, and spread them on the (ungreased) baking sheet.
6. Place the baking sheet on the middle rack in the oven and bake until golden, about 17 minutes. If you like, you can brush the top of the bannock with a dab of butter just after you take it from the oven.
7. Enjoy warm with soups or stews or at tea time with butter and jam.

## VARIATIONS:

Yvonne sometimes replaces a quarter of the flour with oats and throws in a Tablespoon of flaxseeds for fibre. For a sweet bannock, she'll add a few Tablespoons of raisins or saskatoon berries. For savoury, she adds ¼ cup grated cheese and 1 teaspoon dried herbs. Yvonne says, "My mom made what she called Lazy Bannock. She'd add a bit more liquid and drop it by spoonfuls on a greased baking sheet." And last but not least, when Yvonne wants to turn bannock into fry bread, she adds a lightly beaten egg with the water. After she flattens the dough, she cuts it in squares, slices the squares almost the whole way through the middle crosswise, and then deep-fries the butterflied pieces until golden, 5 to 10 minutes, in vegetable oil heated to 350°F. Her final word on bannock? "Have fun with it!"

# Morel Mushroom Cheese Spread

**MAKES** 8 to 12 servings
**TAKES** 30 minutes' hydrating time + 20 minutes' active time + 4 hours' chilling time
**RATING** All levels

Eric and Michelle Whitehead are foragers extraordinaire. They are based out of St. Albert and own Untamed Feast, which specializes in the sustainable harvesting of Canada's wild foods. Fifty percent of their mushrooms come from Alberta's boreal forests. This morel-based dip is an absolute flavour bomb that's going to be your new favourite to take to parties and potlucks. You can use morels or a mix of wild mushrooms. I love using pure morels.

**WHAT YOU NEED TO GATHER**

Measuring cups and spoons
Small bowl
Knife
Cutting board
Frying pan
Wooden spoon
Spatula
Plastic wrap

1 cup (approximately 20 grams) dried morel or mixed wild mushrooms
½ cup hot tap water
2 Tablespoons butter or olive oil
½ cup diced onion
2 cloves garlic, minced
8-ounce (250-gram) package cream cheese, goat cheese, or spreadable vegan substitute
¼ teaspoon salt
Pinch pepper
Edible flowers and fresh herbs, for garnish (optional)

**WHAT YOU NEED TO DO**

1. Put the mushrooms in a small bowl and cover with the hot water. Let sit until soft, about 30 minutes, then squeeze them gently over the bowl to remove the water. Reserve the water. Finely chop the mushrooms and set them aside.
2. Heat the butter (or oil) in a frying pan over medium heat, add the onion, and cook until golden, about 5 to 10 minutes, then add the garlic and cook until fragrant, about 30 seconds.
3. Stir in the chopped, rehydrated mushrooms and cook, stirring occasionally, until dry.
4. Stir in the reserved mushroom liquid, reduce the heat to medium-low, and cook down, stirring occasionally, until dry again. This is the key step. The slower you let this happen, the more mushroom flavour you will get.
5. Remove from the stove once all the liquid is absorbed, and let the mixture cool.
6. Soften the cream cheese with a wooden spoon, add the mushroom mixture, salt, and pepper, and blend well. Use a spatula to transfer it to a plastic wrap–lined bowl, press it evenly, cover with more wrap, and refrigerate until firm, at least 4 hours.
7. Invert the cheese spread onto a serving platter and sprinkle with fresh herbs and edible flowers, if desired.
8. Enjoy it with bread, crackers, or chips; on a potato, burger, pork chop, or steak—or just eat it with a spoon.

## PRO TIP FROM MICHELLE AND ERIC:

Make this dip ahead. The flavour develops more fully if it sits for a day in the refrigerator before eating.

# Forest Mushroom Barley Salad

**MAKES** 4 to 6 servings
**TAKES** 30 minutes' hydrating time + 20 minutes' active time
**RATING** All levels

This recipe comes from one of my favourite restaurants in Alberta, Twisted Fork in St. Paul. Its delightful chef/owner, Deb Poulin, has both Red and Blue Seal certifications and close to 40 years' experience as a culinary professional and instructor. Poulin has her finger on the pulse of what the 200-plus farmers in Alberta's Lakeland region are growing. It's her mission to bring those flavours, and those of her Métis heritage, to the table in her restaurant. This recipe celebrates Alberta's bountiful barley supply and our access to wild mushrooms. Enjoy it on its own or as a side with beef, poultry, fish, or Bison Meatloaf with Cranberry Barbecue Glaze (page 113).

**WHAT YOU NEED TO GATHER**

Bowls
Medium saucepan
Measuring cups and spoons
Knife
Cutting board
Frying pan
Wooden spoon
Whisk
Zester

*For the salad*

½ cup dried wild mushrooms (morels, chanterelles, oyster, or a mix of your favourites)
½ cup hot tap water
2 cups cold water
1½ cups quick-cooking barley
2 Tablespoons butter
2 cups mushrooms (cremini, button, oyster, morels, or a mixture of your favourites), finely diced
2 stalks celery, finely diced
1 red onion, finely diced
1 clove garlic, minced
½ teaspoon dried or 1 teaspoon chopped fresh thyme
½ teaspoon dried or 1 teaspoon chopped fresh oregano
4 ounces dry white wine
Salt and pepper

*For the vinaigrette*

½ cup canola oil
¼ cup white balsamic vinegar
1 lemon, juiced and zested
2 teaspoons dried or 2 Tablespoons finely chopped fresh chives
Salt and pepper
Zest of 1 lemon, for garnish

## PRO TIP:

I always save mushroom water to add to soups and sauces.

### #EATALBERTAFIRST TIP:

I buy my quick-cooking barley from Innisfail Growers (page 359).

**WHAT YOU NEED TO DO**

*For the salad*

1 Put the mushrooms in a small bowl and cover with the hot water. Let sit until soft, about 30 minutes.
2 Pour 2 cups of cold water into a medium saucepan, add the barley, and bring to a boil over medium-high heat. Reduce the heat to medium and cook until tender, about 15 minutes. Drain and set aside to cool.
3 Drain the softened mushrooms and dice them.
4 Melt the butter in a frying pan over medium heat, stir in the fresh mushrooms, celery, and onion, and cook until soft, about 5 minutes, then add the reconstituted wild mushrooms and minced garlic and cook, stirring, for about 5 minutes more. You want most of the juices to evaporate.
5 Stir in the thyme and oregano, followed by the wine, and season with salt and pepper to taste. Cook for 2 to 3 minutes more, just to warm everything through and allow the flavours to meld. Remove from the heat, and let cool.

*For the vinaigrette and assembly*

1 Whisk the oil, balsamic, and lemon juice with the chives in a medium bowl. Season with salt and pepper. Set aside.
2 Combine the reserved barley and mushroom mixture in a large bowl and stir in the vinaigrette. Toss lightly. Taste and adjust the salt and pepper as needed.
3 Garnish with the lemon zest.

BIG BEEHIVE IN THE FOREGROUND WITH MT. LEFROY (BEHIND RIGHT) AND MT. ABERDEEN (LEFT) NEAR LAKE LOUISE

# Bison Meatloaf with Cranberry Barbecue Glaze

**MAKES** 6 servings
**TAKES** 30 minutes' active time + 60 minutes' baking time
**RATING** All levels

This recipe comes from my friend Cindy Lazarenko, who is a Métis chef. Cindy's one of my favourite people to cook with because she has a wonderful taste memory and knows how to put flavours together: in this case, the essential umami of Alberta bison and the sweet-tart mix of cranberries, mustard, barbecue sauce, and birch or maple syrup. Enjoy with Forest Mushroom Barley Salad (page 109) or Shades of Green Salad (page 129). This also makes fabulous meatloaf sandwiches if you have any left over.

**WHAT YOU NEED TO GATHER**

Loaf pan
Measuring cups and spoons
Knife
Cutting board
Bowls

*For the meatloaf*
2 lb ground bison
2 cloves garlic, minced
1 carrot, grated
½ medium onion, finely chopped
½ cup bread crumbs
1 teaspoon dried sage
1 teaspoon dried thyme
½ teaspoon salt
½ teaspoon pepper
2 eggs, lightly beaten
1 Tablespoon canola oil
1 Tablespoon Worcestershire sauce

*For the glaze*
½ cup highbush cranberry sauce (or regular cranberry sauce)
¼ cup Alberta-made barbecue sauce
2 Tablespoons maple syrup or birch syrup
2 teaspoons Dijon mustard

**WHAT YOU NEED TO DO**

*For the meatloaf*

1. Preheat the oven to 350°F and oil or grease a loaf pan.
2. Mix the bison, garlic, carrot, onion, bread crumbs, sage, thyme, salt, pepper, eggs, oil, and Worcestershire together in a bowl using your hands. Form the mixture into a loaf and place in the prepared pan.

*For the glaze and to bake*

1. Mix the cranberry sauce, barbecue sauce, syrup, and mustard together in a bowl.
2. Spread half the glaze over the top of the meatloaf. Reserve the other half to serve on the side with your meal.
3. Bake until the internal temperature reaches 160°F, about 1 hour.
4. Let the meatloaf rest in the pan for about 10 minutes before slicing.

# Buffalo Trail Bison Burgers

**MAKES** 8 patties
**TAKES** 25 minutes' active time + 5 to 10 minutes' resting time + minimum 2 hours' chilling time for the patties before cooking
**RATING** All levels

Here's another great recipe from chef Deb Poulin. She sources her bison from a ranch called Buffalo Trail. I thought the name was perfect for this recipe too. At Poulin's restaurant, Twisted Fork, they serve this burger with caramelized onions, cheese, spicy Blueberry Jalapeño Jam (page 203), lettuce, and bacon. Those items aren't listed in this recipe, but by all means, go for it. Or when you're in the Lakeland region, do what I do: pop into Twisted Fork and get one hot off the grill. (Even cooks need a day off!)

**WHAT YOU NEED TO GATHER**

Measuring spoons
Large bowl
Plate
Wax paper
Pastry brush
Flipper
Instant-read thermometer

2½ lb ground bison
1 Tablespoon onion powder
1 Tablespoon garlic powder
2 teaspoons minced fresh garlic
1½ teaspoons ground coriander
1½ teaspoons dry mustard
1½ teaspoons ground black pepper
1 teaspoon salt
½ teaspoon dry or 1 teaspoon finely chopped fresh rosemary
1 Tablespoon Worcestershire sauce
Sunflower oil as needed

**WHAT YOU NEED TO DO**

1. Place the bison, onion and garlic powders, fresh garlic, coriander, mustard, salt and pepper, rosemary, and Worcestershire sauce in a large bowl and mix thoroughly with your hands.
2. Divide the meat into 8 equal portions and form them into patties. Place them on a plate, separated with wax paper, and refrigerate for a minimum of 2 hours (the longer the better, up to 8 hours is acceptable) to set.
3. Preheat the barbecue grill so that a medium-hot grill surface of 475°F to 500°F is maintained.
4. Brush some sunflower oil on the top side of the burgers. Quickly grease the preheated grill with a rag or paper towel soaked with more sunflower oil. Place the burgers on the preheated grill, oiled side down.
5. Grill the burgers, keeping the lid closed, for 4 minutes without disturbing them. Flip the burgers and cook on the other side for 3 minutes.
6. Flip the seared burgers twice more over the next 4 to 6 minutes, or until an internal temperature of 135°F to 140°F is reached for a medium-rare burger. Check with an instant-read digital stick thermometer to be sure. After the burgers come off the grill, allow them to rest for 5 to 10 minutes before serving.

## PRO TIP:

Sunflower oil is your best option for this recipe. It tolerates high heat, is neutral-tasting, and won't add a burnt taste to the burgers.

# Tourtière Canadienne

**MAKES** Two 9-inch pies
**TAKES** 1 hour active time + 10 minutes to 24 hours' pastry resting time + 45 minutes' baking time
**RATING** Proficient

Chef Deb Poulin shared her Mère Poulin's Métis recipe for Tourtière Canadienne and it got me thinking about my Robicheau family's Acadian French background. When my grandfather left Meteghan, Nova Scotia, to find work across the Bay of Fundy in New Brunswick during the Depression, he stopped speaking French. But the culture is prominent enough that tourtière is still part of our Christmas traditions. For many years, my mom came to Alberta and made dozens of these savoury meat pies for my friends and me to enjoy over the holidays. This recipe is a blend of Deb's mom's recipe and my mom's recipe. Enjoy with Green Tomato Chow Chow (page 195) and Never-the-Same-Way-Twice Coleslaw (page 139) or Green Beans with Herbs (page 335).

**WHAT YOU NEED TO GATHER**

Measuring cups and spoons
Large bowl
Pastry blender
Metal slotted spoon
Dinner knife
Kitchen knife
Cutting board
Potato peeler
Saucepan
Large frying pan
Wooden spoon
Rolling pin
Two 9-inch pie plates
Small bowl
Whisk
Pastry brush

*For the pie crust*

4 level cups flour, plus more for rolling
½ teaspoon baking powder
¼ teaspoon salt
1 lb chilled shortening
2 cups ice water
1 egg, for egg wash (optional)
1 Tablespoon milk (any type), for egg wash (optional)

*For the filling*

3 or 4 yellow-fleshed potatoes
2 teaspoons olive oil
1 cup diced onion
1 lb ground beef
1 lb ground pork
⅔ cup water
½ teaspoon ground cinnamon
½ teaspoon ground cloves
½ teaspoon celery salt
½ teaspoon dried summer savory
½ teaspoon salt
½ teaspoon white pepper
¼ teaspoon freshly ground black pepper

## MULTIPLY AND/OR MAKE AHEAD:

This recipe multiplies well. Uncooked tourtières can be frozen for up to 3 months. Cook from frozen at 375°F for 60 to 90 minutes.

When it comes to shortening, I generally use regular Crisco when making tourtière pastry but if I'm making fruit pies, I'll often switch it up to 1 cup shortening and 1 cup butter.

#### WHAT YOU NEED TO DO

*For the pie crust*

1 Combine the flour, baking powder, and salt in a large bowl.
2 Blend the shortening into the flour mixture with a pastry blender until it resembles coarse pea-sized lumps. Form a well in the centre and set aside.
3 Use the 2 cups of ice water to pour exactly 250 ml into a measuring cup. Be sure you measure out 250 ml and not just 1 cup, as 250 ml is slightly more. Pour this water into the well you made in the flour mixture and stir with a metal slotted spoon until it comes together as a dough.
4 Use a dinner knife to compress and shape the dough into a mound in the bowl.
5 Let the dough rest in the bowl, covered, in the refrigerator for at least 10 minutes or until the filling is ready (up to 24 hours).

*For the filling*

1 Peel and quarter the potatoes, place them in a saucepan of cold salted water, and bring to a boil on high heat. Once the water is boiling, reduce the heat to a low boil and cook the potatoes until a knife pierces them with ease. Drain and reserve the water. Use enough of the hot potato water to mash the potatoes and remove any lumps. Set them aside to cool. Meanwhile, you can start making the rest of the filling.
2 Heat a large frying pan on medium heat. Add the oil and onions and cook the onions until they turn translucent.
3 Stir in the ground beef, pork, and water and cook until browned, using a wooden spoon to break the meat into fine crumbs. This could take 10 to 15 minutes.
4 Drain off any excess oil and place the meat and onion mixture back in the pan.
5 Stir in the cinnamon, cloves, celery salt, summer savory, salt, and both peppers until well distributed.
6 Mix in the mashed potatoes, remove from the heat, taste and adjust the seasoning as desired, and cool the mixture to at least room temperature.

*For assembly*

1 Get the dough out of the refrigerator. Preheat the oven to 375°F.
2 Cut the dough into 4 unequal pieces. You want 2 slightly larger portions for the bottom crusts.
3 Choose a bottom portion and use your hands to shape it into a disc.
4 Flour a flat surface and roll your rolling pin through the flour.
5 Place the disc on the floured surface and begin to roll it out, pressing lightly with the rolling pin from the centre out. Use very light pressure and move the rolling pin around to keep the dough forming a round shape.
6 Lift the dough as necessary and sprinkle the surface with more flour to keep the dough from sticking. When you reach the diameter of the pie plate you are using, fold the dough over your rolling pin and transfer it to the bottom of one of your pie plates.
7 Add half the filling, roll out a top crust using the same technique described above, and then crimp the 2 crusts together by folding the top over the bottom and pinching the dough lightly between the thumbs and forefingers of each hand as you go around the diameter of the pie.
8 Repeat with the remaining ingredients.
9 Cut vents in the top of each pie and, if you like, brush them with an egg wash of 1 egg whisked with 1 Tablespoon milk.
10 Bake until golden, about 45 minutes.

## VARIATION:

You can use this pie crust recipe for fruit and berry pies. Just fill the base of the pie with fruit until it is mounded and add a mixture of 1 cup sugar, 3 Tablespoons flour, and a few drops of fresh or bottled lemon juice. Depending on the sweetness of the fruit in your pie, you may need a little more or less than the 1 cup of sugar.

# Foraged Mushroom Cream Sauce with Poached Fish

**MAKES** 2 servings
**TAKES** 30 minutes' hydrating time + 30 minutes' active time
**RATING** All levels

The sauce in this recipe is an easy-to-multiply classic. It's got depth of flavour from the umami bomb of the wild mushrooms, the sherry, and, of course, the cream. I've used it here to poach and serve with fish. But it also makes a fabulous sauce for bison, beef, or pork chops. Make your favourite kind of rice to enjoy with the fish or Fluffy Mashed Potatoes (page 331) if you're going the steak or chop route.

**WHAT YOU NEED TO GATHER**

Knife
Cutting board
Measuring cups and spoons
Small saucepan
Sieve
Frying pan with a lid
Lemon juicer and zester

1 cup dried morel or mixed wild mushrooms
1 cup boiling water
2 Tablespoons unsalted butter
1 large shallot, diced
2 Tablespoons dry sherry
½ teaspoon salt
2 teaspoons dried or 2 Tablespoons chopped fresh chives, divided
½ teaspoon dried or 1 teaspoon fresh thyme
1 cup whipping cream
2 Tablespoons lemon juice
Two 4-ounce white fish fillets (halibut, cod, ling cod, or pickerel), washed and dried
Pepper to taste
Zest of 1 lemon
2 sprigs fresh thyme

**WHAT YOU NEED TO DO**

1. Place the morels in a large measuring cup and pour in the boiling water to cover them. Let soak for at least 30 minutes, then drain, reserving the water. Strain the water through a fine sieve into a small saucepan. Simmer over medium heat until reduced to ¼ cup, 10 to 15 minutes. Set aside to cool.
2. Melt the butter in a frying pan over medium heat and cook the shallots until translucent, about 5 minutes.
3. Stir in the mushrooms, reserved mushroom liquid, sherry, and salt and cook until almost dry, about 5 minutes.
4. Stir half the chives, the thyme, cream, and lemon juice into the mushroom mixture, then make a well in the middle and add the fish. Cover the pan with a lid and poach the fish for 5 minutes per inch of thickness.
5. Taste the sauce and adjust the salt and add pepper to taste.
6. Plate the fish topped with the mushroom mixture.
7. Enjoy over rice, garnished with the remaining chives, the lemon zest, and a sprig of thyme.

# Saskatoon and Apple Crumbly Crisp

**MAKES** 6 to 8 servings
**TAKES** 20 minutes' active time + 60 minutes' baking time
**RATING** All levels

Here's another wonderful recipe from Yvonne Jobin. Yvonne loves to pick saskatoon berries in season and dry them for use through the winter just like her mother did before her. Whether you use fresh, dried, or frozen berries in this recipe, the juicy apples will plump them up.

**WHAT YOU NEED TO GATHER**

9 × 13-inch baking dish
Knife
Cutting board
Measuring cups and spoons
Large bowl

*For the filling*

8 cups chopped apple (I like to leave the peel on)
2 cups saskatoon berries
¼ cup packed light brown sugar
1 Tablespoon unbleached all-purpose flour
Zest of 1 lemon

*For the crumbly crisp topping*

1¼ cups quick-cooking oats
1¼ cups unbleached all-purpose flour
¾ cup packed light brown sugar
¼ cup granulated sugar
1 teaspoon ground cinnamon
½ teaspoon salt
¼ teaspoon baking powder
¾ cup unsalted butter, melted

**WHAT YOU NEED TO DO**

1 Preheat the oven to 350°F and butter a 9 × 13-inch baking dish.

*For the filling*

1 Toss the apples and berries with the sugar, flour, and lemon zest in a bowl until evenly coated. Place the mixture in the baking dish, then press on it until it is lightly and uniformly packed into the dish.

*For the topping and to bake*

1 Place the oats, flour, both sugars, cinnamon, salt, baking powder, and melted butter in a large bowl and mix together with your fingers until the butter is evenly distributed.
2 Spread the topping evenly over the fruit filling and bake until the topping is golden and the juices are thick, about 60 minutes.
3 Enjoy with whipped cream or ice cream.

CHAPTER 4

FULL-ON
SUMMER

Spring might creep in, but for the summer part of Alberta's "not-winter" season, nature cranks the sun up to hot and it hits us full on. Most of the days in this season coalesce in July and August. But depending on our proximity to the North or the Rockies, we can still have occasional periods of snow even in these months. One year in Banff it snowed so much EVERY month that my friend Jeffrey Carpenter stopped talking about summer at all. Weather in the Rockies can be fickle at the best of times but that year they were permanently stuck in "Neither Here nor There" and Jeffrey gave up hope of summer and just counted the number of winters they were experiencing that year.

No matter. When we do get summer in Alberta, it's extraordinary and we all take in as much of it as we can. Even the sun. It rises early and lasts late into the night. We cycle, raft, hike, golf, sit on the porch, gather around the fire, stargaze, camp, go RVing, and do road trips. I often feel we live two days in one this time of year. I love it.

If you drive around the province in summer, you'll see fields of gold canola, purple flax, and green barley, oats, and wheat. U-picks open as their crops ripen. Each week at the farmers' markets brings more excitement at the prospect of discovering what's fresh from the fields.

# Celebrating the Bounty of Summer and Food Day Canada

This is the time of year we gorge on berries and greens like grizzlies on a late summer feeding frenzy. Spring's asparagus is the harbinger that Mother Earth's soil is about to perform a summer-long miracle. Farmers sow their seeds and transplants and pray to the weather gods for heat units, moisture, and a season free from hail. July and August deliver a bounty of vegetables. This is true across Canada, and that's why we celebrate Food Day Canada on the Saturday of every August long weekend.

My good friend the late Anita Stewart founded this day in 2003. It was originally called the World's Longest Barbecue (WLBBQ) and was launched countrywide in response to sanctions on beef exports imposed by Canada's largest trading partner. Anita organized chefs and groups across the country to buy Canadian beef and grill it in a show of support for the agricultural communities that were so badly affected by the sanctions. According to Food Day Canada, the day has grown into a celebration "when we share Canada's rich culinary heritage, our delicious Northern bounty and the best managed food system on the planet."

It's fun to plan a bountiful menu for Food Day Canada and any other excuse that comes along to be outside for summer gatherings while we can. The recipes I share in this chapter are designed to help you savour every ounce of summer. They are all about fuelling your next adventure.

# Shades of Green Salad with Alberta Vinaigrette

**MAKES** 6 servings (as a starter or side)
**TAKES** 15 minutes' active time
**RATING** All levels

At Alberta Food Tours, we often create an experience where we change a classic French vinaigrette into an Alberta vinaigrette starring two of Alberta's signature foods, canola and honey. Using an Alberta-made mustard instead of one from Dijon (which ironically is most likely made from Alberta mustard seeds) takes it to another level and makes me absurdly happy. We get our guests to do the whisking, and once they see how easy it is to make their own vinaigrette, they're hooked. And that, my friends, is what it's really all about.

### WHAT YOU NEED TO GATHER

Knife
Cutting board
Measuring cups and spoons
Platter
Medium bowl
Whisk
Tongs

*For the salad*

1 cup watercress, arugula, or pea shoots
2 cups butter lettuce, green frisée, or baby romaine (or a combo of these)
1 green pepper, cut lengthwise in 8 strips and then sliced diagonally
6 baby cucumbers, ends removed and sliced diagonally with skin on
2 ribs of celery, sliced diagonally
1 ripe avocado, halved, pitted, and sliced diagonally
3 scallions, sliced diagonally

*For the vinaigrette*

2 Tablespoons vinegar
Salt
2 teaspoons Alberta honey
2 teaspoons Alberta-made mustard
6 Tablespoons organic canola oil
Pepper

### WHAT YOU NEED TO DO

*For the salad*

1 Arrange the vegetables on a platter, starting with the watercress around the outside and working in with the lettuce leaves in a circular pattern before topping with the green pepper, cucumbers, celery, avocado, and finally the scallions.

*For the vinaigrette*

1 Whisk the vinegar with a pinch of salt in a medium bowl until the salt dissolves.
2 Add the honey and mustard to the bowl and whisk to a smooth paste.
3 Drizzle the oil into the mix slowly, whisking continuously until the dressing is thick and creamy.
4 Season with pepper to taste.
5 Drizzle the vinaigrette over the salad on the platter just before serving.

## VARIATIONS:

- Make it a Hungry Bear Salad by adding a handful of fresh berries and chopped grilled salmon or trout as desired.
- Add 1 to 2 Tablespoons of mixed chopped herbs like dill, parsley, tarragon, mint, basil, or chives to the dressing to create an Alberta Herb Vinaigrette.

# Creamy (No Cream) Asparagus Soup

**MAKES** 4 to 6 servings
**TAKES** 40 minutes' active time
**RATING** All levels

The potatoes give this soup a creamy texture once it's puréed. It freezes well, so don't worry if you have leftovers. I buy one of Edgar Farms' 5-pound bags of imperfect asparagus and quadruple this recipe to make enough to get me through the long Alberta winter.

**WHAT YOU NEED TO GATHER**

Large stockpot with lid
Measuring cups and spoons
Knife
Cutting board
Vitamix or other high-speed blender

1 teaspoon extra virgin olive oil
1 teaspoon butter (or olive oil for a vegan soup)
1 yellow onion, finely chopped
3 stalks celery, chopped
1 clove garlic, chopped
4 cups chicken or vegetable broth
2 medium-sized yellow-fleshed potatoes, peeled and chopped
1 bunch asparagus, cleaned and chopped in 2-inch pieces (save a few of the tips for a garnish)
1 small head romaine lettuce
Salt and pepper
Chive or other edible flowers, for garnish (optional)

**WHAT YOU NEED TO DO**

1. Heat the stockpot over medium heat. Add the oil and butter, followed by the onion and celery, and cook until the onion is translucent, about 10 minutes.
2. Stir in the garlic and cook just until fragrant, about 1 minute. Then add the broth and potatoes. Cover with a lid, raise the heat to medium-high, and simmer briskly until the potatoes are tender, about 15 minutes.
3. Add the asparagus, and cover, reduce the heat to medium again, and cook until fork-tender, about 5 minutes. Add the romaine lettuce (this is the secret ingredient that keeps your soup bright green) and cook for 2 more minutes or until heated through.
4. Transfer the contents of the soup pot to a Vitamix and purée until smooth. Depending on the size of your blender, you may have to do this in batches.
5. Return the soup to the pot, add salt and pepper to taste, and reheat.
6. Garnish with a few of the asparagus tips you saved and some chive blossoms or other edible flowers, if desired.
7. Enjoy hot as is or drizzle with a bit of cream if you like a thinner consistency.

# Hot Pepper Cornbread

**MAKES** 12 large pieces or muffins
**TAKES** 20 minutes' active time + 20 to 25 minutes' baking time + 10 minutes' cooling time
**RATING** All levels

I love how moist this cornbread is. Though the recipe calls for making it in a square baking pan, I've also used a cast-iron pan, a 12-cup muffin tin, and two small loaf pans. I like to toast any leftover slices and drizzle them with honey. I find this keeps my inner Pooh Bear very happy. Enjoy as a side with Lip-Smacking, Finger-Licking, Messy, Good Ribs (page 157), Chipotle Bison Chili (page 227), or Trail's End Classic Beef Stew (page 231).

**WHAT YOU NEED TO GATHER**

8 × 8-inch baking pan or 12-cup muffin tin
Parchment paper
Measuring cups and spoons
Large bowl
Wooden spoon
Can opener
Wire rack

1½ cups flour
1 cup cornmeal
¼ cup cane sugar
4 teaspoons baking powder
½ teaspoon salt
2 large eggs, lightly beaten
14-ounce (398 ml) can creamed corn
1 cup skim milk
¼ cup whipping cream or 2 teaspoons canola oil
½ cup diced pickled banana peppers
½–1 jalapeño, seeded and diced (optional)

**WHAT YOU NEED TO DO**

1. Preheat the oven to 425°F and line the baking pan with parchment and spray with cooking spray.
2. Stir the flour, cornmeal, sugar, baking powder, and salt together in a large bowl and make a well in the centre.
3. Pour the eggs, corn, milk, and cream into the well and stir until everything is just mixed and moist. Fold in the banana peppers and jalapeño (if using).
4. Pour the mixture into the prepared pan and bake until golden brown, 20 to 25 minutes.
5. Cool in the pan for 10 minutes, then use the parchment paper to lift the cornbread to a wire rack to finish cooling, or cut and serve while still warm.

# Cold Asparagus Salad with Sesame Ginger Vinaigrette

**MAKES** 6 servings
**TAKES** 20 minutes' active time
**RATING** All levels

I've taken a few busloads of people to Edgar Farms to enjoy their asparagus patch, which is the largest in Alberta. Elna and Doug Edgar love to share how they harvest the crop with the three-person asparagus-picking mobile Doug invented. Elna's a walking encyclopedia of delicious ways to use their sweet-as-fresh-green-peas asparagus. We made this salad for one event where we cooked a lamb and asparagus dinner for fifty out in the fields. I've made it every summer since, and each time I do, it's like I'm tucking into all the tastes of that sunny day on the farm once again.

**WHAT YOU NEED TO GATHER**

Measuring spoons
Frying pan
Large pot
Large bowl with ice
Paper towels
Serving platter
High-speed blender

1 Tablespoon sesame seeds
1 bunch Edgar Farms' fresh asparagus
1–2 cloves garlic
2 teaspoons minced fresh ginger
2 Tablespoons rice vinegar or mirin
2 Tablespoons orange juice
2 Tablespoons organic canola oil
2 teaspoons sesame oil
2 teaspoons soy sauce
½ teaspoon sambal oelek

**WHAT YOU NEED TO DO**

1. Pour the sesame seeds into a frying pan and cook over medium heat just until fragrant and golden. This will take only a minute or two. Watch them carefully as they can go from golden to burnt quickly. Remove from the pan and set aside to cool.
2. Bring a large pot of water to boil, add the asparagus, and cook on medium-high until it turns bright green and is tender-crisp, 3 to 5 minutes.
3. Drain the asparagus and then plunge the spears into a large bowl of ice and water. Leave it until it's cool and then drain it. Dry it on paper towels and then arrange it on a serving platter and set aside.
4. Put the garlic, ginger, rice vinegar, orange juice, canola oil, sesame oil, soy sauce, and sambal oelek in a blender and blend until smooth.
5. Pour this dressing evenly over the asparagus and sprinkle with the reserved toasted sesame seeds.
6. Enjoy as a fantastic side with grilled meats or fish.

## VARIATION:

Chop the cold asparagus and add it and the dressing to cooked noodles and chopped tofu to create a great summer salad meal.

## #EATALBERTAFIRST TIP:

Elna and Doug Edgar were the first to grow asparagus commercially in Alberta. Elna hid the first acre in the back 40. Asparagus is a perennial that takes about 3 years to establish. It can then last for 20 or so years. Elna wanted to keep her asparagus patch a secret until she knew whether or not it would grow in Alberta's climate. Now, Edgar Farms has over 30 acres of asparagus and several other growers have sprouted around the province. The season lasts for only 6 weeks, so get it while you can.

# Never-the-Same-Way-Twice Coleslaw

**MAKES** 8 to 10 servings
**TAKES** 30 minutes' active time
**RATING** All levels

I truly never make coleslaw the same way twice. Here's my formula for winging it.

See Sesame Slaw (page 141) for a tasty example of how to bring it all together.

*For the slaw*
Start with 1 or more **kinds of cabbage**, add a **complementary crunch**, a **surprise vegetable or fruit**, a member of the **onion** family, and some **herbs**. Finish with some **nuts, seeds, or dried fruit.**

*For the dressing*
Start with ½ cup **mayonnaise**, add ½ cup of **another fat**, add a few teaspoons or Tablespoons of an **accent flavouring**, sprinkle in some fresh or dried **spices**, add a bit of **heat**, complement with something **sweet**, and add a bit of **acid** with citrus or vinegar. Always finish by tasting and adjusting with good old **salt and pepper**.

Here are some examples for each type of ingredient:

- **CABBAGE:** green, purple, napa, or Savoy cabbage, or bok choy
- **COMPLEMENTARY CRUNCH VEGETABLES:** celery, fennel bulb, and/or carrots
- **SURPRISE VEGETABLES OR FRUITS:** bell peppers, cucumbers, apples, citrus wedges, or pomegranate arils
- **ONIONS:** scallions, shallots, or red, Vidalia, or yellow onions
- **HERBS:** parsley, fennel fronds, cilantro, chives, dill, or tarragon
- **NUTS, SEEDS, OR DRIED FRUIT:** walnuts, pecans, roasted peanuts, hazelnuts, toasted or black sesame seeds, pepitas, sunflower seeds, dried cranberries, or raisins
- **FATS:** Greek yogurt, plain yogurt, mayonnaise, or olive, canola, or avocado oil
- **ACCENT FLAVOURING:** sesame oil or mustard
- **SPICES:** ground cumin, fennel, or chopped ginger or garlic
- **HEAT:** sambal oelek, gochujang, or chili sauce, or 1 chopped jalapeño
- **SWEET:** runny honey, jam, sugar, or maple syrup
- **ACID:** lemon or lime juice, or apple cider or rice wine vinegar

# Sesame Slaw

**MAKES** 8 to 10 servings
**TAKES** 30 minutes' active time
**RATING** All levels

Enjoy this as a side dish for almost anything but especially for the Broek Pork Acres' Pulled Pork (page 155).

**WHAT YOU NEED TO GATHER**

Knife
Cutting board
Bowls
Measuring cups and spoons
Whisk
Serving bowl

*For the slaw*

4 cups loosely or finely chopped green cabbage
1–1½ cups diced or diagonally sliced celery
1 cup or more sliced oranges
1 cup grated carrot
1 red bell pepper, diced
1 medium onion, finely diced, or 1 bunch scallions, sliced on the diagonal
3 Tablespoons finely cut cilantro
1 Tablespoon minced ginger
1–2 teaspoons or Tablespoons sesame seeds

*For the dressing*

½ cup mayonnaise
½ cup Greek yogurt
2 Tablespoons lime juice
2 Tablespoons sesame oil
1 Tablespoon runny honey
1 Tablespoon sambal oelek
1 teaspoon ground cumin
1 teaspoon minced ginger
1 teaspoon pepper
½ teaspoon salt

**WHAT YOU NEED TO DO**

1. Place the cabbage, celery, oranges, carrot, red bell pepper, onion, cilantro, ginger, and sesame seeds in a large bowl.
2. Whisk the mayonnaise, yogurt, lime juice, sesame oil, honey, sambal oelek, cumin, ginger, pepper, and salt in another bowl. Add about half to the vegetables in the large bowl and stir it through.
3. Add half of the remaining dressing and then assess if you need it all to get the creaminess you desire. Then taste the salad to see if you need to adjust any of the other elements.
4. Transfer the salad to a serving bowl.

### PRO TIP:

Store any leftover dressing in an airtight jar in the refrigerator to use as a sandwich spread.

# Zesty Potato Salad

**MAKES** 4 servings
**TAKES** 30 minutes' active time + cooling time for the eggs and potatoes
**RATING** All levels

I like my potato salad to have a little personality. This one, with its mixture of zippy radish, tangy pickles, and spicy mustard and chili powder, fits the bill. Enjoy with grilled meats, or Six Ways to Sunday (Dinner) Beer Butt Chicken (page 163), or the Lip-Smacking, Finger-Licking, Messy, Good Ribs (page 157) in particular.

**WHAT YOU NEED TO GATHER**

Saucepans
Knife
Cutting board
Large bowl
Measuring cups and spoons
Whisk

*For the salad*

4 eggs, boiled, peeled, and sliced (reserve a few pieces for garnish, if desired)
2 cups boiled, cooled, new red baby potatoes, sliced in coins or quarters
1 cup freshly shelled garden peas, blanched and cooled
1 cup diced radish
1 cup diced baby cucumber
½ cup diced celery
½ cup diced scallions
¼ cup diced red onion
¼ cup diced gherkins or dill pickles

*For the dressing*

½ cup mayonnaise
½ cup grainy Alberta mustard
1 teaspoon dry mustard
½ teaspoon ground cumin
½ teaspoon ground coriander
¼ teaspoon chili powder
1 Tablespoon vinegar or pickle juice
1 teaspoon dried or 2 teaspoons finely chopped fresh dill, parsley, or tarragon
Salt and pepper
Pinch of paprika (optional)

I recommend new red baby potatoes for this salad because they're waxy and hold together.

**WHAT YOU NEED TO DO**

1. Place the eggs, potatoes, peas, radish, cucumber, celery, green and red onions, and gherkins in a large bowl.
2. Whisk the mayonnaise, both mustards, cumin, coriander, chili powder, vinegar, dill, and salt and pepper together in another bowl. Stir this into the potato mixture.
3. Garnish with egg slices and a pinch of paprika (if desired).

## #EATALBERTAFIRST TIP:

Look for potatoes from The Homestead Farm, Upper Green Farms, Poplar Bluff Organics, Eagle Creek Farms, Sparrow's Nest, Sundog Organic Farm, Serben Farms, and Redcliffe Farms.

GRAN DEPOSITO
ACETO BALSAMICO
GIUSEPPE GIUSTI
GIUSTI

# Beet Carpaccio Salad

**MAKES** 4 servings (as a lunch or starter)
**TAKES** 20 minutes' active time + 1 hour to bake the beets
**RATING** Competent

Beets and berries are twin rubies glimmering in this salad. They're as pleasing to the eye as they are to the palate. Add in the crunch of the pistachios, the creaminess of the goat cheese, and the beauty of edible flowers and you have a fantastic showcase of an Alberta signature food.

**WHAT YOU NEED TO GATHER**

Roasting pan
Aluminum foil
Knife
Cutting board
Measuring cups and spoons
Serving plates

2 cups tender young salad greens
4 cups red, golden, or candy cane (Chioggia) beets (or a mix), cooked, peeled, sliced thinly, and dried
4 ounces fresh goat cheese, crumbled
1 Tablespoon balsamic glaze
1 Tablespoon extra virgin olive oil
Salt and pepper
½ cup edible flowers (nasturtiums, pansies, violas, rose petals)
¼ cup chopped unsalted pistachios
¼ cup toasted sunflower seeds
40 or so fresh raspberries, blackberries, or a mix

**WHAT YOU NEED TO DO**

1. Divide the lettuce to line 4 plates and arrange the beet slices on them.
2. Scatter the goat cheese on top.
3. Drizzle with the balsamic reduction and olive oil.
4. Sprinkle with salt and pepper to taste.
5. Garnish with the edible flowers, pistachios, sunflower seeds, and berries.

This recipe doubles and triples well, so it's ideal when you want to feed a crowd.

**PRO TIP:**

The easiest and least messy way to cook beets that I know is to remove the top and bottom of the beets, line a roasting pan with foil, sit the beets in it, add 1 inch of water, and then wrap the foil around them and bake until fork-tender, about 1 hour. Once they cool, simply slide the peels off under cold running water and use as desired.

Progressive

# Roasted Potato and Root Vegetable Fries

MAKES 6 servings
TAKES 25 minutes' active time + 35 minutes' baking time
RATING All levels

This quick and easy side dish is a great way to celebrate one of Alberta's signature foods: root vegetables. Enjoy as a side with Berbon Glazed Ham (page 311), Cedar-Planked Prime Rib Roast of Alberta Beef (page 159), or Six Ways to Sunday (Dinner) Beer Butt Chicken (page 163).

### WHAT YOU NEED TO GATHER

1 large rimmed baking sheet or 2 smaller ones
Parchment paper
Large bowl
Knife
Cutting board
Measuring spoons

6 carrots, scrubbed, but not peeled, and halved lengthwise
6 parsnips, scrubbed, but not peeled, and halved lengthwise
3 large potatoes, scrubbed, but not peeled, cut in wedges
6 shallots, peeled and quartered
2 Tablespoons organic canola oil
2 teaspoons dried or 2 Tablespoons chopped fresh rosemary
1 teaspoon dried thyme
Salt and pepper
2 Tablespoons Alberta runny honey

### WHAT YOU NEED TO DO

1. Preheat the oven to 400°F and line a baking sheet with parchment paper.
2. Put the vegetables in a large bowl and toss them with the oil and herbs, then spread them out on the baking sheet and sprinkle with salt and pepper. Leave plenty of space between the vegetables so they get crisp. You may need to use 2 baking sheets.
3. Bake for 25 minutes (use convection if you have it), turn the vegetables and drizzle them with the honey, and continue to bake until golden and crisp, another 10 minutes or so.

# Dynamite Dick's Five Bean Beans

**MAKES** 12 servings (as a side dish)
**TAKES** 20 minutes' active time + 6 to 8 hours in a slow cooker or 2 hours in an oven
**RATING** All levels

These beans are named for a former neighbour, Richard Wyman, who made them for a Stampede party one year. I said, "Those beans were dynamite, Dick," and they've been Dynamite Dick's ever since. The more beans you eat, the more farmers you support. Over 6,500 Alberta farmers grow pulses (dried peas, beans, chickpeas, lentils, soybeans, and fava beans). In 2021, 2.4 million acres of pulses were planted and 1.97 metric tons harvested, 80 percent of which were exported at a value of $723.8 million. Now that's something to toot about. Enjoy with grilled meats, especially Turn Coat Steaks (page 151), with Highwood Crossing Oat Buns (page 243) and Never-the-Same-Way-Twice Coleslaw (page 139).

**WHAT YOU NEED TO GATHER**

Can opener
Slow cooker or large Dutch oven
Knife
Cutting board
Measuring cups and spoons
Saucepan
Wooden spoon

19-ounce (540 ml) can lentils
19-ounce (540 ml) can red kidney beans
19-ounce (540 ml) can chickpeas
19-ounce (540 ml) can romano beans
19-ounce (540 ml) can lima beans
1 cup bacon bits (omit if you want it to be vegetarian or vegan)
1 onion, diced
1 cup tomato juice
⅓ cup packed brown sugar
⅓ cup fancy molasses
¼ cup chili sauce
2 teaspoons dry mustard
1 teaspoon ground ginger
1 teaspoon pepper

I chose to use lentils, red kidney beans, chickpeas, romano beans, and lima beans for this recipe but you get the idea—just use 5 cans of various beans!

**WHAT YOU NEED TO DO**

1. If you're using a Dutch oven, preheat your oven to 325°F.
2. Drain and rinse all the beans, and put them in a slow cooker or large Dutch oven.
3. Heat a saucepan on medium heat and add the bacon bits and onion. Cook until the onion is translucent, about 3 to 5 minutes.
4. Stir in the tomato juice, sugar, molasses, chili sauce, mustard, ginger, and pepper until well combined, then bring to a simmer before adding to the beans.
5. Cook on low for 6 to 8 hours in your slow cooker or at 325°F for 2 hours in a Dutch oven in the oven.

# Turn Coat Steaks with Hasselback Potatoes

**MAKES** 4 servings
**TAKES** 30 minutes' active time + 24 to 48 hours' marinating time for the steak; 10 minutes' active time plus 50 minutes' baking time for the potatoes
**RATING** Competent to proficient

The Turn Coat in the title of this recipe doesn't refer to a lack of loyalty to Alberta's amazing beef; it's simply short for grill, turn, and coat the steaks. Hasselback potatoes were invented in the 1940s at a restaurant in Stockholm, Sweden, named Hasselbacken. They're surprisingly easy, and I think they're the perfect accompaniment for this classic Alberta meal. (Note that you have to start this at least one day before you plan to eat it.)

**WHAT YOU NEED TO GATHER**

Paper towel
Knife
Cutting board
Glass baking dish
Measuring cups and spoons
Bowls
Whisk
Wooden spoon
Parchment paper
Baking sheet
Pastry brush
Instant-read thermometer
Wire rack
Aluminum foil

*For the steaks*

2 lb top sirloin steak, about 1½–2 inches thick
2 Tablespoons horseradish
4 Tablespoons grainy mustard

*For the marinade*

½ cup finely diced onion
2 cloves garlic, minced
½ teaspoon hot pepper flakes
½ cup balsamic vinegar
¼ cup canola oil

*For the potatoes*

4 large Yukon Gold, russet, Agria, or Kennebec potatoes
4 Tablespoons butter, melted
Salt and pepper
Sweet paprika

**WHAT YOU NEED TO DO**

*For the marinade*

1 Rinse the steak under cold water and pat it dry with a paper towel. Make shallow slits on both sides of the meat and place it in a glass baking dish.
2 Whisk the onions, garlic, hot pepper flakes, balsamic vinegar, and oil together in a bowl and pour over the steak, turning it to coat both sides evenly. Cover and marinate in the refrigerator for 24 to 48 hours.

### PRO TIP:

A couple of hours before you want to grill the meat, set it out on the counter and bring it to room temperature. It will cook more evenly.

*For the potatoes*

1. Wash the potatoes, pat them dry, and set them on a cutting board. Make slits in each with a sharp knife about ¼ inch apart, stopping before you reach the cutting board. You want to leave the bottom of the potato intact and create a fan or accordion effect. You may find it helpful to position the potato against a flat wooden spoon handle to help your knife stop at the right depth.
2. Preheat the oven to 425°F.
3. Set the potatoes on a parchment-lined baking sheet and use a pastry brush to baste the outside of each potato with 1½ teaspoons of butter, then sprinkle with salt and pepper.
4. Bake for 30 minutes and then baste with another 1½ teaspoons of butter per potato once the wedges have opened.
5. Continue baking until the potatoes are crispy on the outside and cooked through on the inside, about 20 minutes, depending on the size of the potato.
6. Meanwhile, start cooking your steaks.
7. Sprinkle the potatoes with a pinch of paprika just before serving.

*For the steaks*

1. Preheat the grill to medium-high.
2. Combine the horseradish and mustard in a bowl and set aside.
3. Place the meat on the grill and cook until it lifts easily, about 3 to 5 minutes.
4. Flip the steak and slather the top with a thick layer of the horseradish and mustard coating.
5. Cook to an internal temperature of 135°F for medium-rare.
6. Remove from the grill, tent with foil, and let stand for 10 minutes on a wire rack before slicing into 1-inch-thick slices.
7. Enjoy with horseradish-laced mayonnaise on the side and those crispy on the outside and soft and buttery on the inside hasselback potatoes.

# Broek Pork Acres' Pulled Pork

**MAKES** 8 to 10 servings
**TAKES** 10 minutes' active time + 8 to 12 hours' slow cooker time
**RATING** All levels

My friend Joanne Vanden Broek shared this recipe in 2011 when I took a group of city folk to Joanne and Allan's Broek Pork Acres farm to learn how much TLC they put into growing pasture-raised Berkshire hogs. Joanne made this pulled pork for our alfresco lunch for forty. Trust a mother of nine to have a tasty recipe like this up her sleeve. You can easily double it as well. You'll just need either a bigger slow cooker or two slow cookers. Enjoy on fresh buns with Never-the-Same-Way-Twice Coleslaw (page 139) and a cold Alberta craft beer.

**WHAT YOU NEED TO GATHER**

Paper towels
Measuring cups and spoons
Bowl
Slow cooker
2 forks

4–5 lb pork shoulder or rump roast
¼ cup packed brown sugar
4 Tablespoons sweet paprika
3 Tablespoons kosher salt
3 Tablespoons pepper
2 teaspoons garlic powder
2 teaspoons onion powder
2 teaspoons celery seed
1 teaspoon cayenne pepper

**WHAT YOU NEED TO DO**

1. Rinse the roast, dry it with paper towels, and place it in a slow cooker.
2. Combine the sugar, paprika, salt, pepper, garlic and onion powders, celery seed, and cayenne pepper in a bowl and then rub all over the surface of the meat.
3. Cook on high for 8 hours, or on low for 12 hours, turning once at the halfway mark. I like to throw this together in the morning and serve it for dinner. Just before serving, use 2 forks to pull the tender meat apart and let it soak up the juices that have accumulated.

### PRO TIP:

Substitute an equal weight of jackfruit for the pork to make this vegan, and reduce the cooking time to 2 hours.

# Lip-Smacking, Finger-Licking, Messy, Good Ribs

**MAKES** 4 to 6 servings
**TAKES** 90 minutes' active time + minimum 2 hours' marinating time or marinate overnight and grill the next day
**RATING** Competent to proficient

My sister Laurie got the recipe for Phil's Original BBQ ribs when she lived in Toronto. When she and my brother-in-law, Zig, saw the light and moved to Jasper, she always made them when we visited. I loved all those messy, good times and have continued to make the ribs over the years, only changing the sauce a bit. Enjoy these succulent ribs slathered with lots of the sauce, along with Zesty Potato Salad (page 143), Shades of Green Salad (page 129), and Hot Pepper Cornbread (page 135).

**WHAT YOU NEED TO GATHER**

Large stockpot
Measuring cups and spoons
Skimmer
Whisk
Saucepan
Knife
Cutting board
Roasting pan

*For the meat*

5 lb pork side ribs
2 garlic cloves with skins on, smashed
¼ cup red pepper flakes
2 Tablespoons whole black peppercorns
8 bay leaves

*For the sauce*

2 cloves garlic, minced
1½ cups ketchup
½ cup chili sauce
2 Tablespoons lemon juice
2 Tablespoons soy sauce
2 Tablespoon honey
1 Tablespoon Worcestershire sauce
1 teaspoon onion powder
Sunflower oil for the grill

## #EATALBERTAFIRST TIP:

As a food journalist since 2006, I've seen many of Alberta's pork farmers opt out of raising factory pork and switch to raising heritage breeds on pasture. Breeds like Berkshire, Red Wattle, Mangalitsa, Tamworth, KuneKune, and Duroc are all thriving in Alberta. Each dollar we spend as consumers determines the food system we get. Because many consumers prefer the idea of pasture-raised pork, a market for this product has been created and larger grocers, like Calgary Co-op, for example, are responding by phasing out caged-pork products.

#### WHAT YOU NEED TO DO

1. Put the ribs in a large stockpot with the garlic, pepper flakes, peppercorns, and bay leaves and add enough cold water to cover.
2. Bring to a boil, slowly over medium heat, and then lower the heat and simmer, uncovered, for at least 1 hour. Remove any scum that floats to the surface with a skimmer. Meanwhile, make the sauce.
3. Whisk together the minced garlic, ketchup, chili sauce, lemon juice, soy, honey, Worcestershire sauce, and onion powder in a saucepan and bring to a simmer over low heat, stirring occasionally, and let thicken for about 10 minutes. Set aside until the ribs are boiled.
4. When the ribs are cooked through and tender, remove them from the cooking liquid and use a knife to remove any outer silver skin. Place them in a large roasting pan or baking dish, and coat all sides with the marinade. Put in the refrigerator and leave for at least 2 hours or overnight.
5. Turn the grill on to low to medium heat, wipe it with oil to prevent sticking, add the marinated racks of ribs, and cook, turning once, until heated through and slightly charred, about 20 minutes.
6. Remove from the grill and slice on a cutting board.

# Cedar-Planked Prime Rib Roast of Alberta Beef

**MAKES** 6 servings
**TAKES** Overnight soaking + 20 minutes' active time + 2 hours' cooking + 30 minutes' resting
**RATING** Competent to proficient

You need to soak a cedar plank in water overnight to make this recipe. Yes, that takes a bit of planning, but it's worth it, because this rendition of Alberta beef impresses the heck out of people. I once served it to friends who own a few of Calgary's steak houses. My husband said incredulously, "You're serving *them* beef!?!" I sure did. And Franca, Peter, Connie, and Gerry loved it. Time for a shout-out: I learned everything I know about planking from former Albertan, and international barbecue champion, Rockin' Ronnie Shewchuk and his book *Planking Secrets*. Enjoy with Roasted Potato and Root Vegetable Fries (page 147) and Shades of Green Salad (page 129).

**WHAT YOU NEED TO GATHER**

Large cedar plank
Measuring cups and spoons
Bowl
Instant-read meat thermometer
Wire rack
Aluminum foil
Knife
Cutting board

*For the roast*

5 lb Alberta prime rib roast with bones attached
6 (each 5 inches long) whole rosemary branches

*For the coating*

3 large cloves garlic, minced
3 shallots, finely diced
1 teaspoon dried or 2 teaspoons finely cut fresh rosemary
1 teaspoon dried or 2 teaspoons finely cut fresh dill
1 teaspoon dried or 2 teaspoons finely cut fresh tarragon
½ teaspoon coarsely ground salt
1 teaspoon pepper
½ cup Alberta grainy mustard
1 Tablespoon organic canola oil

**WHAT YOU NEED TO DO**

*For the roast*

1. Soak the cedar plank overnight in water.
2. About an hour before you plan to start cooking, remove the roast from the refrigerator to bring it to room temperature. This results in more even cooking.
3. Preheat your gas grill on high until the temperature is about 450°F.
4. Remove the cedar plank from the water and pat it dry with a cloth.
5. Lay the rosemary branches across the cedar plank and set the roast on them.

*For the coating*

1 Mix the garlic, shallots, rosemary, dill, tarragon, salt, pepper, mustard, and oil in a bowl and then coat the surface of the roast with it.

*To cook the roast*

1 Turn one side of your grill off, and place the planked roast on that side. Reduce the heat on the other side of the grill to medium or 350°F.
2 Cook the roast until the internal temperature reads 125°F on a meat thermometer, about 1½ to 2 hours. You may need to turn the plank halfway through cooking so that the roast cooks evenly.
3 Remove the roast to a rack when done and tent it loosely with foil. Let it rest for 20 to 30 minutes before carving it.

# Six Ways to Sunday (Dinner) Beer Butt Chicken

**MAKES** 4 to 6 servings
**TAKES** 15 minutes' active time + 1½ to 2½ hours' grilling time + 10 minutes' resting time
**RATING** All levels

Who says chicken dinner is boring? Here are six different rubs to jazz up your routine along with complete instructions for making super-moist beer butt chicken.

**WHAT YOU NEED TO GATHER**

Paper towel
Mixing bowl
Measuring cups and spoons
Cutting board
Knife
High-sided saucepan
Aluminum foil
Thick rubber gloves
Serving platter

*For the chicken*

12-ounce (354 ml) can Alberta craft beer
3–5 lb whole chicken
Rub of your choice

*For a traditional rub*

1 Tablespoon olive oil
1 teaspoon dried summer savory
1 teaspoon dried thyme
1 teaspoon dried sage
Salt and pepper

*For a Korean gochujang rub*

3 Tablespoons gochujang paste (you'll find this at Korean and Japanese grocers)
1 Tablespoon sesame oil
1 teaspoon minced garlic

*For an Indian tandoor rub*

1 teaspoon garlic powder
1 teaspoon onion powder
1 teaspoon ground cumin
1 teaspoon ground coriander
1 teaspoon garam masala
Pinch saffron threads
1 Tablespoon tomato paste
1 Tablespoon plain yogurt
1 Tablespoon olive oil

*For a Chinese five-spice rub*

2 teaspoons Chinese five-spice powder
1 teaspoon finely crushed Sichuan peppercorns
2 Tablespoons hoisin sauce
½ teaspoon soy sauce
½ teaspoon olive oil

*For a Thai coconut rub*

1 Tablespoon red curry paste
1 Tablespoon softened coconut oil
6–10 makrut lime leaves
¼ cup finely diced shallots
2 teaspoons finely diced lemongrass

*For a rancher's rub*

1 Tablespoon olive oil
1 teaspoon smoky paprika
1 teaspoon brown sugar
1 teaspoon chili powder
¼ teaspoon garlic powder
¼ teaspoon onion powder
¼ teaspoon hot dry mustard powder
¼ teaspoon ground cumin
¼ teaspoon ground coriander
¼ teaspoon turmeric
Salt and pepper

Yes, it's worth making a special trip to an Asian grocer for gochujang. I wouldn't send you on a wild goose chase.

WHAT YOU NEED TO DO

*For the chicken*

1 Open the beer and drink a third of it. You're welcome. Set the can aside.

2 Wash the chicken inside and out with cold water, then pat it dry with a paper towel. Now, slather it with one of the following rubs according to your cravings or menu planning.

*For the traditional rub*

1 Coat the bird with the oil and sprinkle the savory, thyme, and sage, plus salt and pepper to taste, all over it.

*For the Korean gochujang rub*

1 Combine the gochujang paste with the oil and garlic and rub all over the outside of the chicken. Smear any extra between the skin and breast meat.

*For the Indian tandoor rub*

1 Mix the garlic and onion powder, cumin, coriander, garam masala, and a few saffron threads with the tomato paste, yogurt, and oil. Rub all over the outside and tuck the extra between the skin and the breast meat.

*For the Chinese five-spice rub*

1 Mix the Chinese five-spice powder with the peppercorns, hoisin sauce, soy sauce, and oil and rub all over the chicken, inside and out.

*For the Thai coconut rub*

1 Mix together the curry paste and coconut oil and rub all over the outside of the chicken. Slide the lime leaves, shallots, and lemongrass in between the skin and breast.

When chopping lemongrass, use only the white bit at the root.

*For the rancher's rub*

1 Coat the chicken with the oil. Mix the paprika, sugar, chili powder, garlic and onion powders, dry mustard, cumin, coriander, turmeric, and salt and pepper together in a small bowl and coat the chicken inside and out with the rub.

*To cook the chicken*

1 Slide the bottom of the rubbed chicken onto the beer can. Place it in a high-sided saucepan so it doesn't tip over while you heat the grill.
2 Preheat one side of your grill on high, then lower it to medium-high and place the beer can on the other side of the grill with no direct heat. A 3 lb chicken will take about 1½ to 2 hours; a 5 lb chicken will take about 2½ hours. Rotate the chicken a few times during this time so it cooks evenly on all sides. You'll know the chicken is done when the legs move easily and the juices run clear. If you're using a meat thermometer (always a good idea), the internal temperature should read 165°F.
3 Clean the saucepan you used earlier and place the chicken and can in it and take it back to your kitchen. Tent it with foil for at least 10 minutes and then carefully remove the chicken from the can. I use a thick pair of rubber gloves to do this and to discard the residual beer from the can.
4 Carve the chicken and arrange the pieces on a platter. Remember to freeze the bones to make Homemade Stock (page 215).
5 Enjoy with sides to complement the rub.

## MAKE-AHEAD TIP:

It's just as easy to cook two chickens as it is one. There's a reason I make this dinner on a Sunday. If you grill (or roast) two chickens on Sunday, you can eat one that day and use the second for sandwiches, quesadillas, curries, pasta dishes, or soups throughout the week.

# Sesame Flank Steak

**MAKES** 8 to 10 servings
**TAKES** 30 minutes' active time + 10 minutes' resting time + 4 to 48 hours' marinating time
**RATING** All levels

The flavours of sesame, soy, honey, lime, chili paste, and garlic seep into the meat during a long marination, yielding a deeply satisfying Asian umami bomb of flavour. I always make more of this than I need because the cold leftovers are excellent in wraps or salad bowls.

**WHAT YOU NEED TO GATHER**

Knife
Cutting board
Glass baking dish
Whisk
Bowl
Saucepan
Pastry brush
Tongs
Wire rack
Aluminum foil

2–3 lb flank steak
8 cloves garlic, minced
½ cup soy sauce
½ cup Alberta honey
¼ cup lime juice
2 Tablespoons toasted sesame oil
1 Tablespoon gochujang or sambal oelek chili paste

**WHAT YOU NEED TO DO**

1. Score the steak with a sharp knife on both sides and place it in a glass baking dish.
2. Smear both sides of the steak with the minced garlic, making sure to get it into the areas you've sliced into.
3. Whisk the soy sauce, honey, lime juice, oil, and gochujang together and pour over the steak, flipping it so all sides are coated. Place in the refrigerator and marinate the meat for at least 4 hours or up to 2 days. Remove the meat from the refrigerator 1 hour before grilling to bring it to room temperature. Lift it from the marinade and pat it dry just before grilling. Reserve the marinade.
4. Pour the marinade into a saucepan, bring it to a boil over medium-high heat, and then reduce to a simmer until syrupy in consistency. You'll use this reduced liquid to brush on the steak as a glaze while it's grilling.
5. Grill the steak for 4 minutes per side for medium-rare (based on 1-inch thickness), basting with the reduced marinade a few times on each side.
6. Remove from the grill, tent with foil, and rest on a wire rack for 10 minutes before slicing it on the diagonal.
7. Enjoy with noodles and sautéed spinach dressed with a drizzle of sesame oil. Or fold it in lettuce cups and top with store-bought kimchi, cucumber slices, and sesame seeds.

Can't find flank steak? Skirt or flat iron steaks also work well in this recipe. If I see any of these steaks on sale, I'll multiply the recipe and freeze the steaks in their portions of marinade. It's great to pull the already marinated steak out of the freezer to thaw for a quick and delicious supper.

# Overnight Rhubarb Sauce

**MAKES** 3 cups
**TAKES** 30 minutes' active time + overnight maceration time
**RATING** All levels

I once did a CBC Radio *Alberta at Noon* column about Alberta's signature foods, and the callers phoning in kept the lines busy because they were absolutely shocked rhubarb didn't make the list. Rhubarb, I've learned, is a most beloved Alberta, and Canada-wide for that matter, food. This recipe comes from my best friend, Shawnee. The overnight maceration of the fruit in sugar results in an intense flavour, decreased simmering time, and one delightfully easy rhubarb sauce. It's a great make-ahead food. You can store it in the refrigerator for up to 2 weeks or freeze it in serving-size portions for up to 6 months.

**WHAT YOU NEED TO GATHER**

Knife
Cutting board
Saucepan
Measuring cups and spoons
Wooden spoon
Storage containers

8 cups chopped rhubarb
1 cup granulated sugar
1 teaspoon vanilla extract

**WHAT YOU NEED TO DO**

1. Place the chopped rhubarb in the saucepan you intend to cook it in.
2. Stir in the sugar and leave it, uncovered, overnight.
3. Bring the rhubarb and liquid to a simmer over medium heat and cook, stirring occasionally, until the juices are thick and syrupy, about 20 to 30 minutes. Turn off the heat, stir in the vanilla, let the mixture cool, and then transfer to glass or plastic storage containers.
4. Enjoy with yogurt, over ice cream, or in Sweet Sourdough Fruit Strudel (page 87).

## #EATALBERTAFIRST TIP:

Walk down the back lanes in any town or city in Alberta and you'll find rhubarb growing in many gardens. It's the first fruit of spring and a most beloved and enduring perennial. If you've got even a small patch of earth, it's worth planting, as you'll be rewarded for years to come.

# Bing Cherry Butter Tarts

**MAKES** 12 tarts

**TAKES** 25 minutes' active time + 20 minutes' baking time + minimum 1 hour (but ideally overnight) resting time for the dough

**RATING** Competent to proficient

This is butter tart perfection. I can say that without bragging because it's based on my friend Michael Allemeier's recipe and he's one of only three Certified Master Chefs in Canada. Born in South Africa and raised in Winnipeg, Michael made his mark as a chef at Vancouver's Bishop's, Kelowna's Mission Hill, and Calgary's Teatro, and now as an instructor at SAIT polytechnic. I never liked this ultra-Canadian dessert until I tasted Michael's version. This crust and maple syrup won me over. Oh, and in my version I may have swapped raisins for luscious Bing cherries and white chocolate.

### WHAT YOU NEED TO GATHER

Large bowl
Whisk
Measuring cups and spoons
Wooden spoon
Wax paper
Muffin tin
Bowl
Whisk
Baking sheet
Wire rack

*For the pastry*

1½ cups flour
¼ teaspoon kosher salt
10 Tablespoons butter, cold, cubed
1 egg yolk
1 teaspoon white vinegar
¼ cup ice water

*For the filling*

½ cup packed brown sugar
1½ teaspoons cornstarch
1 teaspoon kosher salt
½ cup maple syrup
2 eggs
7 Tablespoons butter, melted
1 Tablespoon apple cider vinegar
1 teaspoon vanilla extract
36 pitted Bing cherries
36 white chocolate chips

### WHAT YOU NEED TO DO

*For the pastry*

1. Mix the flour and salt in a large bowl.
2. Rub in the butter with your fingers until the mixture develops a coarse pea-like texture.
3. Whisk the yolk and vinegar together in a measuring cup and add enough water to make a volume of 80 ml in a metric measuring cup.
4. Make a well in the centre of the flour and butter mixture, add the yolk-vinegar mix, and stir with a wooden spoon to bring the dough together. Shape the dough into a log, wrap it in wax paper, and chill for at least 1 hour in the refrigerator. Note: overnight is best.

I've also used preserved and frozen cherries in this recipe with great success. Follow the method as is if you use these. You don't need to adapt the cooking time.

## VARIATIONS:

Instead of cherries and white chocolate, divide ⅔ cup golden raisins or, for an Alberta signature food, ⅔ cup fresh or frozen saskatoon berries among the shells before adding the filling.

5 Preheat the oven to 400°F and butter the cups of a muffin tin.
6 Bring the dough to room temperature before using. Divide it into 12 even pieces and roll each piece into a ball.
7 Place a ball in each cup of the buttered muffin tins and press evenly into the bottom and up the sides to make a tart shell.
8 Cover and set aside until needed.

*For the filling and to bake*

1 Whisk the sugar, cornstarch, salt, maple syrup, eggs, butter, vinegar, and vanilla in a bowl until smooth.
2 Divide the cherries evenly among the tart shells.
3 Spoon the filling over the fruit and place 3 chocolate chips per tart on top.
4 Bake the tarts on a baking sheet in the bottom third of the oven until the filling bubbles and the crust is golden, about 18 to 20 minutes.
5 Remove from the oven. Let the tarts stand in the pan for 5 minutes, then carefully remove them and let them cool on a wire rack. Enjoy as a fabulous dessert in the fresh cherry season.

## PRO TIP:

To remove the tarts from the pans, I loosen the crust around the edges with a knife and then use an offset cake icing knife or pie lifter to extract them with great success.

# Summer's Every Fruit Cake

**MAKES** 10 servings
**TAKES** 20 minutes' active time + 55 minutes' baking time
**RATING** All levels

I once bought a whopping amount of big, fat, juicy, ripe, black Bing cherries at the Penticton farmers' market during an Okanagan vacation. Layering them throughout, I baked them into a light cake with crispy, golden edges. I called it Cheery Cherry Cake and served it to my friend Laura Kowalchuk, who then made it for her friend Gwen Bathgate, who just kept on making it with every fruit, all summer. It became Amazing Apricot, Perky Plum, Pretty Peach, and Perfect Pear. Back home in Alberta, if you can find sour cherries, you can even make it as a Sensational Sour Cherry Cake.

**WHAT YOU NEED TO GATHER**

10-inch springform pan
Stand mixer fitted with paddle attachment
Measuring cups and spoons
Spatula
Whisk
Bowl
Cherry pitter
Cake tester or toothpick

¾ cup butter, softened, plus a little extra to butter the cake pan
¾ cup granulated sugar
½ cup packed brown sugar
3 eggs
¾ cup plain Greek yogurt
1½ teaspoons kirsch liqueur or pure vanilla extract

1¾ cups unbleached all-purpose flour
1 teaspoon baking powder
½ teaspoon baking soda
½ teaspoon ground cinnamon
Salt
2 cups pitted, halved cherries, apricots, plums, or peaches
Whipped cream
1 cup same fruit used above, whole or sliced

**WHAT YOU NEED TO DO**

1. Preheat the oven to 350°F and butter a 10-inch springform pan.
2. Place the butter and both sugars in the bowl of a stand mixer fitted with the paddle attachment and cream together on high speed until fluffy.
3. Add the eggs one at a time, scraping down the sides of the bowl with a spatula and beating well between each addition.
4. Add the yogurt and kirsch and beat on high until incorporated.
5. Whisk the flour, baking powder, baking soda, cinnamon, and a pinch of salt in a small bowl. Add the mixture to the bowl of the stand mixer and beat on low until the batter is smooth.
6. Pour half the batter into the prepared springform pan and use a spatula to smooth it to the outer edges of the pan.

7 Place half the pitted fruit on the top, spreading to cover the surface. Pour the remaining batter over and then arrange the remaining pitted fruit, cut side up, on top.
8 Place the cake in the centre of the oven and bake until the top is golden and the centre is firm, about 50 to 55 minutes. A cake tester inserted into the centre of the cake should come out clean.
9 Remove the cake from the oven and set it on a wire rack to cool.
10 Enjoy with whipped cream and whole or sliced fruit on the side. This cake is especially delicious served warm from the oven.

# Prairie Berry Squares

**MAKES** 24 squares
**TAKES** 15 minutes' active time + 30 minutes' baking time
**RATING** All levels

This is an old Mennonite recipe shared by my friend Ingrid Friesen. We rented cabins side by side for a decade out in BC's Okanagan. Naturally, over the years, we started cooking the evening meal for our families together. Ingrid could make this recipe blindfolded. And ever since she introduced us to it, it's been a keeper in my repertoire of quick and easy go-to recipes.

**WHAT YOU NEED TO GATHER**

13 × 9-inch glass baking pan
Measuring cups and spoons
Bowl
Pastry blender

2 cups + 1 Tablespoon flour, divided
1½ cups sugar, divided
Salt
1 cup butter, softened, plus a bit more for the baking pan
2 cups fresh or frozen berries (saskatoons, haskaps, sea buckthorn, blueberries, huckleberries, or a combo, enough to cover the crust in a single layer)
1 cup unsweetened shredded coconut
3 eggs, beaten
2 Tablespoons butter, melted

**WHAT YOU NEED TO DO**

1. Preheat the oven to 350°F and butter the baking pan.
2. Use a pastry blender or your hands to mix 2 cups of the flour, ½ cup of the sugar, a pinch of salt, and the softened butter in a bowl until the butter is completely distributed. Spread this mixture evenly in the baking pan and press it down to form a crust.
3. Cover the crust with the berries.
4. Sprinkle the berries with the coconut.
5. Mix the remaining 1 cup of sugar and 1 Tablespoon of flour with the eggs and melted butter and pour it over the coconut layer.
6. Place on the middle rack in the oven and bake until golden brown, about 30 minutes.
7. Cool in the pan, cut into squares, and enjoy as a quick and easy dessert any time you need one.

## #EATALBERTAFIRST TIP:

From mid-July to late August, you'll find U-picks across Alberta where you can fill your own buckets with haskaps, saskatoons, and raspberries. Strawberries are often of the everbearing variety and will continue until the first frost happens. At Lethbridge's Broxburn Vegetables and Cafe, that is often not until late September.

# Prairie-Hardy Fruit Muffins with Hazelnut Topping

**MAKES** 12 muffins
**TAKES** 10 minutes' active time + 20 minutes' baking time
**RATING** All levels

I developed this recipe when I presented a CBC Radio column called "Edible Landscapes and Prairie Hardy Fruits." The research was fruitful (groan). I learned that haskaps (honeyberries) are native to swampy parts of Alberta's boreal forests and are now successfully cultivated. You'll see sea buckthorn, originally from Siberia, everywhere, once you know what it looks like. Hazelnuts are native to Alberta's Parkland. But, as my friend Kristin Graves of Fifth Gen Gardens says, "Good luck getting them before the squirrels!" The next time you do any landscaping, maybe you can include one of these Alberta growing zone–friendly plants.

**WHAT YOU NEED TO GATHER**

Muffin tin and liners
Measuring cups and spoons
Bowls
Whisk
Wooden spoon
Spatula
Wire rack

1¾ cups flour
½ cup granulated sugar
3 teaspoons baking powder
½ teaspoon salt
1 cup skim milk
½ cup unsalted butter, melted
1 egg, beaten
1 cup mixed prairie fruits
½ cup hazelnuts, peeled and chopped
2 Tablespoons brown sugar
1 teaspoon ground cinnamon

**WHAT YOU NEED TO DO**

1. Preheat the oven to 375°F and line the cups of a muffin tin with non-stick liners, or butter them or spray with vegetable oil.
2. Whisk the flour, granulated sugar, baking powder, and salt in a large bowl to mix well.
3. Stir the milk, butter, and egg together in another bowl.
4. Stir the fruit into the flour mix and then add the wet ingredients.
5. Stir just until moist (overmixing will result in tough muffins).
6. Distribute the batter evenly to make 12 muffins.
7. Combine the ½ cup of hazelnuts, brown sugar, and cinnamon in a bowl and sprinkle a little over the top of each muffin.
8. Bake until golden brown on top, about 20 minutes, and remove to a wire rack to cool.

For our photo shoot, I used ½ cup each of sea buckthorn and haskaps (honeyberries) but saskatoon and blueberries work well too.

# CHAPTER 5

# HARVEST HURRY-UP

When gardens and markets start spilling over with abundance, it means the next season is here: Harvest Hurry-Up. Grain growers are checking the moisture content of their crops daily to see if the time is right to start combining. Once the harvest is on, everyone knows they have to hurry up and get it done. Life goes into full throttle. Many people work around the clock. If you drive around the province at this time, you'll see the dust of combines at work in the air all day every day. Sunsets are spectacular through the haze. It's a good year when the work gets done before an unexpected snow grinds it all to a painful stop.

Market and home gardeners are also alert. They watch the frost reports and nightly lows. They keep a stash of blankets by the back door, ready to shield summer's bounty should hail or frost threaten it. The definition of a good harvest is that everything is ready all at once. Whether you're picking your own crop or picking the best at your local market, now is the time to preserve summer for all it's worth.

Follow the rule "Never can alone!" and pair up with a friend. In this chapter, I give you a primer on canning and preserving basics and eight detailed recipes to help you fill your cupboards as you capture the goodness of summer in bottles and jars.

# Canning and Preserving Basics

Years ago, I helped lead canning bee workshops for Slow Food Calgary. They were transformational for the participants. The people who came had always wanted to learn how to can but lacked mentorship. Some of them even broke down and cried in gratitude. We kept the canning bees small on purpose. The participants told us they felt a loving transfer of knowledge they'd never had the opportunity to receive in their own families.

I grew up in a family with three generations of great cooks. Every year as summer wound down, it didn't matter whose home you entered, there was some kind of jam, jelly, or pickle making going on. When something is part of the fabric of your life, you learn without knowing it. I never realized how blessed I was until I did that volunteer work for Slow Food.

In this chapter, I'm happy to continue sharing what I know. Food knowledge like this takes you from just surviving to thriving. I'm grateful for the mentorship of my parents, my grandparents, and the Slow Food volunteers I taught with, my friend Penny Marshall and chefs Val Andrews and Dee Hobsbawn-Smith. I've tapped into recipes from my family, the Alberta Food Tours team, and our community. I hope you'll use this chapter as a launch pad into the art of canning. For people who grow up in a small town like I did—with little access to produce in winter—pickles and preserves were always bright spots on our supper table.

Properly sealed jars will keep for years in your pantry but why hoard them? Use them up, share them, and take the opportunity to mentor someone with each batch you make.

Rule number one: If you can help it, NEVER CAN ALONE. Canning is labour-intensive but immensely rewarding. There are few sounds that make a home cook happier than the popping noise lids make when jars of goodies have been properly processed. Still, facing a mountain of tomatoes or spiky little cukes in your kitchen alone can be daunting. Tackling the job arm in arm with a mate keeps your spirits high and the work light. So find a pickling partner and take turns "doing up" each other's bounty.

Now, let's get right to it with some other guidelines to keep in mind.

## ACIDITY LEVELS

First of all, when it comes to canning, foods can be divided into high or low acid.

- **HIGH-ACID FOODS** have a pH of 4.6 or lower. They include most fruits, tomatoes, and some vegetables. High-acid foods may be processed in a water bath canner. Citric acid or lemon juice is usually added to ensure the acidity level is just as it should be. When you're canning vegetables, you also add vinegar and sugar.
- **LOW-ACID FOODS** have pH values higher than 4.6. They should be processed in a pressure canner and include red meats, seafood, poultry, milk, and all fresh vegetables except for most tomatoes. Most mixtures of low-acid and high-acid foods also have pH values above 4.6, so if you're canning a mix, make sure the recipe includes enough lemon juice, citric acid, or vinegar to make them acid foods.

## PECTIN

Naturally occurring pectin comes from the skin, pith, and seeds of fruit. Apples and citrus fruits contain very high quantities of pectin. Commercial pectin is generally made from apple and citrus fruits, with or without the addition of sugar. When heated with sugar, it causes a thickening that is characteristic of jams and jellies. Commercial pectin comes in two forms: dry crystals and liquid. Recipes do not always gel successfully if dry crystals are exchanged for liquid and vice versa. Use the form the recipe calls for.

Jams, jellies, chutneys, conserves, and syrups can be made without the addition of store-bought pectin. However, making preserves without store-bought pectin is more time-consuming and requires more attention. Using commercial pectin saves a lot of time.

Commercial pectins gel in the presence of sugar and acid. These pectins are usually blended with sugar and other additives. They produce a firmer-set product. If you use these products, you must measure the ingredients accurately; otherwise your product may not set.

Other high-acid preserves will set without the addition of commercial pectin and with as little as 0 to 30 percent sugar. But remember, preserving using this method requires extra time and attention.

## POTS, PANS, AND JARS

Use stainless steel or ceramic pots with heavy bottoms. Anything other than stainless steel or ceramic pots may react to the acid/sugar in your batch and cause discoloration or stop your ingredients from setting. Wide, shallow pots and pans are generally better than tall, deep ones.

For sweet preserves it's best to use ½-cup to 1-cup jars. If you use larger jars, there's a greater possibility that the set may break down during the cooling period. This results in a softer set or no set at all.

## STERILIZING JARS FOR PRODUCTS PROCESSED FOR LESS THAN 10 MINUTES

If you're processing jams, jellies, or pickled products for less than 10 minutes, you must use sterilized jars to store them. To sterilize empty jars, put them right side up on the rack of a boiling water bath canner. Fill the canner and jars with hot (but not boiling) water to 1 inch above the tops of the jars. Bring to a boil and boil for 10 minutes at altitudes of less than 1,000 feet. At higher elevations, boil for 1 additional minute per additional 1,000 feet of elevation. Using tongs, remove and drain the hot sterilized jars one at a time and place them on a baking sheet. Put them in the oven on the baking sheet at 200°F to keep them hot. Save the hot water for processing your filled jars.

Once you've filled the jars with food, put the lids on top and tighten the screw band rings.

**IMPORTANT:**

- You don't need to sterilize jars for fruits, tomatoes, and pickled or fermented foods that will be processed for 10 minutes or longer in a boiling water canner. You can simply run them through the dishwasher and then keep them on a baking sheet in the oven as above.
- You don't have to boil lids. They only need to sit in hot water long enough to soften the rubber ring. Five minutes is plenty of time to soften the ring. Never reuse lids.

## VINEGAR

Always use vinegar with a minimum acidity of 5 percent. Anything less and you risk the food spoiling, which can have serious consequences. You'll find the acidity level on the label of the vinegar bottle. Never use homemade vinegar or unlabelled vinegar—if you can't be sure of the acidity, you can't be sure of the safety. Don't buy more-acidic vinegars either. If a vinegar is 10 percent, dilute it by adding the equivalent of half its volume in water.

## WATER

Use distilled, reverse-osmosis, or spring water. Chlorinated water may affect the flavour of your finished product or inhibit the fermentation process. When I discovered this, it was a light bulb moment for me.

## SALT

Use premium-quality sea salt. Do not use iodized salt or table salts, as they contain additives that may cause discoloration and affect the flavour of the finished product.

## SPICES

Use whole spices. Ground spices will cloud your pickling medium. Common pickling spice mixes usually include a combination of bay leaf, mustard seed, coriander, pepper, allspice, juniper, cinnamon, mace, dried ginger, and dill seeds.

## STORING CANNED FOODS

The best storage temperatures for canned and dried foods is between 50°F and 70°F. Foods stored above 95°F may spoil.

# The Water Bath Canning Method

**TAKES** About 30 minutes
**RATING** All levels

This method of canning is normally used for processing high-acid foods like marmalades, jams, jellies, chutneys, and pickles. I describe the process in general here and in detail, with timing, in each recipe. Basically, you fill the jars with the food, seal them loosely with the lid and rings, and then completely submerge them in vigorously boiling water for the prescribed amount of time in the recipe. If something is hot pack, the product must be hot when ladling it into the jars. Cold pack means the food is packed raw but has boiling sauce, syrup, or water added to the jars before processing.

**WHAT YOU NEED TO GATHER**

Jars or bottles suitable for the product, preferably all the same or a similar size
Rimmed baking sheet to set the jars on when in the oven
Water bath canner
Kettle
Pot to heat the lids
Long tongs and a bottle gripper to grip bottles and jars
Wide-mouth funnel
Metal ladle
Glass measuring cups
Clean tea towels (dish towels)
Vinegar
Cooling racks

**WHAT YOU NEED TO DO**

1. Preheat the oven to 200°F and wash the jars.
2. Heat the clean jars in the oven for at least 15 minutes. If you like, you can first place them in a saucepan, cover them with water, and bring to a boil. Turn off the heat and let them sit in hot water until they are ready to use or hold them in a 200°F oven.
3. Fill the canning bath with water to about two-thirds full, as the jars will displace water when you add them, and heat to boiling. Turn the heat to low and keep the water hot on a low simmer—but don't let it boil.
4. Have a large pot or kettle filled with hot water ready to top up the water bath, and place the lids and rings in another pot of boiled water until needed.
5. Once the product you want to can is ready, remove the jars from the oven and place the tray on a heatproof surface.
6. Using a funnel and a ladle or measuring cup, fill the jars with the hot product.
7. Wipe any spills with a clean paper towel or cloth and immediately place the lids on the jars.
8. Fill the jars one batch at a time (a batch = the number of jars that will fill the canner).
9. Place the jars gently into the hot water canner. Add 2 Tablespoons of vinegar to the canning bath to prevent residue buildup on the glass.
10. Bring to a boil, cover the pot, and maintain a gentle boil for the required canning time. Start counting the processing time from when the water starts to boil.

SUNDOG ORGANIC FARM
LUCKY DILL PICKLES

## A FEW POINTS TO NOTE:

- Bottles and jars must be clean and hot
- Ladles and funnels must be as clean as possible
- When you're filling the jars be sure to wipe the rims absolutely clean of any product before applying the lid and screw band
- Always allow for about ¼ to 1½ inches of air space between the rim of the jar and the product you've ladled into the jar
- Do not place a hot product on a cold counter—your jars might crack or even break
- Always check the storage times in a recipe—different products can be stored for different times
- Adding a little vinegar to the water bath's water prevents the minerals in water from adhering to the jar surface and creating an unpleasant and dirty-looking finished product

11 After the appropriate time, turn off the heat, let the jars sit in water for 5 minutes, then remove to the cooling rack.
12 Check the gaskets on the lids the next day. They may take up to 24 hours to seal and they should be sucked down when cool.
13 Got all that? Now you're ready to rock 'n' roll with some of my all-time favourite pickling, canning, and preserving recipes.

# Classic Canned Tomatoes

**MAKES** Twenty-four 1-pint or twelve 1-quart jars
**TAKES** About 2 hours' active time + 45 to 55 minutes' processing time
**RATING** All levels but novice cooks might want to do this with a mentor if possible

My friend Marianne Spoletini once casually mentioned she'd be happy to help me can tomatoes. The first time, we did 40 pounds. While the tomatoes were having their water bath, we sat down to enjoy a cuppa and she asked, "How did you feel about that?" I said that it was AMAZINGLY fast and easy. She chuckled and said, "Just a little tip. If you're going to call in an Italian, you can get A LOT more tomatoes." One year, we did 200 pounds with Marianne's octogenarian mother, Theresa Tudda, who is a legendary Calgary cook, and they didn't break a sweat.

**WHAT YOU NEED TO GATHER**

Large pot
Large bowl
Jars
Rimmed baking sheet
Lids and rings
Small saucepan
Paring knife
Slotted spoon
Canning bath
Towels

25 lb Roma tomatoes
25 sprigs fresh clean basil

**WHAT YOU NEED TO DO**

1. Bring a large pot of water to a boil. Prepare a large bowl of ice cubes and cold water.
2. Heat the clean jars on a rimmed baking sheet in the oven at 200°F for at least 15 minutes. Keep fresh lids and rings at hand in a small saucepan of hot water.
3. Wash the tomatoes under cold running water.
4. Use a paring knife to remove the core at the top and to cut a small "X" in the bottom of each tomato.
5. Immerse the tomatoes, a few at a time, in the boiling water until the skins split, about 1 to 2 minutes.
6. Use a slotted spoon to transfer them to ice and cold water. After a minute or so, slip the skins off the tomatoes using a paring knife and pile the peeled tomatoes into another big bowl.
7. Place 1 sprig of basil in each of the prepared jars and then fill the jars with tomatoes, leaving ½ inch of air space between the tomatoes and the lid. As you fill the jars, occasionally plunge a knife into the tomatoes to remove air pockets and squish as many tomatoes into the jar as possible.
8. Wipe the lip of all the jars once they're stuffed, add the sealer lids, and screw the rings on, being careful not to screw them too tightly.
9. Lower the jars gently into the canning bath.
10. Let the water come back to a boil over high heat and then set the timer for 45 minutes for pint jars and 55 minutes for quart jars.

11 Turn off the heat when the time is up and let the jars sit in the water for 5 minutes before you place them on a countertop lined with towels. Set the jars lid sides down on the towels and then wrap the towels around them and leave for 24 hours. (Mrs. Tudda says this slows down the cooling-off process and improves the success rate of them sealing.) The jars are sealed when the lids are sucked down and immobile.

12 Store the sealed jars in a cool, dry place for up to 2 years. Place any unsealed jars in the refrigerator and use within a few days. Easy-to-Multiply Tomato Soup (page 223) would be a good way to use them.

## #EATALBERTAFIRST TIP:

If you're going to buy 25 lb of Roma tomatoes, you'll find them most affordable in late August or early September when they're most plentiful.

# Green Tomato Chow Chow

**MAKES** Sixteen 1-cup jars
**TAKES** About 4 hours' active time + 20 minutes' processing time + overnight salting
**RATING** All levels

This is an old family recipe that my parents made every fall. Dad grew bushels of tomatoes each year but they rarely all ripened on the vine. We loved this solution to an abundance of green tomatoes. I hope you do too. Enjoy your chow chow with a dab of Greek yogurt on baked potatoes, with Tourtière Canadienne (page 117), and especially with Maple-Brined Roast Turkey (page 325).

### WHAT YOU NEED TO GATHER

Knife
Cutting board
Measuring cups and spoons
Large non-reactive (glass or pottery) bowl
Tea towels
Stockpot
Cheesecloth and kitchen twine
Wooden spoon
Jars
Rimmed baking sheet
Lids and rings
Small saucepan
Wide-mouth funnel
Canning bath
Lifter or tongs

8 lb green tomatoes
5 lb onions
½ cup pickling salt
10 cups loosely packed brown sugar
8 cups white vinegar (or just enough to cover the tomato and onion mix)
1 package pickling mix tied in cheesecloth

### WHAT YOU NEED TO DO

1. Slice the tomatoes and onions horizontally in rounds and layer them in the large bowl, sprinkling each layer lightly with pickling salt.
2. Cover with a tea towel and leave them on the counter overnight, or for at least 8 hours but no more than 12, then drain the accumulated liquid and rinse them in cold water and drain again.
3. Transfer the mixture to a stockpot and add the sugar, enough vinegar to cover (you may need slightly more or less than the 8 cups), and the pickling mix.
4. Bring the mixture to a boil on high heat and then lower the heat to medium-low and simmer, stirring occasionally, until the juices reduce and become thick, sticky, and a rich brown colour, at least 2 hours.
5. Meanwhile, preheat the oven to 200°F and sterilize your canning jars as directed previously. Place them on a rimmed baking sheet in the oven until you need them. Keep fresh lids and rings to hand in a small saucepan of hot water.
6. Fill the sterile jars, leaving ½ inch of air space. Wipe any spillage from the rims with a clean tea towel, top the jars with lids, and lightly twist on the rings, being careful not to screw them too tightly.
7. Process the jars in the water bath for 20 minutes.
8. Remove the jars from the bath and place on clean tea towels on the counter. Cover them and let them settle overnight. The lids should all pop and be sealed within 24 hours.
9. Store the sealed jars in a cool dark place for up to 1 year. Transfer any jars that didn't seal to the refrigerator and use them within 3 weeks.

# Salsa

**MAKES** Twelve 1-cup jars
**TAKES** About 90 minutes' active time + 5 minutes' processing time
**RATING** All levels

This recipe comes from a wonderful cook named Maria Klyzub-Andryo. Maria and her husband, Terry Andryo, are huge supporters of Alberta's local food scene. Maria is a skilled preserver, and I love to follow her progress in canning season. When I saw photos of her salsa on Instagram, it looked so good, I asked if she'd share the recipe. And she said yes. The Andryos also loaned us many of their Ukrainian dishes and linens for our photography. Enjoy with Big-Batch Burritos (page 225), Alberta Sunshine Eggs (page 315), and any Mexican food you like.

### WHAT YOU NEED TO GATHER

Knife
Cutting board
Measuring cups and spoons
Large saucepan
Jars
Rimmed baking sheet
Lids and rings
Small saucepan
Ladle
Magnetic lid lifter
Canning bath
Tea towels

10 medium field tomatoes, skins removed (see page 191)
2 cloves garlic, minced
2 medium onions, finely chopped
3–5 jalapeños, seeded and diced
⅔ cup cider vinegar
Two 5½-ounce (156 ml) cans tomato paste
1 red bell pepper, seeded and diced
1 yellow bell pepper, seeded and diced
1 green bell pepper, seeded and diced
½ cup finely chopped fresh cilantro

### WHAT YOU NEED TO DO

1. Place the tomatoes, garlic, onions, jalapeños, vinegar, and tomato paste in a large saucepan and bring to a boil over high heat.
2. Reduce the heat to medium and let the mixture simmer, uncovered, stirring occasionally, for 10 minutes to reduce the liquid.
3. Stir in the peppers and cilantro and simmer for an additional 10 to 15 minutes for the flavours to meld and the vegetables to cook.
4. Preheat the oven to 200°F and sterilize your canning jars as instructed previously. Place them on a rimmed baking sheet in the oven until needed. Keep fresh lids and rings at hand in a saucepan of hot water.
5. Ladle the mixture into the hot sterilized jars, leaving ½ inch of air space. Wipe any spillage from the rims with a clean tea towel, top the jars with lids, and lightly twist on the rings, being careful not to screw them too tightly.
6. Process in a canning bath for 5 minutes.
7. Turn off the heat and let the jars rest in the water for 5 minutes, then place them on tea towels on your counter and leave them alone for 24 hours. The lids should all pop and be sealed within 24 hours.
8. Store the sealed jars in a cool dark place for up to 1 year. Transfer any jars that didn't seal to the refrigerator and use them within 3 weeks.

# Sweet Pickled Beets

**MAKES** Six 2-cup jars
**TAKES** About 2 hours' active time + 35 minutes' processing time
**RATING** Competent to proficient

I've always loved beets but since I have started making salads with pickled beets, soft chèvre, and candied nuts, I have treasured these ruby gems even more. You can also enjoy them on a charcuterie board, as a condiment, or in sandwiches.

**WHAT YOU NEED TO GATHER**

Large bowl
Knife
Cutting board
Stockpot
Jars
Rimmed baking sheet
Lids and rings
Lifter
Small saucepan
Medium saucepan
Canning bath
Tea towels

6 lb beets
6 teaspoons pickling spice
6 bay leaves
6 cloves (optional)
3 cups apple cider vinegar
2¼ cups water
¾ cup + 3 Tablespoons sugar
1 cinnamon stick
1 Tablespoon + 2 teaspoons salt

**WHAT YOU NEED TO DO**

1. Prepare a large bowl of iced water.
2. Wash and trim the beets, then cook them in a stockpot of boiling salted water on high heat until tender when pierced with a knife, about 15 minutes.
3. Drain off the water, transfer the beets to the iced water to cool, then remove the skins.
4. Slice the beets in ¼-inch rounds or quarters as you please.
5. Preheat the oven to 200°F and sterilize your canning jars as directed previously. Place them on a rimmed baking sheet in the oven until you need them. Keep fresh lids and rings to hand in a small saucepan of hot water.
6. Place 1 teaspoon of the pickling spice, 1 bay leaf, and 1 clove (optional) in each clean jar and layer the beets on top.
7. Make a brine by combining the cider vinegar, water, sugar, cinnamon stick, and salt in a saucepan on medium-high heat. Bring to a boil, reduce the heat to medium, and simmer for a few minutes to infuse the cinnamon flavour. Discard the cinnamon stick.
8. Divide the hot brine evenly among the 6 jars of beets, leaving ½ inch of air space.
9. Wipe any spillage from the rims with a clean tea towel, top the jars with lids, and lightly twist on the rings, being careful not to screw them too tightly.
10. Place the jars in the canning bath and process for 35 minutes. Turn off the heat and let the jars sit in the water for 5 minutes. Place the jars on tea towels on the counter and leave for 24 hours to seal. The lids should all pop and be sealed within 24 hours.
11. Store the sealed jars in a cool dark place for up to 1 year. Transfer any jars that didn't seal to the refrigerator and use them within 3 weeks.

## #EATALBERTAFIRST TIP:

Look for organic beets from Poplar Bluff, Blue Mountain, Eagle Creek, Sparrow's Nest, Riverbend, Sundog, and The Homestead. They just taste better.

# Fresh Dill Pickles

**MAKES** Seven 2-cup jars
**TAKES** 1 to 2 hours' active time + 15 minutes' processing time + 10 hours' soaking time.
**RATING** Competent to proficient

From mid-August to mid-September you can find big nylon bags of pickling cucumbers at markets around Alberta. My friend Val Andrews has a few tips on how to keep your dills crunchy to share: Soak the vegetables in water and a constant supply of ice for up to 10 hours before using. Add a thumb-sized piece of fresh horseradish root or a grape leaf to each jar before adding the cucumbers. And pickle cucumbers within 24 hours of picking them. Enjoy with Buffalo Trail Bison Burgers (page 115), with Zesty Potato Salad (page 143), in egg salad, or in almost any sandwich.

**WHAT YOU NEED TO GATHER**

Large bucket or bowl for soaking
Knife
Cutting board
Measuring cups and spoons
Large saucepan
Jars
Rimmed baking sheet
Lids and rings
Small saucepan
Lifter
Canning bath
Tea towels

30–36 (each 3–4 inches long) pickling cucumbers
3 cups white vinegar
3 cups water
6 Tablespoons sea salt
14 sprigs fresh dill, washed and dried
7 cloves garlic, sliced
10½ teaspoons mustard seed
7 (each 2 inches long) pieces fresh horseradish

**WHAT YOU NEED TO DO**

1. Wash the cucumbers and soak them in a large, clean bucket of iced water for 10 hours. Replace the ice frequently to keep the temperature way down.
2. Place the vinegar, water, and salt in a large saucepan and bring to a boil over high heat to make a brine.
3. Preheat the oven to 200°F and sterilize your canning jars as directed previously. Place them on a rimmed baking sheet in the oven until you need them. Keep fresh lids and rings at hand in a small saucepan of hot water.
4. Put 1 sprig of dill, 1 garlic clove, 1½ teaspoons of mustard seeds, and a piece of horseradish root in each clean jar.
5. Pack the cucumbers tightly into each jar, adding another layer of dill at the halfway mark.
6. Fill the jars with the brine, leaving ½ inch of air space. Clean the rims, place the caps, and screw the rings on, being careful not to screw them too tightly.
7. Place in the canning bath and process for 15 minutes.
8. Turn off the heat, let cool in the water for 5 minutes, and then place on clean tea towels on the counter for 24 hours to seal. The lids should all pop and be sealed within 24 hours.
9. Store the sealed jars in a cool dry place for up to 1 year. Store any that don't seal in the refrigerator and eat within 2 weeks.

# Blueberry Jalapeño Jam

**MAKES** Six 1-cup jars
**TAKES** 60 minutes' active time + 5 minutes' processing time
**RATING** All levels

This is another great recipe from my friend chef Deb Poulin of Twisted Fork in St. Paul, Alberta. Wild blueberries grow in Northern Alberta, and Deb picks them to make this jam. The zip she adds with the jalapeños is a fantastic complement to her famous Buffalo Trail Bison Burgers (page 115) that she shares in chapter 3. You can also use it to liven up your next grilled cheese sandwich.

**WHAT YOU NEED TO GATHER**

Canning jars
Rimmed baking sheet
Lids and rings
Small saucepan
Measuring cups and spoons
Large pot
Wooden spoon
Ladle
Wide-mouth funnel
Canning bath
Lid lifter
Tea towels

4 lb blueberries
2 finely diced jalapeños (including seeds for more spice)
2 cups sugar
½ cup water
1 pouch liquid pectin

**WHAT YOU NEED TO DO**

1. Preheat the oven to 200°F and sterilize your canning jars as directed previously. Place them on a rimmed baking sheet in the oven until you need them. Keep fresh lids and rings at hand in a small saucepan of hot water.
2. Place the blueberries, jalapeños, and sugar in a large pot and add the water. Bring to a boil over medium-high heat and then reduce to medium heat and cook, stirring from time to time, until thickened, about 30 to 45 minutes depending on the moisture content of the berries.
3. Remove the mixture from the heat and stir in the pectin.
4. Ladle the jam into the jars using a wide-mouth funnel and leaving ½ inch of air space. Wipe the jar rims to remove any residue. Apply the lids and rings, being careful not to screw them too tightly.
5. Place the jars in the canning bath and process for 5 minutes. Turn off the heat and let the jars sit in the water for 5 more minutes. Place the jars on tea towels on the counter and cover with towels to let cool slowly over 24 hours. All the lids should seal within 24 hours.
6. Store the sealed jars in a cool dry place for up to 6 months. Store any that don't seal in the refrigerator and eat within 2 weeks.

# Lady Ashburnham Mustard Pickles

**MAKES** Six 2-cup jars
**TAKES** 1 hour active time + overnight soaking + 1½ hours the next day including 15 minutes' processing time
**RATING** All levels

Lady Ashburnam was originally a telephone operator named Maria Anderson. Captain Thomas Ashburnham, the fifth son of the Earl of Ashburnham and the family's problem child, was sent to the colonies (Fredericton, New Brunswick, in this case) to mend his ways. He fell in love with sweet Maria, the telephone operator, just from talking to her and changed his ways. When the couple married, Maria always served her sister Lucy's mustard pickles at their gatherings. After Thomas's four older brothers all died, Thomas became an earl and Maria, a duchess. Ironically, though she never made the pickles herself, they became known as Lady Ashburnham Mustard Pickles. Fortunately, their taste lives up to their great name. Enjoy with Berbon Glazed Ham (page 311), fish, meat, and poultry—especially roast chicken or Maple-Brined Roast Turkey (page 325).

### WHAT YOU NEED TO GATHER

Non-reactive pottery or glass bowl
Knife
Cutting board
Measuring cups and spoons
Tea towels
Large pot
Wooden spoon
Jars
Rimmed baking sheet
Lids and rings
Small saucepan
Ladle
Canning bath
Magnetic lid lifter

6 large field cucumbers, quartered, seeded, and finely chopped
¼ cup sea salt
4 cups finely chopped onions
2 cups sugar
3 Tablespoons flour
1 Tablespoon yellow mustard seeds
1 Tablespoon turmeric powder
1 Tablespoon celery seed
2 cups vinegar

### WHAT YOU NEED TO DO

*Day 1*

1 Layer the cut cucumbers and salt in a large non-reactive bowl, cover with a tea towel, and let stand overnight on the kitchen counter.

*Day 2*

1 Rinse and drain the cucumbers and place them in a large pot with the onions, sugar, flour, mustard seeds, turmeric, celery seed, and vinegar, mixing well.
2 Bring to a boil on high heat, then lower the heat to medium and cook, stirring occasionally, uncovered, for 1 hour.
3 Preheat the oven to 200°F and sterilize your canning jars as instructed previously. Place them on a rimmed baking sheet in the oven until you need them. Keep fresh lids and rings at hand in a small saucepan of hot water.
4 Ladle the hot mixture into the hot sterilized jars, leaving ½ inch of air space. Clean the rims, cover with the lids, and screw on the rings, being careful not to screw them too tightly.
5 Place in the canning bath and process for 15 minutes, then turn off and leave for 5 minutes.
6 Remove from the canning bath and place on tea towels on the counter for 24 hours for the lids to seal. All the lids should seal within 24 hours.
7 Store the sealed jars in a cool dry place for up to 1 year. Store any that don't seal in the refrigerator and eat within 2 weeks.

# Crabapple Jelly

**MAKES** 8 to 10 jars
**TAKES** 1 hour active time + 10 minutes' processing time + a few more hours spread over a few days to pick and prep the apples
**RATING** Proficient

Most apple trees of the good eating variety don't thrive in Alberta but hardy crabapples sure do. Many of us plant trees and shrubs in our yards, so why not plant something that will bear fruit? Crabapples are a great choice because they are hardy and yield pretty, pink, flavourful juice. You can use it straight up, as a base for cocktails, or for my favourite, this jelly recipe. Though this recipe takes a couple of days to complete, there are really only a few hours of active time involved. And looking at a pantry cupboard lined with the glistening ruby jar gem results makes it well worth the time and effort involved.

**WHAT YOU NEED TO GATHER**

Knife
Cutting board
Large stockpot
Cheesecloth
Sieve
Large bowl
Measuring cups and spoons
Canning bath
Jars
Rimmed baking sheet
Lids and rings
Magnetic lid lifter
Small saucepan
Dishcloth
Tea towels

4 lb crabapples
4 cups sugar
1 Tablespoon store-bought bottled lemon juice

**WHAT YOU NEED TO DO**

1. Wash the apples and remove the stem and blossom ends. Halve the apples but do not core them. Put them in a large stockpot and cover with cold water.
2. Bring the mixture to a boil over high heat, stirring frequently, and then reduce the heat and boil gently, stirring and crushing the apples until soft, about 30 minutes.
3. Pour the apple mixture through a cheesecloth-lined large sieve set over a large bowl. Let the juice drip for at least 2 hours, or up to overnight. Though it might be tempting, don't squish it through, as that might cause your juice and subsequent jelly to be cloudy. Note: You need at least 4 cups of juice. If you don't have enough, you can top it up with some regular apple juice.
4. Prepare your canner, lids, and jars. I put my jars in the dishwasher and run them through. When they're done, I put them on a baking sheet in a 200°F oven to keep them warm. I put my lids and rings in a pot of freshly boiled water and lift them out with a magnetic lid lifter (available anywhere canning supplies are).
5. Combine the apple juice with the sugar (don't be tempted to scrimp, as the fruit needs this much sugar to gel properly) and lemon juice in a large stockpot.
6. Bring the mixture to a boil over medium-high heat, stirring to dissolve all the sugar. Boil hard, stirring frequently, until the jelly starts to "sheet." This should take about 25 to 30 minutes.

7 Remove the jelly juice from the heat and skim off any pink foam that has accumulated. Pour the hot jelly juice into the waiting jars, leaving ¼ inch of air space. I find it best to use a glass 1-cup measuring cup with a handle to do this and to have a dishcloth under it to catch any drips.
8 Wipe the rims of all your jars and apply the lids and the rings, being careful not to screw them too tightly.
9 Place the jars in the canning bath all at once, ensuring they are completely covered. Cover the canner with a lid and bring the water to a boil over high heat. Process for 10 minutes once it reaches the boiling point.
10 Remove the canner lid, wait 5 minutes, then remove the jars to a counter lined with tea towels. Cover with towels to let cool slowly over 24 hours. All the lids should seal within 24 hours.
11 Store the sealed jars in a cool, dark place for up to 1 year. Place any unsealed jars in the refrigerator and eat within 2 months.

## PRO TIPS:

- Gather 4 lb of crabapples from your own tree after the first frost. Or ask a neighbour for some of their crabapples in return for jelly.
- To detect if the apple juice is ready to "sheet" and become jelly, use a cold metal spoon to pick up some of the jelly juice, then turn the spoon sideways. If the jelly falls off in drops, it's not done. If it falls off in a single sheet, it's done.

CHAPTER 6

FALL
BACK

The first frost is your clue that fall is back. By October, the kids have been back in school awhile and activities are going full tilt. Families are crunched for time. Batch-cooking Saturdays or Sundays are a great way to help folks cope with life's demands. While the fresh local berries and the last of the Okanagan peaches have disappeared from the markets, crisp juicy apples and pears of all sorts are stacked row upon row. Pumpkins and squashes, root vegetables, and cold crops like green and purple cabbages and Brussels sprouts are stepping forward to take their turn in the limelight. It's time to stock up on these and get your turkey order in as well, because our Canadian Thanksgiving lands smack in the middle of this season. It's a time to be outdoors as much as possible until the snow flies.

Days spent roaming hiking trails, admiring golden larch needles and aspen leaves, and getting in the last few road-biking spins for the season all feel like gifts. Parents cross their fingers for a Halloween without snow and sub-zero temperatures. The daylight hours are waning as we head to the date we all fall back. Maybe it's the chill in the air. Maybe it's that sudden shift on the clock that brings nightfall to our door an hour earlier, but this is a time for comfort food. The batch-cooking recipes in this chapter are all about cooking comfort for you, your family, friends, and community. This kind of food is the essence of the sentiment that sharing is caring. It was that way long before any social media guru came up with the phrase. It's time to gather round whatever your modern-day hearth looks like and get cooking.

# The Joy of Batch-Cooking

Freezers filled with batch-cooked foods are a source of help and comfort for neighbours and friends in need when life's calamities hit. Alberta has seen its share of forest fires and floods. Everybody knows someone with a new baby or who has had a frightening diagnosis or who is going through something. Dropping a gift of food from your batch-cooking stash is a timeless custom that transcends seasons. But this season, with markets full of harvest's cornucopia of produce, is the best season for batch-cooking. This section arms you to face whatever comes your way.

The recipes in this chapter are the ones I turn to time and again when my own joyous life gets busy and to help friends in need. Mastering them will prepare you for anything and everything. The first recipe is for a clear and flavourful homemade stock. You can use this to make a variety of soups and sauces and you'll save lots of money while you're at it. All the soups, casseroles, and stews in this chapter are tremendously tasty crowd-pleasers. All of the recipes except the Puffed Wheat Squares and carrot cake freeze well. The snacks and desserts are as easy as they are drool-worthy.

We all experience hard times to one degree or another in life, but the recipes in this chapter can help us through them, even in the smallest way.

# Homemade Stock

**MAKES** 16 cups
**TAKES** 5 to 10 minutes' active time + about 4 hours' simmering, packaging, and cleaning time
**RATING** All levels

Making homemade stock is one of the most frugal things you can do as a cook—and you control the amount of salt, which is a major health bonus. Store-bought versions are often loaded with the stuff. And they often don't come in the size a home cook might need. I like to divide what I freeze into 1-, 2-, and 4-cup containers. Beyond all that, breathing in the smell of stock simmering away on the stove for an afternoon followed by slowly and steadily ladling it into storage containers for your future convenience is a very satisfying way to spend time.

**WHAT YOU NEED TO GATHER**

Large stockpot
Cheesecloth and twine or tea ball
Strainer
Large bowl
Storage containers

3 bay leaves
1 Tablespoon whole black peppercorns
1 teaspoon dried thyme or 6 sprigs fresh thyme
1 teaspoon dried summer savory
3–5 lb chicken, turkey, or beef bones
3 stalks celery
3 carrots, whole but peeled
2 onions, halved, and any extra onion skins you've collected (they add a nice brown colour)
1 apple, any type (skin on), halved
6–8 quarts cold water

**WHAT YOU NEED TO DO**

1. Tie the bay leaves, peppercorns, thyme, and savory in a cheesecloth tied with kitchen twine.
2. Place the bones, celery, carrots, onions, apple, and bag of herbs in the stockpot and add enough cold water to cover everything by 1 inch, about 6 to 8 quarts.
3. Slowly bring it to almost the boiling point on medium-high heat, but don't let it reach a boil, because that causes a cloudy stock. Once the first bubbles start to appear, reduce the heat to low and let it warm through for 3 to 4 hours. Strain the broth and discard any solids.
4. Return the broth to simmer over low heat for an additional 30 minutes if you desire a more intense flavour. Otherwise, transfer to storage containers, cool, then freeze until needed.

## HOT TIPS FOR MAKING STOCK:

- Keep 2 plastic bags in your freezer. Add chicken or turkey carcass bones to one—all chicken parts are suitable but you'll get more flavour from the dark meat wings, legs, and necks—and key vegetable bits from your cutting board remnants to the other. I save celery hearts, washed leek ends, scallions, carrot ends, and onion skins.
- You can make beef broth this way too. Just place the beef bones on a baking sheet and bake them at 350°F for about an hour before placing them in the stockpot. This will deliver far more flavour.
- When you have about 3 to 5 lb of one kind of bones (could be poultry or beef but don't mix them) you are ready to make stock.
- Use only cold water to make stock. Hot water can seal the bones and lock the flavour inside.
- Your goal is to produce a clear stock, so simmer and do not boil the stock. Boiling causes the fat to emulsify into a cloudy, fatty-tasting stock.
- Always use dried herb leaves or whole spices and herbs, as ground ones will cloud the stock.
- Avoid adding salt to stock. Use your homemade stock in the dish you'll make and add salt to taste to the finished dish instead.
- Store stock in an airtight container in the refrigerator for up to 4 days. After that, it will sour and need to be reboiled. Or store it in 1-, 2-, or 4-cup containers in the freezer and thaw as you need them.

# Chicken and Wild Rice Soup

**MAKES** 6 servings
**TAKES** 20 minutes' active time + 45 minutes' simmering time
**RATING** All levels

Now that you've got all that glorious homemade stock (page 215) on hand, here's a tasty way to use it. After Thanksgiving or Christmas turkey dinner, you can easily make a variation of this soup using turkey stock and meat. Enjoy with Highwood Crossing Oat Buns (page 243) or Sweet Sourdough Biscuits (page 85).

### WHAT YOU NEED TO GATHER

Large stockpot
Knife
Cutting board
Measuring cups and spoons

1 teaspoon olive oil
1⅓ cups diced onion
⅓ cup diced carrot
⅓ cup diced celery
1 clove garlic, minced
8 cups chicken stock (page 215)
½ cup wild rice
1 cup chopped cooked chicken meat
1 cup chopped zucchini
1 cup chopped fresh tomatoes, skin on
1 cup fresh or frozen corn niblets
1 teaspoon dried summer savory
1 Tablespoon fresh curly parsley (optional)
1 teaspoon pepper

### WHAT YOU NEED TO DO

1. Heat the oil in a stockpot over medium heat and add the onions, carrots, and celery. Cook, stirring constantly, until translucent.
2. Add the garlic and cook until fragrant, about 30 seconds, before stirring in the stock and then the rice. Bring to a boil over medium-high heat and then turn the heat to low to simmer until the wild rice splits and is tender to chew, about 45 minutes.
3. Add the chicken, zucchini, tomatoes, corn, and savory. Heat through, about 10 to 15 minutes.
4. Garnish with fresh parsley, if desired, and add pepper to taste.

### VARIATION:

If you can't find wild rice, you can substitute any long-grain rice or other grain. Just cook it separately and add it at the end.

# Triple "S" Soup with Sausage, Squash, and Spinach

**MAKES** 4 to 5 quarts (enough for 8 to 12 servings)
**TAKES** 10 minutes' active time + 10 to 15 minutes' simmering time
**RATING** All levels

Keeping these ingredients in your spice drawer, pantry cupboard, and freezer means you can always make something tasty at a moment's notice. And the best part is that this makes a lot and freezes well, so you can enjoy it again or share it with someone who needs a little TLC. Depending on the spiciness of the sausage you use, you can create a mild or zippy broth to suit your palate. Enjoy with Sweet Sourdough No-Knead Bread (page 75) and Shades of Green Salad (page 129).

**WHAT YOU NEED TO GATHER**

Large soup pot
Knife
Cutting board
Wooden spoon
Measuring cups and spoons
Can opener

1 Tablespoon olive oil
1 onion, roughly chopped
1 lb frozen chicken or turkey sausage, thawed
½ cup white wine
28-ounce (796 ml) can whole tomatoes
2 cans water
19-ounce (540 ml) can beans (your choice), drained and rinsed
10-ounce (300-gram) package frozen chopped spinach
10-ounce (300-gram) package frozen butternut squash
1 teaspoon dried oregano
1 teaspoon dried basil
Salt and pepper

**WHAT YOU NEED TO DO**

1. Heat the oil in a soup pot on medium heat and then add the onions. Cook, stirring, until translucent.
2. Slice the sausage into rounds (or remove the meat from the casings and use a wooden spoon to break it up) and brown it, then add the wine. Stir well and scrape the brown bits off the bottom of the pan.
3. Add the tomatoes and their juice and use the empty can to measure out 2 cans of water. Add the beans, spinach, squash, oregano, and basil, and simmer until heated through, 10 to 15 minutes.
4. Taste the soup and season it with salt and pepper as desired.

### #EATALBERTAFIRST TIP:

Look for Alberta sausage makers like Spolumbo's, Meuwly's, Otto's, Sunterra, Spragg's, Old Country, Empire Provisions, and TK Ranch.

# Easy-to-Multiply Tomato Soup

**MAKES** 2 servings
**TAKES** 10 minutes' active time + 5 minutes' simmering time
**RATING** All levels

This recipe is one of the first things I taught my son, Cole, to cook. He quickly got creative with it. To this day, he loves to wing it. He'll add chili flakes or harissa and throw in leftover pasta or rice and vegetables. During university, if his local Italian market put their 3-litre cans of tomatoes on sale, he'd snap one up, make a huge batch of this soup, eat some, and freeze the rest. Follow Cole's lead and multiply this as you wish. Paying yourself forward by batch-cooking not only delivers delicious dividends, but also saves you money.

### WHAT YOU NEED TO GATHER

Saucepan
Wooden spoon
Can opener
High-speed blender

1–2 Tablespoons olive oil
½ cup chopped onion
1 teaspoon minced garlic
28-ounce (796 ml) can whole tomatoes or 4 cups Classic Canned Tomatoes (page 191)
2 Tablespoons tomato paste or basil or sun-dried pesto sauce
¼–½ cup cream of choice or milk of choice (optional)
Salt and pepper
Fresh basil or curly parsley, for garnish (optional)

### WHAT YOU NEED TO DO

1. Heat the oil in a saucepan on medium heat and add the onions. Cook until translucent. Stir in the garlic and cook until fragrant, about 30 seconds.
2. Pour in the tomatoes and their juice and the tomato paste and mix well.
3. Transfer the tomato mixture to a blender, purée to your desired smoothness, then return to the saucepan and heat through, about 5 minutes.
4. Add the cream (if using).
5. Season with salt and pepper to taste.
6. Garnish with fresh basil (if using).
7. Enjoy with a classic sandwich like egg salad, grilled cheese, or a tuna melt.

# Big-Batch Burritos

**MAKES** 16 burritos
**TAKES** 45 minutes' active time + 15 minutes' simmering time
**RATING** All levels

These burritos make a tasty, super-quick meal for people (especially families with kids in sports at suppertime) on the go. The recipe comes from our Alberta Food Tours' operations manager, Callandra Caufield. She always keeps them on hand and says that her kids, who are both busy with competitive swimming, even love them for breakfast. Callandra also likes to get creative with the fillings using different beans, grains, and veggies—especially mushrooms.

**WHAT YOU NEED TO GATHER**

Measuring cups and spoons
Bowl
Large frying pan
Wooden spoon
Can opener
Plastic wrap
Freezer bag

*For the seasoning*

2 Tablespoons chili powder
1½ teaspoons smoked paprika
1½ teaspoons cornstarch
1½ teaspoons salt
1 teaspoon ground cumin
1 teaspoon garlic powder
1 teaspoon onion powder
½ teaspoon oregano leaves
½ teaspoon black pepper
¼ teaspoon cayenne pepper

*For the filling*

2 lb ground beef, pork, chicken, or your favourite sausage
2 cups diced onion (about 1 large)
1 red bell pepper, seeded and diced
19-ounce (540 ml) can cooked lentils or black beans, drained and rinsed
1½ cups canned or frozen corn niblets
2 cups cooked long-grain white or brown rice

*For assembly*

16 whole wheat tortillas
4 cups grated cheddar, havarti, or Monterey Jack cheese
Toppings: hot sauce, salsa, guacamole, and sour cream

## PRO TIP:

If you're cooking the rice from scratch for this recipe, rather than using leftover rice, 1 cup of uncooked rice will give you 2 cups of cooked.

### WHAT YOU NEED TO DO

*For the seasoning*

1. Combine the chili powder, paprika, cornstarch, salt, cumin, garlic and onion powders, oregano, black pepper, and cayenne pepper in a bowl. Set aside.

*For the filling*

1. Heat a large frying pan over medium heat and brown the ground meat.
2. Stir in the onions and peppers and cook until the onions are translucent, about 5 minutes.
3. Stir in the lentils and corn, followed by the rice and the reserved seasoning mixture, reduce the heat to low, and simmer, stirring frequently, until heated through, about 10 to 15 minutes.

*For assembly*

1. Lay the tortillas on the counter and assemble the burritos by sprinkling ¼ cup of cheese down the centre of each one, followed by a heaping ½ cup of the burrito mixture. Add any and all of the toppings, if desired. Fold the short ends around the filling, then the long ends over each other, nice and tight.
2. Enjoy immediately.

## MAKE-AHEAD TIP:

After filling and folding the burritos, but before adding any toppings, you can wrap them in plastic wrap and freeze them in a large freezer bag. When you want to enjoy them from frozen, simply pull out a burrito, remove the plastic wrap, and microwave on high for about 1½ to 2 minutes.

# Chipotle Bison Chili

**MAKES** 7 quarts
**TAKES** 1 hour active time + 2 to 3 hours' simmering time
**RATING** Competent to proficient

This recipe was built for batch-cooking and feeding a crowd because it makes a huge amount. It comes from my friends Tanya Guetre and Michelle Kozy. They used to have a lovely little store and catering company called Savour. When they made this chili, I'd buy it by the gallon. When they closed their store, they very kindly shared the recipe so I could continue to enjoy it. I've adapted it a little bit and I'm thrilled to share my version as a way to enjoy Alberta bison with southwestern flare—in big batches—with you. Enjoy with a side of Hot Pepper Cornbread (page 135), Shades of Green Salad (page 129), or Never-the-Same-Way-Twice Coleslaw (page 139).

**WHAT YOU NEED TO GATHER**

Knife
Cutting board
Can opener
Measuring cups and spoons
Large frying pan
Stockpot or slow cooker

1 Tablespoon olive oil
1½ lb bison steak/roast, cut in 1-inch cubes
1½ lb extra-lean ground bison
4 carrots, peeled and diced
2 large onions, diced
3 stalks celery, diced
2 cups green, yellow, or orange bell peppers, seeded and diced
2 Tablespoons garlic paste
2 chipotle peppers in adobo, diced
2 heaping Tablespoons chili powder
1 Tablespoon ground cumin
1 teaspoon dried oregano leaves
1 teaspoon ground cinnamon
2 ripe tomatoes, chopped (with skins on)
Two 28-ounce (796 ml) cans whole tomatoes
19-ounce (540 ml) can red kidney beans
19-ounce (540 ml) can pinto beans
19-ounce (540 ml) can black beans
10-ounce (300-gram) package frozen chopped spinach
¼ cup tomato paste
2 Tablespoons dried or ½ cup chopped fresh Italian parsley
1 cup packed fresh cilantro leaves, measured then chopped
1 Tablespoon dried or ½ cup fresh chopped basil
4 cups low-sodium V8 juice
1½ teaspoons sea salt
1½ teaspoons pepper
¼ cup molasses
¼ cup lime juice
1½ Tablespoons hot sauce
Toppings: sour cream, guacamole, grated cheese, lime slices, and cilantro leaves

#### WHAT YOU NEED TO DO

1. Heat the oil in a large frying pan over medium heat, add the bison in small batches and brown the meat over medium-high heat, until most of the pink is gone. Transfer each browned batch to a very large stockpot or slow cooker until all the meat is cooked. Then, in the same frying pan, cook the carrots, onions, celery, and peppers over medium heat until just softened. Add a splash more oil if necessary to prevent the vegetables from sticking and burning.
2. Stir in the garlic and cook it until fragrant, about 30 seconds. Add the chipotle peppers followed by the chili powder, cumin, oregano, and cinnamon. Stir in the fresh tomatoes and allow their moisture to deglaze (loosen the sticky bits) at the bottom of the pan. Once the tomatoes are soft, add this mixture to the stockpot and set the big frying pan aside to soak in the sink.
3. Add the canned tomatoes and their juice, all the beans, the still-frozen spinach, tomato paste, parsley, cilantro, basil, and V8 juice to the stockpot and mix well.
4. Turn the heat to medium-low, bring to a simmer, and then add the sea salt, pepper, molasses, lime juice, and hot sauce. Adjust the herbs and spices to taste.
5. Simmer for approximately 2 to 3 hours to allow all the flavours to meld and the meat to become tender. Taste and adjust seasoning again before serving.
6. Garnish with sour cream, guacamole, grated cheese, lime slices, and fresh cilantro leaves.

### #EATALBERTAFIRST TIP:

Alberta bison producers include HGB Bison in Olds, Mount Bison and Cattle Company in Caroline, YR Bison Ranch in Red Deer, Thundering Ground Bison near Edmonton, First Nature Farms near Grande Prairie, Sweetgrass Bison in Southern Alberta, and Backwoods Buffalo in Woodlands County.

# Trail's End Classic Beef Stew

**MAKES** 6 to 8 servings
**TAKES** 30 minutes' active time + 4 hours' oven time
**RATING** All levels

This recipe comes from Rachel Herbert of Trail's End Beef. She says, "This is a classic in our kitchen, and when I say 'classic,' I mean that I cook it often but change it always. It's a nourishing one-pot meal and a great way to use up anything in the refrigerator. Most recently, that included sprouting potatoes, deformed carrots, and virtually empty jars of grainy mustard, salsa, and ketchup swished out with water for seasoning. And the best part is, you can do all the prep and walk away!" That's great advice from one of the busiest ranching women I know. Enjoy in big bowls with a hunk of Sweet Sourdough No-Knead Bread (page 75) or Sweet Sourdough Biscuits (page 85).

**WHAT YOU NEED TO GATHER**

Knife
Cutting board
Measuring cups and spoons
Bowl
Dutch oven or heavy flame-proof casserole with lid
Wooden spoon

1–2 lb grass-fed stewing beef, cut in 1-inch cubes
⅓ cup flour
Salt and pepper
Sweet paprika
3 Tablespoons butter or bacon grease
6–8 medium white or yellow potatoes, peeled and chopped bite-size
6–8 carrots, peeled and chopped bite-size
3 stalks celery, diced
1 large onion, peeled and diced
8 cloves garlic, peeled and left whole
4 cups grass-fed beef stock and/or vegetable stock, red wine, or beer
Generous dash Worcestershire sauce
1 teaspoon dried or 1 Tablespoon fresh finely chopped rosemary
1 teaspoon dried or 1 Tablespoon fresh thyme leaves
1 teaspoon dried or 1 Tablespoon fresh finely chopped sage leaves

### #EATALBERTAFIRST TIP:

Though Trail's End Beef typically sells out their sides of beef, they usually always have ground meat, sausages, pepperoni sticks, and broth for sale at their farm-gate store. Check it out if you are down Nanton way. Just call and make an appointment (see page 366 for contact details).

How long to stew? Rachel says, "There's no magic length of time to cook a stew. The stew is done when the beef melts in your mouth and the vegetables are fork-tender and buttery. If you wish to thicken the sauce, simply grab a fork and mash some of the potatoes."

### WHAT YOU NEED TO DO

1. Preheat the oven to 350°F.
2. Pat dry the beef cubes. Put the flour, a pinch of salt, a pinch of pepper, and a pinch of paprika in a mixing bowl, add the beef, and toss to coat.
3. Heat the butter in a Dutch oven over medium-high heat and brown the beef in batches until golden brown on all sides.
4. Remove the browned beef in its pot from the heat and add the potatoes, carrots, celery, onions, and garlic. Pour in the stock and Worcestershire sauce, then add the rosemary, thyme, sage, and salt and pepper to taste. Give everything a quick stir with a wooden spoon.
5. Place a lid on the Dutch oven and pop it in the oven on the middle rack. Cook for at least 4 hours and stir it at least once at the half-way mark, adding extra liquid if it appears dry.



SCOTTISH LUING CATTLE AT REDTAIL FARMS IN CASTOR

# Chunky Pasta Sauce with Hot Italian Sausage

**MAKES** 6 quarts
**TAKES** ½ hour active time + 2 to 3 hours' simmering time
**RATING** All levels

This truly makes a big batch, freezes beautifully, and can be used in a variety of ways. Serve it over your favourite pasta or as the meat component in lasagna. You can even add a few different cans of drained and rinsed beans and some chili powder for a quick and easy chili. This sauce served over a big plate of pasta is my family's favourite meal to come home to after a long fall day of outdoor work or fun, especially with a Shades of Green Salad (page 129) on the side.

**WHAT YOU NEED TO GATHER**

Knife
Cutting board
Non-stick frying pan
Paper towels
Plate
Measuring cup and spoons
Large stockpot

2½ lb hot Italian sausage
1 Tablespoon olive oil
2 onions, chopped
3–4 cloves garlic, minced
2 small zucchinis, chopped into bite-sized pieces
2 large green bell peppers, chopped into bite-sized pieces
1 large yellow bell pepper, chopped into bite-sized pieces
30–40 cremini mushrooms, halved
Two 28-ounce (796 ml) cans whole tomatoes
4 cups (1 L bottle) tomato sauce
5½-ounce (156 ml) can tomato paste
1 Tablespoon dried parsley
1 Tablespoon dried basil
1 Tablespoon dried oregano
3–4 dried bay leaves
10-ounce (300-gram) package frozen chopped spinach

**WHAT YOU NEED TO DO**

1. Remove the meat from the sausage casings and brown it in a non-stick frying pan over medium heat, breaking it up into a fine crumble as it cooks.
2. Drain the fat from the pan and put the meat on a plate between layers of paper towel to absorb the remaining fat from the meat. Set the meat aside.
3. Heat the oil in a large stockpot over medium heat and add the onions. Cook until translucent and then add the garlic and cook just until it becomes fragrant, about 30 seconds.
4. Stir in the zucchini, bell peppers, mushrooms, tomatoes, tomato sauce and paste, parsley, basil, oregano, bay leaves, and still-frozen spinach, adjust the heat to low, and bring to a slow steady simmer for 2 to 3 hours. And that's as hard as it gets!

# Sweet Potato Coconut Curried Lentils

**MAKES** 8 servings
**TAKES** 20 minutes' active time + 15 to 20 minutes' simmering time
**RATING** All levels

Dee Hobsbawn-Smith was my mentor when it came to taking city folk to meet farm folk. Long before there were Alberta Open Farm Days, Dee and our mutual friend Gail Norton, the then publisher of *City Palate* magazine, dreamed up the idea of daylong Foodie Tootles. When Dee moved to Saskatchewan, I took over as lead. We'd always visit three or four farms and cook the produce from each place for a big feast at the end of the day. Dee always served lentils and I carried on the tradition. After ten trips to India, I've put my own spin on the spicing.

**WHAT YOU NEED TO GATHER**

Knife
Cutting board
Measuring cups and spoons
Large, heavy-bottomed wok or Dutch oven
Lid

2 Tablespoons organic canola oil
1 teaspoon black mustard seeds
2 Tablespoons ginger paste
1 Tablespoon garlic paste
1 Tablespoon ground cumin
1 Tablespoon ground coriander
1 Tablespoon Kashmiri chili powder
1 teaspoon ground turmeric
1 leek, washed, greens trimmed, halved and cut finely
1 large carrot, diced
1 stalk celery, diced
1 onion, diced
1 medium yam, diced
1 cup uncooked or two 19-ounce (540 ml) cans green or brown lentils
1 apple, cored and diced, not peeled
¼ cup sultana or golden raisins
2 cups water
19-ounce (540 ml) can coconut milk
1 Tablespoon garam masala
1 teaspoon fenugreek leaves (kasoori methi)
¼ cup Alberta honey (approx)
¼ cup lime juice (approx)
Salt
Pinch chili flakes
2 Tablespoons fresh cilantro leaves, for garnish (optional)
Lime wedges, for garnish (optional)
Cashews, for garnish (optional)

## #EATALBERTAFIRST TIP:

When shopping for root vegetables like those in this recipe, always check the bag to make sure you are getting ones grown in Alberta. After all, they're an Alberta signature food, they'll be fresher, and you'll be supporting our local food system.

#### WHAT YOU NEED TO DO

1. Heat the oil in a large, heavy-bottomed wok or Dutch oven over medium-high heat.
2. Add the mustard seeds and leave them until they pop and splutter. Lower the heat to medium, add the ginger and garlic pastes, and cook, stirring constantly, until fragrant, about 30 seconds.
3. Stir in the cumin, coriander, chili powder, and turmeric and cook until fragrant, adding a little more oil (about 1 teaspoon at a time) if needed to prevent the spices from sticking or burning.
4. Stir in the leeks, carrots, celery, onions, and yams, place a lid on the pot, and cook until tender, about 5 to 10 minutes.
5. Lower the heat to medium-low, add the lentils, apple, raisins, and water, and simmer, stirring frequently, until the lentils are tender, about 15 to 20 minutes.
6. Stir in the coconut milk, followed by the garam masala and fenugreek, and heat through. Taste and adjust the flavours to balance sweet, sour, salt, and heat with the honey, lime, salt, or chili flakes.
7. Garnish with cilantro, lime wedges, and cashews, if desired.
8. Enjoy with basmati rice and roti or naan.

# Slow-Cooked Alberta Bison on the Silk Road

**MAKES** 6 to 8 servings
**TAKES** ½ hour active time + 8 hours' slow cooker time
**RATING** Competent to proficient

As this Alberta bison simmers the day away in a slow cooker, it will fill your home with warm scents of spices from the Silk Road. I like to prepare it one evening, pop it in the refrigerator overnight, and then turn it on to slow cook the day away when I leave the house the next morning. It's truly wonderful to come home to. Enjoy with Fluffy Mashed Potatoes (page 331) or polenta.

### WHAT YOU NEED TO GATHER

Measuring cups and spoons
Knife
Cutting board
Frying pan
Slow cooker
Wooden spoon

2–3 Tablespoons olive oil
3½–4 lb bison round or cross rib roast
3 carrots, finely chopped
2 stalks celery, finely chopped
1 onion, finely chopped
2 cups mushrooms, stemmed and halved
4 cloves garlic, finely chopped
1 star anise
1 teaspoon pepper
1 teaspoon ground cinnamon
½ teaspoon ground cloves
½ teaspoon ground allspice
2 cups bold red wine (Cabernet, Merlot, Malbec, Zinfandel)
28-ounce (796 ml) can whole tomatoes
Salt and pepper
1 Tablespoon chopped fresh Italian parsley

### WHAT YOU NEED TO DO

1. Heat the oil in a large frying pan over medium heat.
2. Add the meat and brown all sides, about 10 to 15 minutes.
3. Transfer the meat to a slow cooker.
4. Add the carrots, celery, onions, and mushrooms to the frying pan and cook over medium heat until lightly browned (you may need a bit more olive oil), about 10 minutes.
5. Add the garlic and cook until fragrant, about 30 seconds, then add the star anise, pepper, cinnamon, cloves, and allspice. Stir to distribute them evenly among the other ingredients.
6. Pour the wine into the pan and scrape the pan with a wooden spoon to get all the brown bits from the bottom.
7. Add the tomatoes, bring to a boil, and then pour the contents of the frying pan over the meat in the slow cooker.

8 Refrigerate overnight at this point or begin cooking on low until the meat falls apart easily when tested with a fork, about 8 hours.
9 Season with salt and pepper to taste once the meat is ready.
10 Transfer to a serving dish and garnish with a sprinkle of parsley.

FYI FOR NOVICE COOKS: The process of pouring liquid into a hot pan and scraping all the brown bits from the bottom is known as deglazing the pan. It's how you get ALL the flavour.

# Highwood Crossing Oat Buns

**MAKES** 2 dozen buns
**TAKES** about 30 minutes' active time + 2 to 4 hours' proofing and baking time
**RATING** Competent to proficient

Who doesn't love homemade buns? These come from Penny Marshall, a professional home economist and co-owner of Highwood Crossing Organic Foods. Penny develops all the recipes for Highwood Crossing's website, and this one's particularly versatile (see the sidebar for variations). You can make the dough a day ahead and bake the buns fresh the day you want to eat them. This recipe can be easily multiplied. I once made ten dozen when I was bringing a busload of people to the farm to meet Penny and her husband, Tony.

**WHAT YOU NEED TO GATHER**

Stand mixer
Measuring cups and spoons
Large bowl
Wooden spoon
Two 9 × 13-inch baking pans or muffin tins or 2 loaf pans
Tea towel

4–5 cups flour, divided
1 cup quick-cooking oats
½ cup granulated sugar
2 Tablespoons granular yeast (traditional or fast-rising)
2 teaspoons salt
2 cups lukewarm water
¼ cup organic cold-pressed canola oil
1 egg
Butter or canola oil for greasing baking pans, a large bowl, and your hands

Organic cold-pressed canola oil has the same deep yellow of its ubiquitous Alberta acres of flower. It gives the buns a pretty golden colour.

**WHAT YOU NEED TO DO**

1. Add 2 cups of the flour, the oats, sugar, yeast, salt, water, oil, and egg to the bowl of a stand mixer fitted with the paddle attachment. Mix on low to medium speed until it just comes together, about 2 minutes. Or mix by hand with a wooden spoon in a large bowl.
2. Switch to the dough hook attachment and mix in 2 to 3 cups more flour, ¼ cup at a time. The dough should go from sticky to not sticky and be easy to handle.
3. Transfer the dough to the large greased bowl, turning once so the loaf is coated in the butter or oil. Cover with a tea towel and either place in the refrigerator overnight or set in a warm place to double to use on the same day.
4. Deflate the dough once it has doubled. This can take 1 to 3 hours, depending on the temperature, moisture in the dough, the development of the gluten, and the ingredients.
5. Cut the dough into 24 golf ball–sized pieces. (Note: If you're using it the next morning, remove from the refrigerator, gently deflate the dough, and proceed as follows.)
6. Use the butter or oil to grease the baking pans. Rub some butter on your hands and shape the dough pieces into rounds. Place them in the prepared pans and set in a warm place, cover with a tea towel, and wait until doubled again, about 30 minutes.
7. Preheat the oven to 400°F when the buns are almost done doubling.
8. Bake until golden, about 10 to 13 minutes.

## VARIATIONS:

- My secret name for this recipe is Penny's Play Dough. Penny often replaces a cup of the unbleached all-purpose flour with whole wheat flour or throws in a few Tablespoons of flax, sesame, or sunflower seeds. Sometimes she uses part of the dough for cinnamon buns.
- You can also change up the size of the buns, making hamburger or sandwich size instead. I like to make 12 buns and 1 loaf of bread. To make the pull-apart buns that are pictured here, cut each of the dough balls in 3 little pieces and put them seam side down in a 24-cup muffin pan (or two 12-cup pans, of course). They'll cook in roughly the same amount of time as noted above.

## PRO TIP:

If your oven has a proof setting, you can use that for proofing the dough.

# Refrigerator Bran Muffins

**MAKES** 4 dozen
**TAKES** 30 minutes' active time + 20 to 25 minutes' baking time
**RATING** All levels

I've been tweaking this recipe for years, and this is my favourite version. You can keep the mix in your refrigerator for up to 3 weeks and bake the muffins up when the notion strikes. Or you can make them all at once, wrap them individually in plastic wrap, and freeze them for snacks. Anyone I know who has a new baby gets these. That's my way of tossing a lifesaver to new parents getting up for middle-of-the-night feedings. We all know it takes a village to raise a child. It's nice when that manifests as baking.

### WHAT YOU NEED TO GATHER

Muffin tins
Measuring cups and spoons
Large bowls
Stand mixer
Wire rack

2 cups boiling water
5 teaspoons baking soda
4 cups All-Bran cereal (the original one with strands, not flakes)
2 cups natural bran
½ cup wheat germ or hemp hearts
½ cup sunflower seeds or pumpkin seeds
1 lb (2 cups) chopped dates or mix of dates and raisins
1 cup unsalted butter, softened, plus extra to grease the muffin tins
1½ cups Alberta honey
4 eggs
5 cups whole wheat flour
2 teaspoons ground cinnamon
1½ teaspoons salt
4 cups buttermilk

### WHAT YOU NEED TO DO

1. Preheat the oven to 400°F. Butter the cups of the muffin pans.
2. Pour the water into a large (2- or 4-cup) measuring cup. Stir the soda into the water (it should fizz). Set aside.
3. Place the All-Bran, natural bran, wheat germ, sunflower seeds, and chopped dates in a very large bowl and pour the water and soda mix over it, stirring to moisten the ingredients evenly. Set aside.
4. Cream the butter and honey together in the bowl of a stand mixer fitted with the paddle attachment and then beat in the eggs one by one, scraping the sides of the bowl after each addition.
5. Combine the flour, cinnamon, and salt in a bowl and add half to the mixer, followed by half the buttermilk. Mix on a medium to low speed until evenly distributed. Repeat with the remaining dry ingredients and buttermilk.
6. Pour this into the big bowl of bran and fruit and stir until just distributed. Be careful not to overmix or you'll have tough muffins.
7. Fill the cups of each muffin pan two-thirds full with batter.
8. Bake the muffins until they are golden brown and spring back when touched, 20 to 25 minutes. Cool on a wire rack.

### PRO TIP:

Keep whole wheat flour fresher in the freezer if you don't use it often.

# Hit the Trail Cookies

**MAKES** 12 large or 24 smaller cookies
**TAKES** 15 minutes' active time + 15 to 17 minutes' baking time
**RATING** All levels

These cookies are good. They're even bordering on good for you, if a cookie ever really could be good for you. They're loaded with bran flakes and have white cheddar for protein and chewy dried cranberries to contrast with the crispy crunch of the baked bran and whole wheat flour. They freeze well and are the perfect thing to grab whether you're running late for a meeting or heading out to hit the trail.

**WHAT YOU NEED TO GATHER**

2 baking sheets
Parchment paper
Measuring cups and spoons
Stand mixer
Tablespoon
Fork

½ cup butter
¾ cup sugar
1 egg
1 cup whole wheat flour
½ teaspoon baking soda
2 cups bran flakes
6 ounces white cheddar, cubed small
¾ cup dried cranberries
2–4 Tablespoons water

**WHAT YOU NEED TO DO**

1. Preheat the oven to 350°F and line 2 baking sheets with parchment paper.
2. Using a stand mixer fitted with the paddle attachment, cream the butter with the sugar on medium-high speed until fluffy.
3. Add the egg and beat again until fluffy.
4. Add the flour and soda and mix well on low speed.
5. Stir in the bran flakes, cheddar, and cranberries.
6. Add the water a Tablespoon at a time, if you need to, to bring the mix together.
7. Drop by well-rounded Tablespoonfuls, a few inches apart, onto the baking sheets.
8. Flatten the mounds with the tines of a fork and bake until crispy at the edges, 15 to 17 minutes.
9. Leave the cookies on the pan until firm and cool. Store them in an airtight container or wrap individually with plastic wrap and freeze.

# Alberta Energy Bites

**MAKES** 24 bites
**TAKES** 15 minutes' active time + 10 to 12 minutes' baking time
**RATING** All levels

These nutrient-dense, gluten-free morsels of energy are loaded with Alberta-grown ingredients that give them their sweet flavour and chewy texture. Enjoy as a snack or take a few for breakfast on the run. They freeze well in an airtight container.

**WHAT YOU NEED TO GATHER**

24-cup mini muffin tin
Measuring cups and spoons
Small saucepan
Food processor
Wire rack

Cooking spray
¼ cup red quinoa
½ cup water
1¾ cups organic Alberta rolled oats, divided
¼ cup sugar
¼ cup dried apricots
¼ cup golden raisins
¼ cup ground organic Alberta flaxseed
¼ cup unsalted sunflower seeds
¼ cup unsweetened shredded coconut
2 Tablespoons chia seeds
¼ teaspoon baking soda
¼ cup Alberta honey
¼ cup unsalted butter, melted
¼ cup organic Alberta canola oil
½ teaspoon vanilla extract
72 frozen saskatoon berries

**WHAT YOU NEED TO DO**

1. Preheat the oven to 350°F and spray a 24-cup mini muffin pan with cooking spray.
2. Put the quinoa in the saucepan and add the water. Bring to a boil over high heat, give it a quick stir, then reduce the heat to medium and simmer, uncovered, until the water is absorbed. Remove from the heat, cover, and let it steam for 5 minutes. You'll have twice what you need, so freeze the other half for the next time you make this or use it in a grain salad.
3. Pour 1 cup of the oats into the bowl of a food processor fitted with the steel blade and pulse until it becomes oat flour.
4. Add the quinoa, remaining oats, sugar, apricots, raisins, flaxseed, sunflower seeds, coconut, chia seeds, and baking soda and pulse until the apricots are small bits.
5. Add the honey, melted butter, oil, and vanilla and pulse until just combined.
6. Divide the batter among the muffin cups, poke 3 saskatoon berries on the top of each, and bake until golden brown, 10 to 12 minutes.
7. Cool completely in the pan on a wire rack.

# Puffed Wheat Squares

**MAKES** 15 large squares
**TAKES** 15 minutes' active time + 20 minutes' cooling/firming time
**RATING** All levels

Few people realize this chewy chocolate Canadian Prairie classic was invented in Red Deer. The maker, A.J. Russell, was originally from New Brunswick (like me). He'd had a confectionery in Saint John, but he couldn't resist the lure of the West (also like me). He arrived in 1913 (not like me) and had to get really creative with his candy making because of rationing during the First World War. He swapped out sugar for molasses and replaced traditional grains with puffed wheat to make this treat. When he entered the squares (the original was more brittle-like) in a contest, they won, and they've been popular ever since. In my version, the use of brown sugar and corn syrup means these treats are a breeze to make.

**WHAT YOU NEED TO GATHER**

9 × 13-inch baking dish
Measuring cups and spoons
Large non-stick saucepan
Wooden spoon
Sifter
Knife

1 cup lightly packed brown sugar
¾ cup butter, plus a bit more to butter the baking dish
⅔ cup corn syrup
½ cup Dutch processed cocoa, measured then sifted (see page 52)
1 teaspoon vanilla extract
8–9 cups puffed wheat

**WHAT YOU NEED TO DO**

1. Grease the baking dish with butter.
2. Put the sugar, butter, corn syrup, and cocoa in a large non-stick saucepan over medium heat and stir continuously until it comes to a boil. Boil for 1½ minutes, remove from the stove, add the vanilla, and then stir in the puffed wheat.
3. Transfer the mixture to the prepared baking dish and press into the pan. Let sit at room temperature until firm, about 20 minutes. Score and slice into squares and transfer to an airtight container for storage.

# Sheet Pan Chocolate Chippity-Chunk Cookie Bars

**MAKES** 15 huge bars or up to 60 smaller bars
**TAKES** 20 minutes' active time + 10 minutes' baking time
**RATING** All levels

My college roommate, Diane Bell, gave me this recipe in 1983 and I've treasured it ever since. There are lots of chocolate chip cookie recipes out there. This one is my all-time favourite. I hope it becomes yours too.

### WHAT YOU NEED TO GATHER

12 × 16-inch rimmed baking sheet
Measuring cups and spoons
Stand mixer
Spatula
Bowl
Whisk

1 cup unsalted butter, softened, plus more to butter the baking sheet
1 cup granulated sugar
¾ cup packed brown sugar
3 eggs
3 teaspoons vanilla extract
3 cups flour
1½ teaspoons baking soda
1½ teaspoons salt
3 cups semi-sweet chocolate chips and chocolate chunks (50:50 mix)

### WHAT YOU NEED TO DO

1. Preheat the oven to 375°F and butter the baking sheet.
2. Place the butter and both sugars in the bowl of a stand mixer fitted with the paddle attachment and beat on medium-high until light and fluffy. Stop and scrape down the sides of the mixer with a spatula.
3. Add the eggs all at once with the vanilla and beat again until smooth and fluffy.
4. Whisk the flour, baking soda, and salt together in a bowl and then add to the mixer, beating on low until thoroughly mixed.
5. Add the chocolate chips and chunks and beat on low just until evenly distributed.
6. Spread the dough evenly onto the rimmed baking sheet.
7. Bake until golden, about 10 minutes, then cool in the baking sheet before cutting into bars.

**LEFT TO RIGHT:** JODI WILLOUGHBY, HELEN MCINTYRE, AND CAROLYNE MCINTYRE-JACKSON

# Double Chocolate Oatmeal Cookies

**MAKES** About 30 cookies
**TAKES** 20 minutes' active time + 10 to 13 minutes' baking time
**RATING** All levels

My friends Carolyne McIntyre-Jackson and Jodi Willoughby are the founders and owners of Crave Cupcakes. They grew up on a ranch near High River where people were always dropping by to see what their mom, Helen, had in her cookie tins. Whatever Helen does, she does it with finesse, and her daughters are the same. Lots of Crave's goodies are recipes that have been in the McIntyre family for generations. When I asked Carolyne to share a favourite, this is the one that popped into her mind. I'm so pleased to share it with you.

**WHAT YOU NEED TO GATHER**

2 baking sheets
Parchment paper
Measuring cups and spoons
Bowls
Stand mixer
Spatula
Wire rack

1¼ cups flour
2 Tablespoons Dutch processed cocoa
½ teaspoon baking soda
½ teaspoon salt
1¼ cups butter
¾ cup granulated sugar
¾ cup lightly packed brown sugar
1 egg
1 teaspoon vanilla extract
3 cups rolled oats
2 Tablespoons water
1 cup semi-sweet chocolate chips

**WHAT YOU NEED TO DO**

1. Preheat the oven to 350°F and line 2 baking sheets with parchment paper.
2. Whisk together the flour, cocoa, baking soda, and salt in a large bowl and then set aside.
3. Place the butter and both sugars in the bowl of a stand mixer fitted with the paddle attachment and beat on medium-high speed until light and fluffy.
4. Scrape down the sides of the bowl, add the egg and vanilla, and mix again on low to medium speed until well combined.
5. Add the flour mixture to the butter mixture and beat on low speed until just combined.
6. Alternate adding the oats and water, starting and ending with the oats. (You'll make 3 additions of oats and 2 of water.)
7. Add the chocolate chips and mix on low just until evenly distributed. Drop by the tablespoon and flatten with your hands into even rounds 2 inches apart.
8. Bake until cookies have spread out and are crisp at the edges, 10 to 13 minutes.
9. Let cool on the pan for a few minutes before transferring to a wire rack to cool completely.

# Aunty M's Farmhouse Carrot Cake

**MAKES** 12 servings
**TAKES** 20 minutes' active time + 35 to 45 minutes' baking time + cooling time before icing
**RATING** All levels

Sometimes, when I'm on a farm in Alberta, I catch sight of a tire swing and my mind races back in time. I see the little girl I was, swinging with all her heart on the swing that hung from the bowed branches of an old willow at my aunty Muriel's farm. You can make this carrot cake in a sheet pan. But for birthdays, Aunty M baked it triple-layered with oodles of luscious icing. Twirling, twirling, twirling, whenever I make this cake, I ice it with swirls and twirls and remember again the joy of time on a family farm.

## WHAT YOU NEED TO GATHER

9 × 13-inch glass baking dish or three 9-inch round cake pans
Parchment paper
Box grater
Measuring cups and spoons
Bowl
Stand mixer
Spatula
Cake tester or toothpick
Wire racks
Offset icing knife

*For the cake*

3 cups grated carrots (about 12 large carrots)
2 cups flour
2 teaspoons baking soda
1 teaspoon ground cinnamon
2 cups sugar
1¼ cups canola or sunflower oil
4 large eggs
1 teaspoon vanilla

*For the cream cheese icing*

8-ounce (226-gram) package cream cheese
½ cup unsalted butter
2 teaspoons vanilla extract
3–4 cups icing sugar

## WHAT YOU NEED TO DO

*For the cake*

1 Preheat the oven to 350°F.
2 Line the baking dish with parchment paper or butter three 9-inch round cake pans and then line the bottoms with parchment paper.
3 Combine the carrots, flour, baking soda, and cinnamon in a large bowl and stir to coat all the carrots evenly. Set aside.
4 Place the sugar and oil in the bowl of a stand mixer fitted with the paddle attachment and beat on medium until smooth.
5 Add the eggs one at a time, beating until smooth and scraping down the sides of the mixer with a spatula between each addition.
6 Add the vanilla, followed by the carrot mixture, and beat again until smooth.

7. Pour the batter into the baking dish, or divide it among the 3 cake pans, and bake on the middle rack until a cake tester inserted in the middle comes out clean, about 45 minutes (if using the 3 cake pans, place them all on the middle rack and cook them for 35 to 40 minutes—you don't need to rotate the pans during baking).
8. Place the cake(s) in their pan(s) on racks to cool for 10 minutes, then lift the sheet cake using the parchment paper or remove the layer cakes from the pans by inverting them and peeling off the parchment paper.
9. Let the cake(s) cool completely on the wire racks before icing.

*For the cream cheese icing*

1. Place the cream cheese and butter in the bowl of a stand mixer fitted with the paddle attachment and beat on high speed until creamy and smooth.
2. Add the vanilla, then slowly add the icing sugar in 3 or 4 additions, beating until smooth between each addition. (I use between 3 and 4 cups of icing sugar, but adapt the amount to suit your preferences.) Allow at least about 5 minutes for this.
3. Ice the cake with generous swirls and twirls. There will be enough for the sheet pan or layer cake. Use any leftover frosting as a special addition to the Sweet Sourdough Cinnamon Rolls (page 81).

CHAPTER 7

# CELEBRATIONS, FEASTING, AND ENTERTAINING THROUGH THE YEAR

This final chapter is about looking for any and all reasons to be festive throughout the year, no matter the season. By now, you likely agree that Alberta's seasons are wonky. They can bring us T-shirt and sunglasses weather at Lunar New Year or down coat and toque weather at a July cookout. Sometimes at Thanksgiving we have appetizers in the backyard while we bask in the scarlet rays of the setting sun and other times we have to dash out and shovel a path through freshly fallen snow as guests slip and slide their way to the front door. We take what we get weather-wise, but when it comes to feasting and entertaining, it's good to keep calm and celebrate on. The diversity of annual cultural celebrations in Alberta is a great source of inspiration for this.

I grew up in a tiny "vanilla" town in the Maritimes and quickly fell in love with the diversity of Alberta. As a young nurse in Calgary, I tagged along with Filipino and Pakistani co-worker friends to their homes to learn about their food and customs. Having lived beside generous Chinese friends with a hospitality background for many years, Lunar New Year has become part of my life. Cooking with Ukrainian friends helped me learn about their food customs and celebrations. Writing an Indian cookbook and travelling to India taught me about Diwali and Eid. My family has always celebrated Easter while dear friends celebrate Passover Seder.

I've taken a close-up look at a few of Alberta's diverse cultures to share some of my all-time favourite recipes from those groups. This chapter roughly follows those celebrations through a calendar year. Dishes to celebrate Ukrainian Christmas (January 7) start the year followed by a sumptuous sampling of Lunar New Year (first new moon of the lunar year) staples. Dishes for an Easter brunch are presented next, followed by a Passover Seder feast of lamb (March or April). The turkey dinner feast presented here could be served for Thanksgiving, Christmas, or New Year's. Noorbanu's Butter Chicken (page 345) and Festive Vegetable Biryani (page 347) are wonderful post-Ramadan treats at Eid (the date varies widely). The year ends on a sweet note with a recipe for Date Halva Balls (page 353) to give at Diwali (late fall), which celebrates the sweetness of friendship and the triumph of good over evil.

If the thought of entertaining and cooking any or all of these dishes is overwhelming for you, you are not alone. The pandemic has made our entertaining and socializing skills a little rusty, so I open the chapter with Top 10 Tips for Organizing, Cooking for, and Hosting Festive Parties, a few easy dips, and a special oatcake recipe to get you back on top of your game.

# Top 10 Tips for Organizing, Cooking for, and Hosting Festive Parties

Before we get into the nitty-gritty of this chapter, let me share the overarching principle I live and entertain by: There's no such thing as PERFECTION. If you wait for everything to be perfect before you start entertaining, you'll miss out on a lifetime of fun. So, forget about perfection—but do make a plan.

## #1 MAKE A MASTER TO-DO LIST

Make lists of the shopping, decorating, and cooking that you traditionally do before any holiday or celebration. Work backwards from the dates of your gatherings and assign completion times for tasks. Absorbing these known entities into the routines of family life builds holiday rituals and fun instead of creating a last-minute frenzy.

Plan for the unknowns and the unexpected by stocking your refrigerator and pantry with plenty of crackers, cheeses, meats, pickles, and preserves. Then you can easily whip up a charcuterie platter (see page 271) if someone drops by unexpectedly. And always have a bottle of bubbly chilling in the refrigerator.

## #2 KEEP SPIRITS BRIGHT AND MOODS MELLOW

Candles, candles, and more candles. Whether you're gathering during our long, dark, and deep winter nights or our full-on summer evenings around a campfire, candles brighten spirits, show you paid attention to the details, and add a certain softness to everyone's mood. If you're worried about fire hazards, choose battery-powered candle lights with flameless wicks.

Make your own ginger syrup: Place 1 cup of sugar and 1 cup of water in a saucepan with 1 cup of finely grated peeled ginger. Bring the mixture to a boil on medium-high, stirring constantly until the sugar dissolves, cover, lower the heat to medium, and keep on a steady simmer for 15 minutes. Turn off the heat and leave the syrup for 1 hour. You can strain it but I don't, because I like the texture of the ginger in my drinks. Store in an airtight bottle in the refrigerator for up to 1 month.

## #3 OUTSOURCE THE MUSIC PLAYLISTS TO TECH-SAVVY RELATIVES OR FRIENDS

Get the young adults in your family involved in the gathering by delegating the music to them. My son was a DJ in high school and loved having this responsibility. If you're on your own for this task, use technology for good with digital music services. Choose your genre and let it play all night.

## #4 OUTSOURCE SOME OF THE FOOD TO PROS (AND FAMILY) AS YOUR BUDGET ALLOWS

Get a cheese board from your favourite cheesemonger. Pick up Mediterranean appetizers from a deli. Get a sushi tray, salad rolls, or samosas from your favourite takeout places. If holiday baking isn't your thing, why stress about it? Order from your favourite bakery. Just do it well in advance. At Christmas, bakery order cut-offs are often December 1. Another great tip is to delegate the making of some of the food to adult children and family members. Give them all a "specialty" to bring. My dear mother-in-law always calls me the week before a holiday to ask, "The usual?" and I am very happy for her support when she arrives with her fabulous dressing and tomato aspic. Teamwork for the win, always.

## #5 HAVE A GREAT PUNCH LINE

I always have a non-alcoholic punch when I host a party. Now, with increasingly strict drinking-and-driving laws, it tends to disappear fast. The general rule for making punch is to combine five items: pop or sparkling water, juice or syrup (or both), bitters, spicing or fruit, and ice. My favourite is what I call the Mild Mannered Mule: 2 quarts sparkling water, 1 to 2 cups ginger syrup (see sidebar above) depending on how sweet you like it, 1 quart limeade, a dash of Angostura bitters, lime wedges, cranberries, and ice. It makes about 12 servings.

## #6 HAVE A SIGNATURE DISH FOR EVERY KIND OF PARTY

Having a go-to dish saves any stress you might feel over menu planning. Here are some ideas for you: Lip-Smacking, Finger-Licking, Messy, Good Ribs (page 157) for Grey Cup, Chipotle Bison Chili (page 227) for a skating party, Noorbanu's Butter Chicken (page 345) for après-ski, or Alberta Sunshine Eggs with Billionaire's Bacon (page 315) for weekend brunch. You get the idea.

## #7 HAVE A SIGNATURE DISH FOR HOLIDAYS THROUGHOUT THE YEAR

Signature dishes for holidays throughout the year are what this chapter is all about. While it is fun to try new things and experiment, the holidays are not the best time to do so. People will look forward to your classics, and as you repeat your repertoire you will get a routine down. Someday, with practice, you'll be making celebratory feasts with ease. Life is short. Find something to celebrate and give thanks for your food every day.

## #8 BUILD A BUFFET

This is one of the most low-stress ways I know to entertain. Set out the plates, wrap the utensils in napkins with bows, and set your guests loose to serve themselves. With a large group, it's infinitely easier than serving the meal family-style, when half the people at the table can't seem to adhere to the "dishes are passed from left to right" rule of etiquette.

## #9 WHENEVER YOU ENTERTAIN, MAKE EXTRA AND LOVE THE LEFTOVER LIFE

I always cook our big Christmas feast on Christmas Eve. After a lazy Christmas Day brunch of Alberta Sunshine Eggs with Billionaire's Bacon (page 315), we go skating, watch movies, do puzzles, or curl up with a book and enjoy an even lazier supper of leftovers. We splurge on fine wine to keep any house guests happy. As much as I love to entertain, I love a lazy day of leftovers to follow.

## #10 GRANT FLEX TIME TO FAMILY

Cherishing your family every day of the year and making plans to see them regularly outside of holidays will allow you to be more flexible about these few "special" days of the year. When you have young adults and they begin to want to spend time with their partner and their own family, for example, you will make life a lot easier for everyone by being gracious about this.

# Build Your Own Charcuterie Board in 10 Easy Steps

**MAKES** Plan for 1 to 2 ounces of cheese per person
**TAKES** 15 minutes' active time
**RATING** All levels

Loading a rugged (or refined) charcuterie board with local goodness is one of the easiest ways I know to get a party started. Here's how to build one from the board up (and see pages 275–81 for a few simple recipes to add to the board).

### #EATALBERTAFIRST TIP:

Sunterra Market has a new charcuterie factory in Acme, Alberta, where they make Italian prosciutto and salami under the brand name Soleterra. Spragg's Meat Shop in Rosemary makes incredible farmer's sausages. Meuwly's and Menno's in Edmonton and VDG, Pioneer, Empire Provisions, and Illichmann's in Calgary are noteworthy sausage makers as well.

1. **LAY THE FOUNDATION:** Choose a beautiful board and then at least 3 contrasting styles of cheeses.
   - **A HARD CHEESE:** This could include something from Canada's most award-winning cheese artisan, Sylvan Star Cheese, who are renowned for their Goudas. Their Grizzly Gouda is a sweet, caramelized flavour bomb I frequently use instead of imported parmesan. You could also go for a Canadian cheddar or classics like Comté or Gruyère.
   - **A SOFT CHEESE:** Go for a local spreadable chèvre from Fairwinds Farm or Noble Meadows. Or a soft, gooey Brie, Camembert, Neufchâtel, or labneh.
   - **A BLUE OR STINKY CHEESE:** This adds balance. Try a blue Benedictine from Quebec, original Roquefort from France, Stilton or Shropshire from England, or Cambozola or Gorgonzola from Italy.
2. **ADD SOMETHING SWEET:** A little pot of honey, fruit paste, jam, or jelly will do.
3. **SPRINKLE SOME NUTS:** Try Marcona almonds, candied pecans, or spiced cashews.
4. **PLACE SOME DRIED FRUITS:** Dried cherries, apricots, figs, and prunes are great.

5 **LAY IN SOME CHARCUTERIE:** Soleterra from Acme makes prosciutto and salamis. Meuwly's in Edmonton makes incredible sausages, as do Pioneer, VDG, Empire Provisions, and Illichmann's in Calgary. Be sure to include a wedge of pâté.

6 **PILE IN SOME GREAT BREAD AND CRACKERS.**

7 **ADD ASTRINGENCY:** A dollop of mustard or a little pile of pickles will add some pucker to cut through the fat of the cheese.

8 **SQUEEZE IN VEGETABLES:** And a dip that you love too.

9 **WEDGE IN FRESH FRUIT:** Apples, pears, and figs are all made for this.

10 **BEAUTIFY WITH FRESH EDIBLE FLOWERS.**

# Red Lentil and Sun-Dried Tomato Hummus

**MAKES** 1½ cups
**TAKES** 15 minutes' active time + 20 minutes' simmering time
**RATING** All levels

Dwayne Ennest led the chef team at Calgary's famous River Café for its first 10 years. He and his wife, Alberta, had several successful restaurants where guests got to #EatAlbertaFirst. They even hired a farmer to exclusively grow the produce for their menus. Virginia Christopher was an Alberta art icon and Alberta Ennest's mother. Her art gallery was home to the Ennests' Vue Cafe where a few dozen seats snuggled up to a bar and open kitchen. We had a lot of fun there on various Alberta Food Tours and this is my version of one of my favourite menu items. Enjoy it with fresh bread wedges, pita chips, fresh vegetables, or a combo.

**WHAT YOU NEED TO GATHER**

Measuring cups and spoons
Sieve
Medium saucepan
Non-stick frying pan
Spice grinder
Food processor

1 cup red lentils
2 cloves garlic, smashed
1½ cups water
1 teaspoon cumin seeds
1 teaspoon coriander seeds
1 teaspoon smoked paprika
½ cup sun-dried tomatoes, plus a few more for garnish
¼ cup canola oil
1–2 Tablespoons fresh lemon juice
Salt and pepper
Zest of 1 lemon
Chopped fresh curly parsley

**WHAT YOU NEED TO DO**

1. Rinse the lentils in a sieve under cold running water and sort through them to remove any debris. Place them in a medium saucepan with the garlic and water. Bring the mixture to a boil over high heat, reduce the heat to medium-low, and simmer until the water is completely absorbed and the lentils are dry and tender, about 20 minutes. Meanwhile, prepare the cumin and coriander seeds.
2. Heat a non-stick frying pan over low heat, add the cumin and coriander seeds, and pan-toast them, stirring frequently until golden and fragrant, about 5 minutes. Remove the pan from the heat, let the seeds cool a bit, then place them in a spice grinder and pulse until they're finely ground.
3. Transfer the lentil mixture to the bowl of a food processor fitted with the steel blade and add the ground seeds, paprika, sun-dried tomatoes, oil, and lemon juice. Pulse until smooth.
4. Taste and adjust the seasoning with salt and pepper if necessary.
5. Transfer to a serving bowl and garnish with a few chopped sun-dried tomatoes, the lemon zest, and parsley to taste.

# Homemade Ricotta with Lemon Zest and Chili Flakes

**MAKES** 2 cups
**TAKES** 25 minutes' active time + 10 to 30 minutes' straining time
**RATING** Competent to proficient

My friend Cindy Lazarenko taught me how to make this cheese for one of the Foodie Tootle farm tours I used to lead for Calgary's *City Palate* magazine. Whether you use cow or goat milk, be sure to use whole milk. Enjoy with Mrs. Beaton's Oatcakes (page 279).

### WHAT YOU NEED TO GATHER

Sieve
Cheesecloth
Large bowl
Measuring cups and spoons
Heavy-bottomed saucepan
Lemon zester

8 cups whole cow or goat milk
⅓ cup store-bought lemon juice
Zest of 1 lemon
½–1 teaspoon chili flakes
Drizzle extra virgin olive oil
Pepper

### WHAT YOU NEED TO DO

1. Line a sieve with a few layers of cheesecloth and place it over a large bowl.
2. Pour the milk into a heavy-bottomed saucepan on medium-high heat and slowly bring it to the point where the milk begins to boil and foam up to the top of the saucepan, stirring continuously. This takes about 15 to 20 minutes. Immediately pour in the lemon juice, remove from the heat, and stir the mixture as the curds and whey separate, then strain the mixture through the cheesecloth-lined sieve.
3. Leave the curds to drain for 10 to 30 minutes, depending on how soft and fluffy you like your ricotta. I like the moisture and fluffiness at the 10-minute mark. By 30 minutes, the cheese will be quite firm.
4. Transfer the curds to a bowl and stir in the lemon zest and chili flakes. You can eat it straight away or make it ahead and store it in an airtight container in the refrigerator for 2 to 3 days at this point.
5. Enjoy the ricotta drizzled with a little extra virgin olive oil and some freshly ground pepper.

### #EATALBERTAFIRST TIP:

Cheese only tastes as good as the milk you make it with, so I use Rock Ridge Dairy's whole milk. It's also known as "ring of gold" milk because it comes from Jersey cow milk with golden globules of fat that float to the top as you heat it. You can also use their organic goat milk. Either way, the resulting cheese is rich and delicious.

## PRO TIPS:

- Use store-bought lemon juice in the recipe to be sure the pH level is right for the milk to separate into curds and whey.
- Save the whey for use in puddings or smoothies.

## VARIATIONS:

Change this up with the addition of a teaspoon or two of your favourite chopped fresh herbs. Or swirl a mixture of apricot jelly and 1 teaspoon of chili flakes through it.

# Mrs. Beaton's Oatcakes

**MAKES** 3 to 4 dozen
**TAKES** 35 minutes' active time + 10 to 12 minutes' baking time
**RATING** Competent to proficient

Mrs. Elizabeth Beaton's oatcakes were something I enjoyed for many years without ever having to make them. You see, her daughter Janice had a wonderful cheese shop in Calgary. And Mrs. Beaton would faithfully make oatcakes each week and mail them from Mabou in Cape Breton to Janice's cheese shop. Our friend Anita Stewart published a version of these in her iconic *Anita Stewart's Canada* and said they were "laced with love." I hope when you make your batch that you'll remember that lacing food with love is the most important step in any recipe.

**WHAT YOU NEED TO GATHER**

2 unrimmed baking sheets
Parchment paper
Bowl
Measuring cups and spoons
Pastry blender
Fork
Rolling pin
3-inch cookie cutter

2 cups flour, plus more for rolling
2 cups Scottish oatmeal
1 cup steel-cut oats, plus more to sprinkle on top
⅓ cup packed brown sugar
1 teaspoon salt
1¼ cups cold butter, cut into small cubes
1 teaspoon baking soda
⅓ cup boiling water

**WHAT YOU NEED TO DO**

1. Preheat the oven to 380°F and line 2 baking sheets with parchment.
2. Stir together the flour, oatmeal, steel-cut oats, sugar, and salt in a large bowl.
3. Use a pastry blender or a couple of knives to cut the butter into the flour mixture until it resembles pea-sized crumbs.
4. Dissolve the soda in the boiling water in its measuring cup and stir it into the oat mixture. Combine with a fork until all the liquid is incorporated.
5. Use your hands to gently gather the dough into a ball and transfer to a lightly floured surface.
6. Using light strokes with a rolling pin, roll the dough to ¼-inch thickness. Try for a rectangular or square shape if you're using the traditional rectangular-shaped cookie cutter of oatcakes (Mrs. Beaton saves and cleans a corned beef tin for this).
7. Cut the dough into your desired shapes. Take any leftover bits of dough, reform a ball, reroll, and recut to use it all up.
8. Transfer the cut oatcakes to the prepared baking sheets, sprinkle the tops with more steel-cut oats, and bake on the middle rack until golden, about 10 to 12 minutes.
9. Let cool completely on the pans. Once cool, store in an airtight container.

## PRO TIP:

- I divide the dough into 2 balls and roll them separately.
- Scottish oatmeal is made of oats that are slowly ground between 2 millstones where regular oatmeal is steamed and rolled.
  In porridge it creates a very smooth texture and in these cookies, it provides a smooth base to contrast the crispness of the steel-cut oats.

# Ukrainians in Alberta

In 1891, the first Ukrainians arrived in Edmonton. A quarter million others had immigrated to Canada by the 1930s. They settled in farming communities across the Prairies, and today, the Ukrainian population in Canada (about 1.3 million) is third only to that in Russia and Ukraine itself. The largest number of Ukrainian Canadians live in and around Edmonton, where 16 percent of the city's population claims Ukrainian heritage.

With this history, it's easy to understand why Ukrainian food is so much a part of Alberta's food identity. At Ukrainian Christmas twelve dishes, representing the twelve apostles, are served. At Easter there are beautiful breads and pork dishes and of course, pysanky, the intricately decorated eggs. There are whole cookbooks devoted to these dishes. To give you a taste of the culture, I'm including four favourite Ukrainian dishes shared by dear friends for you to try.

**LEFT TO RIGHT:** ERIC AND DEBORAH ANZINGER AND SHARON YEO MAKING PEROGIES WITH BRAD SMOLIAK

# Holubchi (Cabbage Rolls)

**MAKES** 8 to 10 servings
**TAKES** 1 hour active time + 3 hours' cooking time
**RATING** Competent to proficient

The practicality of this Ukrainian dish made it a homesteading staple across the Prairies. Today, we have hothouses and global supply chains, but imagine eating only cold local crop vegetables like cabbage from your root cellar all winter. Whether there was meat to add or just a bit of rice and tomato sauce, this recipe made it all taste better. This version comes from my friend Helen McIntyre. Helen likes to use Bravo cabbage from Innisfail Growers "because they have nice big leaves that are perfect!" This freezes well at the point before you put it in the oven. Enjoy with Pirohy (page 286) and a great kielbasa.

**WHAT YOU NEED TO GATHER**

Knife
Cutting board
Large pot with lid
Baking tray
Measuring cup
Large frying pan
Roasting pan
Aluminum foil

1 large green cabbage
1 lb lean hamburger
1 lb extra-lean hamburger
2 cups long-grain white rice
28-ounce (796 ml) can stewed tomatoes
2 green bell peppers, sliced (optional)
48-ounce (1.36 L) can tomato juice

**WHAT YOU NEED TO DO**

1. Core the cabbage, cut about ¼ inch off the top of the head, put the cabbage in a large pot of water that's on a low boil, and cover with a lid. After about 2 minutes, remove the lid, lift out the cabbage, and peel off the softened leaves (they have to be soft enough to make a roll). Place the cabbage back in the water and repeat this process until all the leaves are removed. Have a baking tray ready to keep the leaves on. Meanwhile, you can also fry the meat. They're side by side on the stove, so it's easy to attend to both.
2. Brown and break up the meat to a fine crumb in a large frying pan over medium heat. Drain any fat, let the meat cool a bit, and then stir in the 2 cups of rice.
3. Preheat the oven to 350°F.
4. Use your hands to make oblong-shaped meat and rice rolls that will fit into the cabbage leaves, and fold each leaf around the meat. My Ukrainian friends tell me that each cabbage roll should not be longer than your baby finger (roughly 3 inches long by 2 inches wide) to give you an idea of the size you are aiming for.
5. Lay the rolls seam side down in a large roasting pan. Repeat this until all the meat mixture is used.
6. Cover the cabbage rolls with the stewed tomatoes, slices of green pepper (if using), and enough of the tomato juice just to cover.
7. Cover with foil and bake until the internal temperature reaches 160°F and a sharp knife slips easily through the cabbage, about 3 hours.

# Pirohy (Perogies) with Potato and Onion or Duck and Mushroom Filling

**MAKES** About 3 dozen
**TAKES** 1½ to 2 hours' active time
**RATING** Proficient

One of my favourite chefs to cook with is Brad "The Smo" Smoliak of Kitchen by Brad in Edmonton. The Smo is fun. He's cooked for Queen Elizabeth II but he remains grounded because his passion comes from time spent as a youth in his baba's kitchen. Before anyone could eat at her table, she gave thanks and named everyone who grew the food she cooked. That stuck with Brad. I learned to make pirohy under his tutelage. This is his baba's dough recipe. One filling is humble, the other fit for a queen. And that's how it rolls with The Smo. These are fantastic alongside Holubchi (page 285), Vegan Borscht (page 291), or Nalysnyky (page 293).

**WHAT YOU NEED TO GATHER**

Knife
Cutting board
Grater
Measuring cups and spoons
Frying pans
Wooden spoon
Bowl
Stand mixer
Rolling pin
3-inch round cookie cutter
Large stockpot

*For the potato and onion filling*

2 Tablespoons butter
2 Tablespoons grated onion
3 cups mashed potatoes (at room temperature)
Salt and pepper

*Or*

*For the duck and mushroom filling*

2 Tablespoons butter
½ cup finely chopped onions
1 cup finely chopped mixed mushrooms (oyster, shiitake, and cremini work well but avoid portobello as they turn the filling grey)
2 duck confit legs (about 1 cup), shredded (see sidebar on page 288)
½ cup dried cranberries
½ teaspoon dried or 1 teaspoon chopped fresh thyme leaves
½ cup demi-glace or turkey or chicken gravy
1 teaspoon garlic paste

*For the dough*

4 cups unbleached all-purpose flour, divided
3 cups sour cream

*For frying*

Butter
6–10 fresh sage leaves

## PRO TIP:

You can buy duck confit canned at specialty stores. I got mine at the Cookbook Co. Cooks in Calgary. If you can't find it, you can substitute dark turkey or chicken meat.

**WHAT YOU NEED TO DO**

*For the potato and onion filling*

1. Melt the butter in a frying pan over medium heat, add the onions, and cook, stirring frequently, until soft.
2. Stir in the mashed potatoes. Season with salt and pepper to taste. Set aside to cool.

*Or*

*For the duck and mushroom filling*

1. Heat the butter in a heavy frying pan over medium heat until the foam subsides, then add the onions and cook until soft.
2. Stir in the mushrooms, and cook until all the moisture is gone and the mushrooms have begun to caramelize, about 10 minutes.
3. Add the duck, followed by the cranberries, thyme, demi-glace, and garlic. Cook until the filling sticks together, about 10 to 15 minutes. Transfer to a bowl and chill in the refrigerator for 30 minutes.

*For the dough*

1. Mix 3 cups of the flour and the sour cream together in a stand mixer fitted with the dough hook on low speed until a soft dough forms. If necessary, add ¼ cup more flour at a time until the dough is no longer sticky and comes away from the bowl cleanly.
2. Roll the dough out to about ½-inch thickness on a well-floured surface.
3. Use the cookie cutter to cut out circles of dough. You should get about 36 circles. Reroll any dough scraps until all the dough is used up.
4. Place 1 Tablespoon of your filling of choice inside each circle, fold the dough over it, and pinch the half-moon shape closed. To get the look of the pirohy in the photo, make successive folds around the edges.
5. Repeat until all the filling and dough are gone. You may have extra of one or the other.
6. Cook the pirohy in a large pot of gently boiling water, until they float to the surface, about 5 minutes.

*For frying*

1. Drain the pirohy and then pan-fry them in butter with a few sage leaves, about 5 minutes per side if you like them golden and slightly crispy.
2. Enjoy with the pan sauce of butter and sage and a dollop of sour cream, if desired.

# Vegan Borscht

**MAKES** 10 to 12 servings
**TAKES** 2 hours' active time including about 45 minutes' simmering time
**RATING** All levels

This was a staple at my friend Cindy Lazarenko's Culina Highlands restaurant in Edmonton. She says, "We served a lot of this soup, with a dollop of sour cream and a fresh dill garnish. I got the recipe from a friend who passed it along from her mom. Her instructions for cooking the cabbage and onions were 'You have to think, I burnt it!' Then you know it's ready for the rest of the ingredients. That deep caramelization is what gives this vegetarian soup so much flavour. I have shared this recipe countless times over the years. It's a keeper!"

**WHAT YOU NEED TO GATHER**

Measuring cups and spoons
Large soup pot
Knife
Cutting board
Small saucepan
Potato masher

*For the soup*

¼ cup vegan margarine
1 Tablespoon canola oil
1 medium onion, diced
1 small head of cabbage cut in ½-inch pieces (about 4 cups)
1 teaspoon salt
½ teaspoon pepper
10 small beets, peeled
4 carrots, peeled
2 medium white or red table potatoes, peeled
1 green bell pepper
8 cups vegetable stock or water
28-ounce (796 ml) can whole tomatoes
2 Tablespoons vinegar
1 bunch finely chopped fresh dill (about ½ cup)

*For the slurry*

2 medium white or red potatoes, peeled and halved
1 cup scalding-hot oat milk

*For the garnish*

Vegan sour cream
Pepper
Chopped dill

**WHAT YOU NEED TO DO**

*For the soup*

1 Heat the margarine and oil in a large soup pot over medium heat and stir in the onions and cabbage. Add the salt and pepper and cook, stirring occasionally, until caramelized to a very dark brown (almost burnt) colour, about 1 hour.
2 Meanwhile, cut the beets, carrots, potatoes, and bell pepper into bite-sized pieces and add them to the pot when the cabbage is ready.
3 Stir the vegetable mixture well and season to taste with more salt and pepper.
4 Add enough stock to cover the vegetables by a few inches and then add the canned tomatoes with their juice.

5 Bring to a boil over medium-high heat and reduce to a simmer over medium-low heat, stirring occasionally until the vegetables are tender, about 45 to 60 minutes.

*For the slurry*

1 While the vegetables are simmering, make the slurry. Boil the 2 potatoes in a small saucepan on medium-high until fork-tender, then drain and mash them with the hot milk. The mixture should be quite runny. Add more milk, 1 Tablespoon at a time, if necessary.
2 Stir the potato slurry into the soup when the vegetables are cooked to thicken it.
3 Add the vinegar, taste and adjust the seasoning as you like, then add the fresh dill and stir well.

*For the garnish*

1 Enjoy hot, garnished with a dollop of sour cream, a pinch of freshly ground black pepper, and more chopped dill.

Freeze (without the sour cream) for up to 6 months. To serve from frozen, thaw in the refrigerator overnight. Reheat and add a bit of water or stock to loosen it up if it's too thick.

# Nalysnyky (Crêpes) with Mushroom and Cranberry Cream Sauce

**MAKES** 4 to 6 servings
**TAKES** 30 minutes' active time + 30 minutes' baking time
**RATING** Proficient

Nalysnyky (pronounced NAL-YES-NAH-KEH) are scrumptious little cheese-filled Ukrainian crêpes that are great at breakfast or any time you crave them. You can bake them straight away or make them ahead and freeze them before they go in the oven. When you bake them, they puff up and are ready to soak up the savoury mushroom and cranberry cream sauce. There are a lot of reasons to make them but mostly, I just like saying "nalysnyky."

**WHAT YOU NEED TO GATHER**

Stand mixer
Measuring cups and spoons
Crêpe pan or low-sided frying pan
Spatula
Bowl
Frying pan
2-quart casserole dish
Aluminum foil

*For the crêpes*

2 eggs
½ cup whole milk
3 Tablespoons water
½ cup sifted flour
¼ teaspoon salt
Sunflower or other neutral-tasting vegetable oil for the pan

*For the filling*

2 cups cottage cheese
2 egg yolks
2 Tablespoons whipping cream
¼ teaspoon salt

*For the mushroom and cranberry cream sauce*

2 Tablespoons butter
½ cup diced shallots or onion
1 cup diced cremini mushrooms
2 Tablespoons dried cranberries
2 teaspoons diced fresh sage leaves
½ teaspoon dried or fresh thyme leaves
¼–½ cup whipping cream
Salt and pepper

*For baking*

½ cup butter, melted

**WHAT YOU NEED TO DO**

*For the crêpes*

1. Crack the eggs into the bowl of the stand mixer fitted with the paddle attachment and beat on medium speed until frothy and white. Add the milk and water and beat again until well incorporated.
2. Add the flour and salt and beat on low speed until smooth. The batter will be quite thin.

25415VH

3 Heat a large crêpe pan on medium-high heat. It must be hot enough to cook the crêpes quickly with bottoms that are light brown, not pale and heavy, but not so hot that the bottom is dark brown and the top is unset. When it's hot, grease it with about a teaspoon of the oil.

4 Ladle ½ cup of the batter into the centre of the pan and swirl it around to create a thin layer. When it's light brown on the bottom and firm to the touch on top, about 45 to 60 seconds, remove the crêpe to a warm plate. Continue frying in this manner until all the batter is used up. Apply more oil between each crêpe as needed. Set aside.

*For the filling*

1 Put the cottage cheese, egg yolks, whipping cream, and salt in the bowl of a stand mixer fitted with the paddle attachment and beat on medium speed until smooth. Set aside.

*For the mushroom and cranberry cream sauce*

1 Heat the butter in a frying pan over medium heat and add the shallots. Cook until translucent, then add the mushrooms, cranberries, sage, and thyme and cook, stirring occasionally, until the liquid evaporates fully, about 5 to 7 minutes.

2 Reduce the heat to low and stir the cream into the mushroom mixture. Slowly bring it back to a simmer and let the flavours meld and the sauce thicken. Season with salt and pepper to taste and set aside (in the refrigerator if you won't be eating them right away), and reheat when the nalysnyky are ready.

*For assembly*

1 Preheat the oven to 325°F and butter the casserole dish.

2 Spread each crêpe with a few Tablespoonfuls of filling and roll them up so the light brown part is on the outside.

3 Arrange them in layers in the casserole, drizzling with a little of the melted butter between each layer and on top.

4 Cover with foil and bake for 30 minutes. You know they are ready when they puff up.

5 Enjoy with a spoonful of the mushroom and cranberry cream sauce on top.

# From Chinese Western to Today's Pan-Asian Lunar New Year Celebrations

The first Chinese immigrants arrived in Alberta as railway workers during the 1880s. They stayed after the railway was completed to work as launderers, market gardeners, and cooks. For a long time they faced much prejudice.

From 1885 to 1923, they paid a head tax to immigrate—the only immigrants in Canadian history ever to do so. From 1923 to 1946, they suffered through an era of exclusion thanks to the Chinese Immigration Act, which saw all Chinese barred from entering the country. It created a bachelor society for the many men who had come ahead of their families. It was not until 1967 that the race-based restrictions of the Chinese Exclusion Act were removed from immigration laws and families unified.

The early cooks from China opened restaurants in every little town the railway stopped in. They were Chinese owners serving a Western menu, and the Chinese Western restaurant became an icon across the Prairies. Many of these restaurants have now been in service for over 100 years, and in 2013 the Royal Alberta Museum curated an exhibit called *Chop Suey on the Prairies* to recognize them as part of the fabric of Alberta's culture.

Chinese culture and the menus in the restaurants progressed when more immigrants came in the 1960s. Ginger beef was invented in Calgary's Silver Inn by George Wong in 1975. The 1980s saw a huge influx of money and people from Hong Kong as the British left the region and China reclaimed it. Menus became much more sophisticated.

These days Alberta is home to many immigrants of Asian descent and Lunar New Year is widely celebrated. The date varies each year according to the lunar calendar. Families gather to exchange gifts and usher in happiness, health, and prosperity for a new year by eating certain foods.

Fish is eaten for prosperity in the new year because in Cantonese, "fish" (鱼 yú/yoo) auspiciously sounds like "wishes and abundance." Long noodles are eaten because they represent a nice long life. Greens represent good fortune in your life. Serving a whole chicken is a visual signifier of unity, and since togetherness is the overarching theme of Lunar New Year celebrations, it symbolizes the reunion of family. The more dumplings that a person eats, the more wealth they will acquire, because dumplings are shaped like currency. Citrus fruits represent a round and full life. The meanings of each food may be symbolic but gathering to eat them is a real opportunity to celebrate family and wish each other success in the coming year.

The following recipes come from my friends the Seto family, who are part of this history.

ROCKY MOUNTAIN REFLECTIONS

# Salmon Fillet with Sizzling Oil, Ginger, and Scallions

**MAKES** 4 to 6 servings
**TAKES** 30 minutes' active time + 10 to 20 minutes' baking time
**RATING** Proficient

My friend Richard Seto's father and grandfather had a Chinese Western restaurant called Harry's Café when Macleod Trail at 50th Avenue was the edge of Calgary. Later, they sold Harry's and moved downtown to own and operate Oriental Gardens, the Dynasty, and a continental restaurant called the Three Greenhorns. The Setos hired chefs from China, and Richard grew up flying in and out the back door of the restaurants. He picked up his cooking techniques from the restaurant's chefs and his parents, has a great palate, and is one of the best home cooks I know. I'm thrilled to share a few of his recipes with you. This is a favourite.

**WHAT YOU NEED TO GATHER**

Rimmed baking sheet
Aluminum foil
Knife
Cutting board
Paper towels
Measuring cups
Saucepan

3 (each 2 inches long) knobs ginger root
1 bunch scallions (green onions)
2 lb salmon fillet (sockeye or coho)
Olive oil
Salt and pepper
⅓–½ cup canola or olive oil
½ cup soy sauce

**WHAT YOU NEED TO DO**

1. Preheat the oven to 400°F and line a rimmed baking sheet with 2 pieces of aluminum foil folded in on each side so it becomes a tray to hold the salmon.
2. Peel the ginger. Turn each piece on its side and cut it into ⅛-inch slices. Then, cut the slices into ⅛-inch-wide by 1-inch-long matchsticks. Set aside.
3. Clean and chop the tops and bottoms off the scallions and then slice them thinly on the diagonal. Set aside.
4. Rinse the salmon under cold running water and pat it dry with a paper towel. Lay it skin side down on the foil, rub it with a little olive oil, and sprinkle it with salt and pepper to taste.
5. Place the baking sheet with the salmon on the middle rack of the oven and bake for 10 minutes per inch of thickness. Meanwhile, slowly heat the canola oil in a small saucepan over medium heat. You know it is hot enough to pour over the fish when you drop a sliver of ginger in the oil and it sizzles. Do not leave the oil unattended on your stove and do not use high heat. If the oil boils or starts to smoke, it's too hot and it might catch fire. So, go low and slow and it will be ready when the salmon is.

6 Remove the salmon from the oven when it's still a bit pink in the middle but otherwise cooked through. Transfer it to a serving platter and spread the ginger in a row down the centre. Carefully pour the hot canola oil over the ginger, sprinkle the scallions over top, and finish by pouring the soy over everything.
7 Enjoy immediately with steamed rice and bowls of chili paste and soy sauce on the side.

# Long Life Noodles with Greens

**MAKES** 4 to 6 servings
**TAKES** 20 minutes' active time
**RATING** All levels

Long noodles in a variety of forms are served at family members' birthdays and at Lunar New Year to wish everyone a long life. This is another of Richard Seto's recipes, and he cooks them in a large wok. The key to success when cooking in a wok is to do all the prep before you start to cook. The dish then comes together in a flash.

### WHAT YOU NEED TO GATHER

Bowls
Large pot
Salad spinner
Measuring cups and spoons
Knife
Cutting board
Paper towel
Whisk
Heavy-bottomed wok
Tongs
Wooden spoon

3–4 cups washed greens (pea shoots, Chinese broccoli, baby bok choy, or a mix)
1 lb (450-gram) package fresh Hong Kong–style chow mein noodles
½ cup sherry
½ cup soy sauce
¼ cup sesame oil
4 teaspoons sugar
2 teaspoons chili paste
2 Tablespoons canola oil
2 cloves garlic, sliced
1 bunch scallions, sliced on the diagonal
2 Tablespoons chopped ginger

### WHAT YOU NEED TO DO

1. Prepare a large bowl of ice and water.
2. Bring a large pot of water to boil over high heat, add the greens, and cook just until they turn bright green, about 2 minutes. Plunge them into the ice water so they stop cooking and retain their colour. Once chilled, drain them and spin them in a salad spinner to remove the excess water. Set them aside.
3. Prepare the noodles by soaking them in a bowl of hot water for 5 minutes, then separate them gently without breaking them, drain, and dry them with a paper towel. Set aside and make the sauce.
4. Whisk the sherry, soy sauce, sesame oil, sugar, and chili paste together in a bowl. Set aside.

### PRO TIP:

When you're frying oil at high temperature in a wok you'll definitely want the hood fan on high.

### WOK THIS WAY:

If I had to choose only one pan for my kitchen, it would be a good carbon steel wok. I've been slowly seasoning mine for 30 years now. Carbon steel can hold the heat, and the more you use it, the more patina it will develop (if properly cared for). The patina makes it non-stick and adds flavour too.

5. Heat a heavy-bottomed wok on high heat and add 1 Tablespoon of the canola oil, tilting to coat the sides, and continuing to heat until it's at the smoke point. Add the noodles and use tongs to turn them until they're a bit crispy and heated through, about 5 minutes. Remove them to a bowl and set aside.
6. Add a little more oil (about a teaspoon) to the wok. Once it returns to full heat, add the garlic, scallions, and ginger. Cook, stirring constantly, for about 10 seconds before adding the greens. Sear for 15 seconds and then cook, stirring constantly until hot, for about 1 minute, before stirring in the noodles.
7. Pour the sauce over the mixture and stir-fry until the noodles are coated and the mixture is heated through, another 2 to 3 minutes.
8. Enjoy immediately as a side or noodle lover's main dish.

# Homestyle Beef and Tomatoes

**MAKES** 4 to 6 servings
**TAKES** 30 minutes
**RATING** All levels

You won't find this on the menu in Chinese restaurants. This is a dish that Richard Seto's parents, Norma and Fong, always made for the family at home. Richard makes it for his friends now. The serving dishes we used for photographing these three recipes came from Harry's Café. I feel very fortunate to share not only these recipes but also a peek into this family's and Alberta's history.

**WHAT YOU NEED TO GATHER**

Measuring cups and spoons
Bowls
Knife
Cutting board
Wok or large frying pan

3–4 Tablespoons cornstarch or tapioca
½ teaspoon salt
½ teaspoon pepper
1½ lb flank or eye-of-the-round steak, cut in 2 × ⅛-inch strips
½ cup oyster sauce, plus more to finish (optional)
8 Tablespoons canola oil, divided
2 yellow onions, cut in wedges
2 Tablespoons finely chopped ginger
8 tomatoes, cut in 4–6 wedges each, depending on the size
1 Tablespoon finely cut fresh cilantro leaves (optional)
2 scallions (green onions), sliced on the diagonal (optional)

**WHAT YOU NEED TO DO**

1. Combine the cornstarch, salt, and pepper in a bowl and set aside.
2. Mix the strips of beef in another bowl with the oyster sauce and 3 Tablespoons of the oil. Let this marinate for at least 15 but not more than 30 minutes at room temperature. Then, sprinkle the cornstarch mixture on top and stir to coat all of the meat. This locks the marinade in the meat and makes the meat look smooth once fried.
3. Heat the wok on high until a drop of water evaporates immediately or the pan begins to smoke.
4. Add 3 Tablespoons of the oil and swirl the wok a bit to coat the sides.
5. Add a third of the beef to the wok and let it sit where it lands for about a minute. This will sear the flavour in. Give it a quick stir-fry and then remove it to a bowl while it's still slightly pink, about 5 minutes total. Repeat this twice to cook the rest of the beef, transferring it all to one bowl. Set aside.
6. Bring the wok to full heat again and add the last 2 Tablespoons of oil, swirling to coat the sides, then add the onions and ginger and stir-fry until the onions become translucent. Break them up as you stir so that the layers separate.
7. Return the beef to the wok and simmer on low heat until it's hot. Stir in the tomatoes right before serving, adding more oyster sauce 1 Tablespoon at a time, if desired.
8. Transfer the beef and tomatoes to a serving dish and garnish with cilantro and scallions, if desired.
9. Enjoy with steamed rice.

To peel ginger, use the bowl edge of a teaspoon to scrape off the skin. You can also use a paring knife, but because the ginger is bumpy, you'll waste a lot of the flesh. Once the ginger is peeled, you can grate it or cut it into rounds, then into strips or dice. Even if you're going to put the ginger in a food processor, slice or cut it into strips first so you don't get long "hairs" of ginger.

# Easter and Passover

Easter and Passover in Alberta come at a time of year when we are still eating winter's roots (vegetables like potatoes, beets, carrots, and parsnips) but are dreaming of spring's shoots (asparagus and fresh greens). Ham is my go-to for Easter dinner or brunch, but Alberta lamb, which is at its finest in spring, is a nice change. It's also part of a traditional Passover Seder.

Eggs are also a big part of Easter, and Alberta's Ukrainian community celebrates with intricately decorated and brightly painted eggs called pysanky. The recipe for Alberta Sunshine Eggs (page 315) in this chapter, along with its side of Billionaire's Bacon, is such a great make-ahead dish that I also serve it on Christmas morning. The Lemon Mascarpone Tart (page 321) is another mix of seasons. Winter's citrus lemon is puckering up to kiss the promise of summer berries. I include it with these lamb and ham recipes because it's as bright as spring sunshine and will work equally well for a brunch or a festive dinner dessert.

# Berbon Glazed Ham

**MAKES** 10 to 12 servings
**TAKES** ½ hour active time + 2 to 2½ hours' basting and baking time
**RATING** All levels

My dear friends Nicole Liboiron-Coles (the lead photographer for this book) and her husband, Warren Coles, are famous for their delicious recipe for bourbon glazed ham. When I discovered Bridgeland Distillery uses Alberta's famous Taber corn to make their award-winning Berbon, I knew this tasty local ingredient would make Nicole and Warren's recipe even more scrumptious. I even started a hashtag: #berbonNOTbourbon. Whether you're celebrating Easter, New Year's, or a special Sunday brunch, this ham's got your butt covered for ease of preparation and delicious results. Enjoy it with Sweet Scalloped Potatoes (page 313), Never-the-Same-Way-Twice Coleslaw (page 139), and Hot Pepper Cornbread (page 135).

**WHAT YOU NEED TO GATHER**

Measuring cups and spoons
Saucepan
Paper towel
Shallow roasting pan and rack
Knife
Cutting board
Pastry brush
Meat thermometer
Aluminum foil

- ½ cup Bridgeland Distillery Berbon (or your favourite bourbon)
- ½ cup Alberta honey
- ¼ cup molasses
- ¼ cup orange marmalade
- 2 Tablespoons Alberta smooth or grainy mustard
- 1 cup orange juice, divided
- 5–6 lb boneless gammon or bone-in ham

**WHAT YOU NEED TO DO**

1. Preheat the oven to 325°F.
2. Stir the Berbon, honey, molasses, marmalade, mustard, and ¼ cup of the orange juice in a small saucepan over medium heat.
3. Rinse the ham under cold, running water, pat it dry with a paper towel, and place on a rack in a shallow roasting pan. Score the surface diagonally in both directions with ½-inch-deep cuts.
4. Use a pastry brush to baste the surface of the ham with a quarter of the Berbon glaze. Pour the remaining ¾ cup of orange juice directly into the roasting pan, place in the middle rack of the oven, and bake until a meat thermometer reads 140°F, 2 to 2½ hours. Baste the ham with more Berbon glaze every 30 minutes while it cooks.
5. Remove from the oven and tent with foil 10 minutes before carving.

# Sweet Scalloped Potatoes

**MAKES** 4 to 6 servings
**TAKES** 10 minutes' active time + up to 55 minutes' baking time
**RATING** All levels

I grew up eating layered russet potatoes with whole milk and onions and a bit of salt and pepper as scalloped potatoes. I still love that dish. We always had it with ham. But one day, when I was getting ready to make Berbon Glazed Ham (page 311), I spied a few sweet potatoes and a can of coconut milk in my cupboard and decided it was time to give that old classic an update. With the subtle addition of nutmeg, it's smooth, sweet and a great accompaniment for many dishes including the Berbon Glazed Ham or any pork or poultry dish with a side of Never-the-Same-Way-Twice Coleslaw (page 139) plus Sweet Sourdough Biscuits (page 85).

**WHAT YOU NEED TO GATHER**

2-quart baking dish
Knife or mandoline
Cutting board
Microplane grater
Spatula

Coconut oil to coat the baking dish
4 cups thinly sliced sweet potatoes or yams (about 1½ lb; try to find ones with similar diameters)
1 onion, sliced in thin wedges
Half a 14-ounce (396 ml) can coconut milk
Freshly grated nutmeg
Salt and pepper

**WHAT YOU NEED TO DO**

1. Preheat the oven to 425°F and coat the baking dish with coconut oil.
2. Arrange the sliced potatoes standing up in rows in the dish, then tuck the onion slices in around the perimeter.
3. Pour the coconut milk over the potatoes and sprinkle with nutmeg, salt, and pepper to taste.
4. Bake, uncovered, on the middle rack of the oven for 30 minutes, then gently press down on the contents to fully submerge them in the coconut milk (use a spatula so you don't scald yourself) and bake until the tops of the potatoes are crispy and the middle is tender, about 20 to 25 minutes more.

# Alberta Sunshine Eggs with Billionaire's Bacon

**MAKES** 6 servings
**TAKES** 15 minutes' active time + 60 minutes' baking time
**RATING** All levels

If this dish has a bit of a southwestern flair, it's because the kind owner of Hacienda del Sol B&B in Taos, New Mexico, gave me the recipe. He called his version Eggs del Sol. I checked, and Alberta surpasses New Mexico for days of sunshine per year. We have 333 to their 310. So I'm calling this version Alberta Sunshine Eggs. The Billionaire's Bacon is a classic recipe from Edmonton chef Brad Smoliak. He serves it at gatherings stacked like a log cabin. Enjoy your Alberta Sunshine Eggs with Billionaire's Bacon along with some Berbon Glazed Ham (page 311), Hot Pepper Cornbread (page 135), and sliced fruit for a deluxe breakfast or brunch.

**WHAT YOU NEED TO GATHER**

10-inch round baking dish
Rimmed baking sheets
Aluminum foil
Rack
Measuring cups and spoons
Cheese grater
Knife
Cutting board
Bowls
Whisk
Wooden spoon
Shallow roasting pan
Plate

*For the eggs*

1 teaspoon softened butter (for the baking dish)
1 cup frozen corn niblets
1 jalapeño, diced (optional)
6 eggs
¼ cup flour
½ teaspoon baking powder
1 cup cottage cheese
½ cup salsa
1 cup grated Monterey Jack
1 cup grated cheddar
1 red bell pepper, sliced thinly lengthwise
1 orange bell pepper, sliced thinly lengthwise

*For the bacon*

½ cup maple syrup
1 cup packed brown sugar (more as needed)
1 lb bacon (any cut will do)

### #EATALBERTAFIRST TIP:

Look for Alberta-made bacon from Pioneer, Irvings Farm Fresh, Twin Oak Farms, Spragg's Meat Shop, or TK Ranch.

#### WHAT YOU NEED TO DO

1. Preheat the oven to 350°F and butter the baking dish. Line a rimmed baking sheet with foil and place a wire rack on top.
2. Spread the corn and jalapeño (if using) over the bottom of the baking dish. Set aside.
3. Crack the eggs into a large bowl and whisk until lightly beaten.
4. Whisk in the flour and baking powder until smooth, then stir in the cottage cheese and salsa.
5. Pour the egg mixture evenly over the corn and top with the grated cheeses.
6. Arrange the bell pepper slices on top to make them look like individual rays of sun.
7. Place the baking dish in a shallow roasting pan and add enough water to the larger pan so it is an inch deep around the smaller dish.
8. Bake until set, about 60 minutes.
9. Meanwhile, pour the maple syrup into a shallow bowl and spread the sugar onto a plate. Dip each slice of bacon in the maple syrup, then press both sides into the sugar. Lay the bacon slices side by side on the wire rack. Place in the oven on a rack below the eggs and cook until crispy, about 30 minutes.

# Lamb Shanks in a Saskatoon and Pinot Noir Sauce

**MAKES** 4 servings
**TAKES** ½ hour active time + 3 to 4 hours' braising in the oven
**RATING** Competent to proficient

Lamb is traditional at a Passover Seder, and this dish is also great for entertaining any time because you prepare it ahead, stick it in the oven, and forget about it until you want to serve it. The perfect side is easy too. Just boil a peeled and chopped buttercup squash and mash it with a bit of butter and a few Tablespoons of brown sugar. It's a warm and mellow complement to the complex flavours of this dish. Alberta lamb is always worth the splurge.

### WHAT YOU NEED TO GATHER

Measuring cups and spoons
Dutch oven
Bowls
Wooden spoon
Tongs
Plate
Aluminum foil
Strainer

⅓ cup olive oil
4 Alberta lamb shanks
Flour for dredging
Salt and pepper
1 yellow onion, chopped
1 leek, mostly the white part, chopped
1 stalk celery, chopped
1 large carrot, chopped
1 clove garlic, minced
1 cup Pinot Noir
1 cup homemade or low-sodium store-bought beef stock
6 sprigs fresh thyme
6 sprigs fresh rosemary
1 cup fresh or frozen saskatoon berries

### WHAT YOU NEED TO DO

1 Preheat the oven to 325°F.
2 Heat the oil in a large Dutch oven on medium-high heat.
3 Dredge the lamb shanks in flour and salt and pepper, shake off the excess flour, add the lamb to the hot oil, and brown on all sides.
4 Add the onions, leeks, celery, carrots, garlic, wine, stock, thyme, rosemary, and berries. Deglaze the pan (see page 240) with a wooden spoon to remove any brown bits. Cover and cook until the meat wants to fall off the bones, about 3 to 4 hours.
5 Use tongs to transfer the lamb shanks to a plate and cover with foil to keep them warm.
6 Pour the liquid in the Dutch oven through a strainer into a large bowl and press on the solids to get all the juices. Discard the solids.

7 Return the liquids to the Dutch oven and heat them over medium heat, stirring occasionally, until reduced to a thick sauce-like consistency.

8 To serve, arrange the lamb shanks on a pillow of mashed buttercup squash and top with a few generous spoonfuls of the sauce. Green Beans with Herbs (page 335) add a pleasant colour and texture contrast to the plate.

# Lemon Mascarpone Tart

**MAKES** 10 to 12 servings
**TAKES** 60 minutes' active time + 42 minutes' baking time
**RATING** Proficient

Many years ago, I asked the founder of Calgary's Brûlée Bakery (now Decadent Brûlée), Marianne Saunders, for this recipe and she willingly shared it. I'm eternally grateful, because it's become a bright thread in the tapestry of our eating year.

Though it might seem like a bit of work up front, making the dough in the food processor and making enough for two tarts (one that you can freeze for later) means it's actually easier than it first appears. Especially the second time around.

## WHAT YOU NEED TO GATHER

10-inch springform pan
Measuring cups and spoons
Food processor
Plastic wrap
Zester
Spatula
Small saucepan
Stand mixer

*For the tart crust*

2¼ cups flour
½ cup granulated sugar
½ cup butter, softened, plus a bit more to butter the pan
1 egg
1 egg yolk
Dash store-bought or fresh lemon juice

*For the lemon curd*

2 large eggs
1 cup granulated sugar
6 Tablespoons fresh lemon juice (2–3 large lemons)
2 Tablespoons lemon zest
¼ cup butter, cubed

*For the filling*

¼ lb cream cheese
¼ lb mascarpone cheese
¼ cup sugar
⅓ cup lemon curd
3 eggs
6 Tablespoons whipping cream
5 Tablespoons fresh lemon juice (2–3 large lemons)

*For the garnish*

Assorted fresh berries and fruit
Icing sugar (optional)
Whipped cream (optional)

## WHAT YOU NEED TO DO

*For the tart crust*

1. Preheat the oven to 350°F and butter the springform pan.
2. Place the flour, sugar, and butter in a food processor fitted with the steel blade and pulse until pea-sized crumbs form.
3. Add the egg, egg yolk, and lemon juice and pulse until the dough comes together.
4. Divide the dough in half. Wrap one half in plastic wrap and refrigerate or freeze it to use another time.

You can make the lemon curd a few days ahead if you like or skip this step and substitute a store-bought lemon curd. Just make sure it's a really good one. If you use store-bought, you'll have about two-thirds of an average jar left for step 4.

5. Press two-thirds of the dough into the bottom of the springform pan, bake it for 12 minutes, then remove it from the oven and let it cool completely.
6. Form a long rope with the remaining dough and press it along the pan's inner circumference to form the edge of the crust. Set this base aside in the refrigerator until you're ready to bake the whole tart.

*For the lemon curd*

1. Whisk the eggs, sugar, lemon juice, and zest together in a small saucepan. Add the butter and cook over low heat, stirring constantly, until thickened, about 20 minutes.
2. Cool completely and store in an airtight container in the refrigerator.

*For the filling and to bake*

1. Place the cream cheese, mascarpone cheese, sugar, and ⅓ cup of the chilled lemon curd in the bowl of a stand mixer fitted with the paddle attachment and beat until smooth and creamy.
2. Add the eggs one at a time, scraping down the sides of the bowl between each addition, and beat until smooth again.
3. Beat in the whipping cream, followed by the lemon juice.
4. Spread the remaining lemon curd evenly across the prepared crust and pour the filling over top.
5. Place the tart on the middle rack in the oven and bake until set, about 20 to 30 minutes. Cool completely and chill in the refrigerator until it's time to serve it.
6. Garnish the tart with fresh berries right before serving. Sprinkle with icing sugar and serve with whipped cream, if desired.

# Thanksgiving and Christmas

Many years ago, I used to lead special Christmas shopping tours for food lovers. Each year had a different theme. One year we were "Christmas Commandos" with a shopping target list. Other years we had a "Homemade Christmas," a "Cowboy Christmas," a "Country Christmas," and both an "International Christmas" and an "Italian Christmas" at different markets around Calgary. The first year, I shared my family's traditional Christmas recipes, and every year after, I added more according to the theme of the year. But people loved my traditional recipes so much that years later, friends and guests would ask me to resend them, so I've put them in this section for you to enjoy too. I make them every Thanksgiving and again at Christmas, and I savour every morsel because these are the only times I make them all together each year. People tell me they've made their lives a lot easier. I hope the same will be true for you.

# Maple-Brined Roast Turkey and Gravy

**MAKES** 6 to 10 servings
**TAKES** 30 minutes' active time + overnight brining + 4 to 5 hours to roast + 1 hour to rest and carve + 30 minutes' active time for the gravy
**RATING** Competent to proficient

Brining a turkey is easy, but you need to start it the evening before you want to cook your bird. The extra effort is worth it, though, because this brine turns the turkey a deep bronze, keeps it moist, and results in a deep brown, rich gravy. The key to a great-tasting turkey is to buy a fresh, local one that's been raised with a healthful feed program and access to fresh air. Enjoy with Wild Mushroom and Apple Dressing (page 329), Rutabaga Puff (page 333), Green Beans with Herbs (page 335), and Cinnamon Orange Cranberry Sauce (page 337).

**WHAT YOU NEED TO GATHER**

Measuring cups and spoons
Very large stockpot
Knife
Cutting board
Kitchen twine
Roasting pan and rack
Meat thermometer
Aluminum foil
Sieve
Large measuring cup
Saucepan

*For the maple brine*

4 quarts water
4 cloves garlic, smashed
2 cups loosely packed brown sugar
¾ cup kosher salt
8 bay leaves
2 teaspoons dried or 2 sprigs fresh thyme
1 Tablespoon whole black peppercorns
2 teaspoons dried sage
2 teaspoons dried summer savory
1 cup soy sauce
1 cup maple syrup

*For the turkey*

25 lb turkey
2 Tablespoons olive oil
2 teaspoons dried summer savory
2 teaspoons salt
½ teaspoon pepper
1 firm apple, halved (Gala or Granny Smith)
1 onion, halved
2 celery stalks, cut in thirds
3 sprigs fresh rosemary
3 sprigs fresh thyme
1 cup apple juice

*For the gravy*

½ cup apple juice
2 cups chicken stock, homemade (page 215) or store-bought
3 Tablespoons butter
¼ cup unbleached all-purpose flour
1 Tablespoon soy sauce
1 Tablespoon lemon juice
1 Tablespoon Worcestershire sauce
½ teaspoon Tabasco sauce

#### WHAT YOU NEED TO DO

*For the maple brine*

1 Put the water in a large stockpot and add the garlic, sugar, salt, bay leaves, thyme, peppercorns, sage, summer savory, soy, and maple syrup. Place over high heat until it boils and the sugar and salt dissolve, about 10 minutes.
2 Remove the pot from the heat and let it cool.

*For the turkey*

1 While the brine cools, remove the giblets and neck from your turkey (reserve for stock if you like). Immerse the turkey in the cooled brine.
2 Store in the refrigerator overnight (but no longer than 12 hours).
3 When you're ready to cook the turkey, preheat the oven to 350°F.
4 Remove the turkey from the pot, rinse it, and pat it dry. Rub the turkey inside and out with the oil and sprinkle with the summer savory, salt, and pepper. Fill the cavity with the apple, onion, celery, rosemary, and thyme. Tie the legs together to close the cavity.
5 Place your turkey on a rack in a roasting pan, pour the apple juice directly into the pan, and roast until a thermometer inserted into the meaty part of the thigh reads 165°F. At 15 minutes per pound for an unstuffed 25 lb turkey, that's about 6 hours, but I find it's usually done at 5 hours so start checking around 4½ hours.
6 Remove the turkey on its rack to a carving board when ready. Set the roasting pan and its juices aside. Remove the fruit and vegetables from the cavity and discard. Cover the turkey with foil and allow it to rest while you make gravy.

*For the gravy*

1. Pour any juices in the roasting pan through a sieve and into a large measuring cup. Place the roasting pan on medium-high heat. Once it's hot, add the apple juice and scrape the bottom of the roasting pan to loosen any brown bits. Pour this liquid through the sieve and into the cup with the juices.
2. Skim and discard any fat from the surface of the juices. You should have at least 1 cup of liquid. Add enough chicken stock to make 3 cups.
3. Heat the butter in a large saucepan over medium heat. Add the flour and cook for a few minutes, just until lightly browned.
4. Whisk in the hot juices and bring to a boil. Add the soy sauce, lemon juice, Worcestershire sauce, and Tabasco sauce. Cook for 5 minutes more, then taste and adjust the seasonings if necessary. Reduce the heat to low to keep the gravy warm until you're ready to serve.
5. Carve the turkey and arrange it on a platter.

### #EATALBERTAFIRST TIP:

I've visited TK Ranch, Sunworks, First Nature Farms, and Winter's Turkeys and I call these places turkey spas because of how well cared for their birds are. They're the gold standard.

# Wild Mushroom and Apple Dressing

**MAKES** 8 to 10 servings
**TAKES** 25 minutes' active time + 45 minutes' baking time
**RATING** All levels

If you bake stuffing on the side, it's called dressing. This is one of the secrets to a moist turkey. With no stuffing, you only have to cook the turkey to 165°F. If the turkey is stuffed, the stuffing must get to 165°F and by then the poor turkey is an overdone 185°F. Like Sally in *When Harry Met Sally*, I like my stuffing as dressing, on the side!

**WHAT YOU NEED TO GATHER**

9 × 13-inch baking dish
Measuring cups and spoons
Knife
Cutting board
Large deep frying pan
Wooden spoon
Aluminum foil (optional)

⅓ cup butter or olive oil
2 onions, finely chopped
2 cloves garlic, finely chopped
3 stalks celery, finely chopped
2 leeks, trimmed and finely chopped
4 cups brown button mushrooms, trimmed and sliced
1 cup wild mushrooms, soaked in 1 cup hot water
2 McIntosh or Pink Lady apples, cored and finely chopped
10 cups crusty 1-inch bread cubes
1 cup turkey or chicken Homemade Stock (page 215)
½ cup chopped fresh curly parsley
1 teaspoon dried or ¼ cup fresh chopped sage leaves
1 teaspoon dried summer savory
1 teaspoon salt
½ teaspoon dried thyme
½ teaspoon pepper

**WHAT YOU NEED TO DO**

1. Preheat the oven to 350°F. Butter a 9 × 13-inch baking dish.
2. Melt the butter in a large deep frying pan over medium-high heat. Add the onions and garlic and cook, stirring occasionally, until fragrant, about 5 minutes. Add the celery and leeks. Cook until softened, about 5 minutes.
3. Stir in the button mushrooms and the wild mushrooms with their liquid and cook, stirring occasionally, until the liquid evaporates, about 10 minutes.
4. Add the apples, bread cubes, stock, parsley, sage, summer savory, salt, thyme, and pepper and combine well. Taste and adjust the seasonings if necessary.
5. Place the stuffing in the prepared baking dish. If you want the top crusty, leave it uncovered. If you want it moist, cover with foil.
6. Bake until thoroughly heated, about 45 minutes.

# Fluffy Mashed Potatoes

**MAKES** 10 to 12 servings
**TAKES** 10 minutes' active time + 20 minutes' simmering time
**RATING** All levels

To achieve fluffy mashed potatoes you need to start with the right potatoes. Choose russets or Yukon Gold. Avoid waterlogging them: No sitting overnight in water, prepped and waiting to be cooked. No leaving them cooked and sitting in water, waiting to be mashed. You'll also need to invest in a potato ricer. This is the secret to getting rid of lumps forever. Enjoy as a side to any meat dish but especially Maple-Brined Roast Turkey and Gravy (page 325).

**WHAT YOU NEED TO GATHER**

Potato peeler
Knife
Cutting board
Large pot
Oven mitts
Small saucepan or microwavable measuring cup
Tongs
Potato ricer or masher
Large bowl
Spatula

5 lb starchy potatoes (russet, Yukon Gold, or Agria potatoes)
2 teaspoons salt, divided
1 cup milk
¾ cup butter, cubed
Pepper
1 Tablespoon finely chopped herbs (parsley, dill, chives, or a mix) (optional)

**WHAT YOU NEED TO DO**

1. Peel and chop the potatoes into equal-sized pieces and place in a large pot with enough cold water to cover. Add 1 teaspoon of the salt, bring to a boil on medium-high heat, then reduce the heat to medium and keep them at a simmer until a knife inserted in the centre comes out without any resistance, about 20 minutes.
2. Drain off the water and return the pot to low heat for just a minute to dry out any remaining liquid. Wearing oven mitts, gently shake the pan for about 1 minute to release some of the steam and moisture from the potatoes. Remove the pan from the heat and set it aside. Your potatoes are now ready to push through a potato ricer or mash.
3. Heat the milk and butter in another saucepan or in a measuring cup in the microwave until the butter is melted and the milk is hot, about 1 to 2 minutes. Add pepper to taste and any herbs, if desired, to this mixture. Set aside.
4. Use tongs to transfer the potato pieces to a potato ricer and squeeze them through in batches into a large bowl. Fold in the milk and butter mixture with a spatula and ideally serve the potatoes right away. If you're not serving them right away, put them back in the pot for up to 20 minutes. If you don't have a potato ricer, mash the potatoes in the pot with the milk and butter mixture. Transfer to a serving dish.

## VARIATIONS:

Be playful. Add cloves of garlic as you boil the water. Substitute cream cheese or sour cream for half the milk. Add bacon bits, diced jalapeño, chopped sautéed kale, grated cheese, or a different selection of herbs. Make a mash with half potatoes and half turnips, celeriac, squash, or sweet potatoes.

# Rutabaga Puff

**MAKES** 8 servings
**TAKES** 30 minutes' active time + 30 minutes' baking time
**RATING** All levels

This smells really good while you're making it thanks to the caramelizing onions. Yum. This is a favourite side at our family feasts for my in-laws, Gail and Erik Anderson. Enjoying rutabagas is another way to enjoy an Alberta signature food, root vegetables. Enjoy with pork dishes and especially with Maple-Brined Roast Turkey and Gravy (page 325), Wild Mushroom and Apple Dressing (page 329), Fluffy Mashed Potatoes (page 331), and Green Beans with Herbs (page 335).

**WHAT YOU NEED TO GATHER**

2-quart casserole dish
Knife
Cutting board
Measuring cups and spoons
Large deep-sided frying pan
Slotted spoon
Food processor
Spatula

¼ cup butter, plus more to butter the casserole dish
1 onion, chopped
1 large rutabaga, peeled and chopped in 2-inch pieces
4 large carrots, peeled and chopped in 2-inch pieces
2 Tablespoons packed brown sugar
1½ cups chicken stock
2 Tablespoons unbleached all-purpose flour
1 teaspoon baking powder
2 eggs, beaten slightly
Salt and pepper
1 cup chopped pecans or pecan pieces
Brown sugar to sprinkle over the top

**WHAT YOU NEED TO DO**

1. Preheat the oven to 350°F. Butter the casserole dish.
2. Melt the butter in a large deep-sided frying pan over medium heat. Stir in the onions and cook until translucent.
3. Add the rutabaga, carrots, sugar, and stock and cook, uncovered, until very tender, about 40 minutes.
4. Using a slotted spoon, remove the vegetables from the stock and transfer to a food processor fitted with the steel blade.
5. Boil the remaining liquid until only 1 Tablespoon remains. Add that reduced liquid to the veggies and process until smooth.
6. Add the flour, baking powder, eggs, and salt and pepper to taste, and pulse until smooth.
7. Transfer to the prepared casserole dish.
8. You can freeze the dish for up to 1 month at this point or store it in your refrigerator for up to 24 hours and then bake as noted below. If freezing, thaw on the counter before baking.
9. When you're ready to bake, arrange the pecans as desired and sprinkle them with sugar.
10. Place the casserole dish in the centre of the oven and bake, uncovered, until it puffs up and turns golden, about 30 minutes.

# Green Beans with Herbs

**MAKES** 6 to 8 servings
**TAKES** 15 minutes' active time
**RATING** All levels

I first had these green beans with roast chicken in the South of France. They were such a nice side dish, I've been making them ever since. You can also enjoy them with roasted meats like the Cedar-Planked Prime Rib Roast of Alberta Beef (page 159), Six Ways to Sunday (Dinner) Beer Butt Chicken (page 163), or, of course, Maple-Brined Roast Turkey and Gravy (page 325).

**WHAT YOU NEED TO GATHER**

Large bowl
Ice and cold water
Large pot
Lettuce spinner
Paper towel
Large frying pan
Measuring cups and spoons

2 lb green beans
2 Tablespoons butter
2 cloves garlic, minced
1 teaspoon dried thyme
½ teaspoon dried summer savory
½ cup sliced roasted red pepper (optional)
¼ cup pine nuts (optional)

**WHAT YOU NEED TO DO**

1. Prepare a bowl of ice water.
2. Bring a large pot of water to a boil over high heat, cook the green beans until tender-crisp, about 3 or 4 minutes, then drain them and plunge them into the ice water.
3. Remove the beans once chilled, spin them in a salad spinner to dry, and wrap them in a paper towel. Place the wrapped beans in a plastic bag in the refrigerator (for up to 4 hours) until just before dinner.
4. Melt the butter in a large frying pan over medium heat, add the garlic, thyme, and savory, and cook until fragrant, about 30 seconds.
5. Remove the green beans from the refrigerator and stir them with the roasted red pepper and pine nuts (if using) in the butter and herb mixture until coated and heated through, about 2 minutes, and serve immediately.

# Cinnamon Orange Cranberry Sauce

**MAKES** 3 cups
**TAKES** 10 minutes' active time
**RATING** All levels

I love having fresh cranberries with a turkey dinner. Of course, I still need a can of jellied cranberries, complete with the ridges from said can, for my husband. I often double this recipe because it keeps well refrigerated in an airtight container for up to a month. Bonus: it's very easy to make. Enjoy with Maple-Brined Roast Turkey and Gravy (page 325) and on turkey sandwiches.

**WHAT YOU NEED TO GATHER**

Zester
Knife
Cutting board
Measuring cups
Microwave-safe bowl
Paper towel
Serving dish or storage container

1 orange
10-ounce (300-gram) package fresh cranberries
1½ cups granulated sugar
2 cinnamon sticks

**WHAT YOU NEED TO DO**

1. Zest the orange. Then use a knife to cut the remaining skin and pith away from the fruit inside. Finely chop the fruit, discarding any seeds.
2. Combine the orange zest and fruit, cranberries, sugar, and cinnamon sticks in a large microwave-safe bowl. Cover with a paper towel and microwave on high for 4 minutes. Stop and stir.
3. Microwave until the cranberries pop, about 3 to 5 minutes. Stir again and transfer to a serving dish or storage container.

# Stonepost Farms' Sugar Pumpkin Pie

**MAKES** Two 9-inch pies
**TAKES** 1 hour active time + 1 hour baking time
**RATING** Proficient

I had never made sugar pumpkin pie filling before Becky Doherty of Stonepost Farms in Wildwood shared this recipe with me. Being a rookie, I overestimated the size of the sugar pumpkin I needed. I ended up filling four pies and still had enough pumpkin left over to make a Thai coconut pumpkin soup. Lesson learned. A small sugar pumpkin will do.

**WHAT YOU NEED TO GATHER**

Measuring cups and spoons
Bowls
Pastry blender
Wooden spoon
Plastic wrap
Knife
Cutting board
Steamer basket
Potato masher
Immersion blender
Rolling pin
Two 9-inch pie plates
Large saucepan

*For the pie crusts*

5 cups flour
2 teaspoons salt
½ teaspoon baking powder
1 lb pork lard
¾ cup ice-cold water
1 egg
1 Tablespoon vinegar

*For the filling*

1 small sugar pumpkin (5 lb should yield 4 cups of mashed pumpkin)
2 cups milk
1 teaspoon salt
½ teaspoon ground nutmeg
½ teaspoon ground ginger
½ teaspoon ground cinnamon
¼ cup butter, melted
1½ cups granulated sugar
4 eggs, beaten

## #EATALBERTAFIRST TIP:

Prairie Gardens in Bon Accord, whose owner, Tam Andersen, raises 50 pumpkin varietals, is Canada's northernmost pumpkin farm. The Jungle Farm near Innisfail, Kraay Family Farm near Lacombe, and Eagle Creek Farms near Bowden are other great places to visit, pick out a pumpkin, and shop at the farm-gate stores.

### WHAT YOU NEED TO DO

*For the pie crusts*

1 Mix the flour, salt, and baking powder together in a large bowl, then, using a pastry blender, cut the lard into the mixture until it resembles pea-sized crumbs.
2 Mix the water, egg, and vinegar together in another bowl, then add to the dry ingredients and bring together in a ball with a wooden spoon. Cover with plastic wrap.
3 Set in the refrigerator to rest and chill while you make the filling.

*For the filling and assembly*

1 Preheat the oven to 350°F.
2 Cut the sugar pumpkin in half, discard the seeds, cut the flesh into small pieces, peel them, and then put them in a steamer basket and steam until tender, about 20 minutes. Transfer the pumpkin to a bowl and mash it. I run an immersion blender through it so it's silky smooth. You should have 4 cups' worth. Set aside.
3 Roll out the chilled dough to fit the two 9-inch pie plates with some overhang. Cut and crimp the crusts, place the pie shells in the oven, and bake until the bottoms turn lightly golden, about 10 minutes. Remove the pie shells from the oven and set aside.
4 Heat the mashed pumpkin in a large saucepan over medium heat and slowly stir in the milk, followed by the salt, nutmeg, ginger, and cinnamon. Now stir in the melted butter, followed by the sugar. Once the sugar is dissolved, stir in the beaten eggs. Once thoroughly mixed, pour the mixture into the waiting pie crusts.
5 Return the filled pie crusts to the oven and bake on the middle rack, still at 350°F, until the filling is golden brown and set, about 1 hour. Remove from the oven and let cool. If you're not eating it right away, store it in the refrigerator.
6 Enjoy with ice cream or whipped cream topped with a little cinnamon.

# Eid

I took my first cooking lesson with the late Noorbanu Nimji in 1996. We stayed in touch and I became her recipe tester in 2006. I cooked at her side for nine years before we published *A Spicy Touch: Family Favourites from Noorbanu Nimji's Kitchen* in 2015. It was a privilege to not only learn about Indian cooking from her but also learn about her Ismaili Muslim culture and Ramadan in particular.

Ramadan is a month when Muslims fast. They eat a pre-dawn meal, suhoor, and break their fast after sunset with iftar. The goals of this holy time are to create room to reconnect with the divine, family, and the state of one's own mind, heart, and habits. Spiritual self-improvement can involve extra recitations of the Qur'an, increased prayers, abstinence from bad habits, or an increased focus on volunteering to help those in need. Approximately 1.8 billion Muslims around the world, including 110,000 in Alberta, observe Ramadan. A traditional greeting at this time is "Ramadan mubarak," which loosely translates to "Have a blessed Ramadan." After the 30 days of fasting, they celebrate with Eid (Eid al-Fitr translates into English as "the festival of the breaking of the fast"). I've included two of the Nimji family's favourite Eid dishes here. As feasting dishes go, they're fairly straightforward. That means you don't have to wait for a special occasion to enjoy them; you can make any occasion special by serving them.

# Noorbanu's Butter Chicken

**MAKES** 6 servings
**TAKES** 45 minutes' active time + from 30 minutes' to overnight marination time
**RATING** All levels

I once tasted eighteen butter chicken dishes when I was judging a *Culinaire* magazine contest. I learned it really is everyone's favourite Indian dish, despite only being invented in the 1950s. This recipe is from *A Spicy Touch: Family Favourites from Noorbanu Nimji's Kitchen*, which I co-authored with my mentor, the late Noorbanu Nimji. It brings back happy memories of sharing it at Nimji family gatherings. It truly is a favourite. Enjoy with basmati rice, naan, and Never-the-Same-Way-Twice Coleslaw (page 139). I usually double or triple this recipe and use any leftovers on naan pizzas.

**WHAT YOU NEED TO GATHER**

Paper towel
Knife
Cutting board
Measuring cups and spoons
Large bowl
Plastic wrap
Blender
Large saucepan or wok
Wooden spoon

*For the chicken and marinade*

1½ lb boneless, skinless chicken breast
3 Tablespoons plain yogurt
2 teaspoons tomato paste
1½ teaspoons garlic paste
1½ teaspoons ginger paste
½ teaspoon chili paste
1 teaspoon ground cumin
½ teaspoon sweet paprika
¼ teaspoon Indian chili powder
¼ teaspoon garam masala
Pinch saffron
¾ teaspoon salt

*For the sauce*

¼ cup roughly chopped onion
½ red bell pepper, roughly chopped
½ green bell pepper, roughly chopped
¾ cup water, divided
¼ cup butter
1 cup tomato sauce
2 teaspoons dried fenugreek leaves (see Pro Tips on page 346)
1 cup half-and-half cream

### #EATALBERTAFIRST TIP:

Look for chicken from TK Ranch, Honest Meat Co., Bowden Farm Fresh Chicken, First Nature Farms, Sunworks, and Field to Fork.

**WHAT YOU NEED TO DO**

*For the chicken and marinade*

1 Rinse the chicken under cold, running water, pat it dry with a paper towel, and cut it into bite-sized pieces. Set aside.
2 Place the yogurt, tomato paste, garlic paste, ginger paste, chili paste, cumin, paprika, chili, garam masala, saffron, and salt in a large bowl. Mix well and then stir in the chicken.
3 Cover the bowl with plastic wrap and marinate in the refrigerator for at least 3 hours, or up to overnight (I have gotten away with as little as 30 minutes and it still tasted great). You can also freeze the chicken in the marinade at this point.

*For the sauce and assembly*

1. Put the onion, green and red bell peppers, and ¼ cup of the water in a blender and purée until smooth. Set aside.
2. Melt the butter in a large saucepan over medium heat. Add the onion and pepper mixture and cook, stirring occasionally, until the onion is cooked through, about 5 minutes.
3. Add the chicken and any remaining marinade and cook, stirring, for about 5 minutes, until the chicken starts to turn white.
4. Add the tomato sauce, fenugreek leaves, and more water, about 2 Tablespoons at a time, as required to keep the dish from sticking or becoming too thick, and continue cooking until the chicken is tender, about 20 minutes.
5. Reduce the heat to low, add the cream, and simmer until heated through, about 5 minutes.

## PRO TIPS:

- To make your own garam masala, use our recipe from *A Spicy Touch*: place ½ cup Sri Lankan cinnamon bark pieces (available at Indian grocers), 2 Tablespoons green cardamom pods, 1 Tablespoon black peppercorns, and 1 Tablespoon whole cloves on a baking sheet and bake at 300°F for 10 minutes. Let the whole spices cool, add to a spice grinder with 1 teaspoon of freshly grated nutmeg, and process to a fine powder.
- Dried fenugreek is also known as kasoori methi because it is methi (fenugreek) from the Kasoor area of Punjab, India. The most common one I see in Alberta (and usually the only one available) comes in a bright yellow box with a blue peacock on it. Now that you know this, you'll easily spot it in the international aisle of your grocery store.
- Pay yourself forward: multiply the chicken and marinade ingredients in this recipe and freeze them in portions suiting your family. I did that for an RV trip to Alaska. It was a real treat in a place where restaurants are as scarce as black spruce is dense.

# Festive Vegetable Biryani

**MAKES** 6 to 8 servings
**TAKES** 45 to 60 minutes' active time
**RATING** Competent to proficient

Biryani originated in Persia. It's a layered dish of rice and vegetables or meat. Cooks for the Mughal emperors in India transformed it into a delicacy by adding spices like saffron, which gives it its characteristic flavour and aroma. Traditionally biryani is reserved for festive occasions like weddings, Diwali, and, for Muslims, Eid. My mentor Noorbanu often made more complicated biryanis with chicken or beef, but this recipe is one that everyone can master with ease. The usual sides are yogurt, chutneys, kachumber (a crunchy salad of chopped carrots, cucumber, tomatoes, and finely cut hot peppers), and coriander leaves tossed with a little vinegar, chili powder, and salt.

**WHAT YOU NEED TO GATHER**

Sieve
Bowl
2 saucepans
Knife
Cutting board
Measuring cups and spoons
Shallow frying pan with lid
Slotted spoon
Paper towel
Rimmed baking sheet
Fork

2½ cups basmati rice
5 cups water
1 teaspoon salt
2 pinches saffron
1 Tablespoon butter or ghee
4 Tablespoons olive oil, divided
6 shallots, sliced thinly and lengthwise
8 chopped fresh curry leaves
2 jalapeños, slit along 1 side lengthwise
1 teaspoon cumin seeds
1 cup carrots, sliced in rounds
1 cup white potatoes, chopped in 1-inch cubes
¾ cup frozen peas
¾ cup cauliflower florets
¾ cup broccoli florets
1 cup chopped tomatoes (1 medium, skin on)
1 teaspoon coarsely ground fennel seeds
1 teaspoon salt
1 cup plain yogurt
2 teaspoons tomato paste
1 teaspoon garlic paste
1 teaspoon ginger paste
1 teaspoon sambal oelek
½ cup chopped green bell peppers
½ cup chopped red bell peppers
1 teaspoon sugar
1 teaspoon finely cut fresh cilantro leaves
½ teaspoon garam masala (see page 346)
1 Tablespoon lemon juice

#### WHAT YOU NEED TO DO

1 Wash the rice in a sieve under running cold water until the water runs clear and then soak it in a bowl of fresh cold water for 10 to 15 minutes. Drain it and put it in a large saucepan on high heat with the water, salt, saffron, and butter. Bring to a boil, boil for 2 to 3 minutes, and then reduce the heat to low. Cover the pot and simmer until all the water is absorbed, about 15 minutes. Even though the water is gone, you still need to check to see if the rice is cooked. If not, add 2 Tablespoons of water and continue to simmer until done. Set aside.

2 Heat 2 Tablespoons of the oil in a shallow frying pan over low heat and fry the shallots until golden brown, about 30 minutes. Remove them with a slotted spoon and spread them over a paper towel–lined baking sheet. They'll darken and become crispier as they cool (as long as they are spread out).

3 Heat the remaining 2 Tablespoons of the oil in a saucepan over medium heat, add the curry leaves, jalapeños, and cumin seeds and cook, without stirring, until the seeds pop and splutter, about 30 seconds.

4 Stir in the carrots, potatoes, peas, cauliflower, and broccoli, and cook for 2 minutes.

5 Stir in the tomatoes, fennel seeds, salt, yogurt, tomato paste, garlic paste, ginger paste, and sambal oelek. Cover and cook, stirring occasionally, until the potatoes are almost cooked, about 15 minutes. Add water about 2 Tablespoons at a time as necessary to keep the mixture from sticking.

6 Stir in the bell peppers, sugar, coriander leaves, and garam masala and cook until the potatoes are tender when pierced with a fork, about 5 minutes more.

7 Add the lemon juice. There should be about 1 cup of liquid in the pot. If not, add enough hot water to make it reach 1 cup.

8 Assemble the biryani by first fluffing the rice with a fork—each grain should separate—then spooning it onto a platter. Top it with the vegetables and then garnish with the crispy fried shallots.

# Diwali

Diwali is a major celebration for millions of Hindus, Sikhs, and Jains in India and the world over. It's known as the festival of lights and comes from the Sanskrit word *deepavali*, meaning rows of lit lamps. Along with family gatherings and the giving of sweets, people decorate their homes and streets with small lamps called diyas. They also light fireworks, where allowed, to scare away evil spirits and celebrate the triumph of good over evil.

The origins of Diwali are based in Hindu mythology. It is said that Lord Rama defeated the demon king Ravana and returned to his homeland, after 14 years in exile, to find the villagers had lit the paths with little lamps to welcome him home. The goddess of wealth, prosperity, and fertility, Lakshmi, is supposed to have chosen her husband, Lord Vishnu, on this night as well.

Diwali dates vary according to the lunar calendar and fall between mid-October to mid-November. It's viewed as a time to make a fresh start, make peace, and settle debts. Whether I'm in India at this time or visiting an Indian market in Alberta, people are busy shopping for mithai (sweets). The markets overflow with colourful boxes of ladoos (fruit and nut confections), jalebis (fried dough with syrup), barfis (fudge), and dried fruit and chocolates. Exchanging sweets is a way for friends and family to celebrate the goodness in life and friendship and to bring love and light into the world. I can't imagine a better sentiment to close this chapter.

# Date Halva Balls

**MAKES** 24 balls
**TAKES** 30 minutes' active time + at least 2 hours' chilling time
**RATING** All levels

These Date Halva Balls come together in a jiffy and package beautifully. Outside of Diwali, they make great energy balls for all your life pursuits.

**WHAT YOU NEED TO GATHER**

Measuring cups and spoons
Saucepan
Wooden spoon
Small bowl
Baking sheet
Plastic wrap
Airtight container

1 lb chopped pitted dates
1 Tablespoon packed brown sugar
1 cup whipping cream
2 cups mixed unsalted nuts (almonds, cashews, pistachios)
1 cup shredded unsweetened coconut

**WHAT YOU NEED TO DO**

1. Combine the dates, sugar, and cream in a saucepan over medium heat, and cook, stirring constantly, until thick and shiny when patted with a spoon, about 10 minutes.
2. Stir in the nuts and cook, stirring, for another 5 minutes.
3. Cool the mixture enough to handle and divide it into 24 equal pieces.
4. Roll the pieces into balls and roll each one in a small bowl of desiccated coconut.
5. Place them on a baking sheet, cover with plastic wrap, and freeze for 2 hours. Once they're frozen, you can transfer them to an airtight container and put them back in the freezer for up to 1 month.
6. Remove them from the freezer about 10 minutes before you want to serve them.

Package these in a jar or pretty box to give as gifts at Diwali or other holidays throughout the year.

Eat (and drink) Alberta first by supporting these food artisans.

**APPENDIX:**

# FOOD ARTISANS OF ALBERTA

## NORTHERN ALBERTA

### BAKED GOODS, TEA, AND COFFEE

- Crooked Creek General Store and Donut Food Truck | Hwy 43 near Grande Prairie | Kayanne and Nolan Raber | facebook.com/Crookedcreekstore
- Ole Smokes Coffee | Grande Prairie | Tim Sanford | olesmokescoffee.com

### BEES AND HONEY

- Simply Bee Market/Lazy Bee Apiary | Irma | Jennifer, Meeghan, and Tanya Ford | simplybeemarket.com
- Wolfe Peace River Honey | Guy | Gilbert and Sharon Wolfe | peaceriverhoney.co

### CHARCUTERIE AND SAUSAGES

- Europa Deli and Sausage Hut | Grande Prairie | Srijohn Mandal | europadelisausagehut.ca

### CHEESE AND DAIRY

- The Cheesiry | Kitscoty | Rhonda Zuk Headon | thecheesiry.com
- Nonay Family Lakeside Farmstead | Sturgeon County | Jeff Nonay with cheesemaker Ian Treuer | lakesidefarmstead.com
- Old School Cheesery Ltd. | Vermilion | Patrick Dupuis and Valerie Roberts | oldschoolcheesery.com

### COOKING SCHOOLS AND SPECIALTY FOODS

- Chickadee Farm Organic Herbs | Flatbush | Elizabeth and Eckehart Boschma | chickadeefarmherbs.ca

### CRAFT BEER, CIDER, FRUIT WINE, MEAD, AND DISTILLERIES

- Anohka Distillery | Parkland County | Gurpreet Ranu | anohka.ca
- Apex Predator Brewing | Edson | Andrew Kulynych | apexpredatorbrewing.com
- Broken Tine Orchard (Haskap Honey Wines) | Rio Grande | Kreg Alde | brokentineorchard.ca
- Cold Lake Brewing and Distilling | Cold Lake | Dusty Kiziak | coldlakebrewingdistilling.com
- Copper Cork Distillery | Vermilion | Rod and Randy Fadden, Todd Ree, and Tom Hartwell | coppercorkdistillery.ca
- Dog Island Brewing | Slave Lake | Ben Fiddler and Chad Paulson | dogislandbrewing.com
- Grain Bin Brewing Company | Grande Prairie | Dalen Landis | grainbinbeer.com
- Lakeland Brewing Company | St. Paul | Colin Porozni | lakelandbrewing.wixsite.com/beer/home
- Latitude 55 Distillery | Grande Prairie | Nick Kebalo | latitude55.ca
- Peace River Brewing | Peace River | Tyrell Kehler and Medrey Bond | peaceriverbrewing.ca
- West of The 5th Distillery | Barrhead | Daniel and Nathan Zdrodowski | westofthe5th.com

#### FRUITS, FUNGI, AND VEGETABLES

- Broken Tine Orchard (Haskaps) | Rio Grande | The Alde Family | brokentineorchard.ca
- The Homestead Farm | Goodfare | Lisa Lundgard and Donovan Kitt | thehomesteadfarm.ca (also meat, see below)
- Lakeland Wild Rice Ltd. | Athabasca | aptolemy17@gmail.com
- Northern Lights Fruits & Vegetables | Manning | Louise and Dan Brister | northernlightsproduce.com

#### MEAT, POULTRY, AND PORK

- Backwoods Buffalo Ranch | Woodlands County | Chad and Laurie Trigg | backwoodsbuffalo.com
- Chatsworth Farm | Vermilion | The Wasylik Family | chatsworthfarm.ca
- First Nature Farms | Goodfare | Owner Jerry Kitt is now succession planning with his son Donovan Kitt and daughter-in-law Lisa Lundgard of The Homestead Farm—hooray! | firstnaturefarms.ab.ca

LISA LUNDGARD AT THE HOMESTEAD FARM IN GOODFARE

- Hog Wild Specialties | Mayerthorpe | Earl Hagman | hogwild.ab.ca
- Meadow Creek Farms | Waskatenau | Mandy Melnyk | meadowcreekfarms.ca
- Nature's Way Farm | Grimshaw | Peter and Mary Lundgard | 780-338-2934
- Serben Farms | Smoky Lake | Jared and Julia Serben | serbenfarms.com

## EDMONTON

#### ARTISAN PRODUCTS

- Culina To Go | Edmonton | Brad Lazarenko | culinafamily.com/culina-to-go/
- Fruits of Sherbrooke | Edmonton | Volunteer Board | fruitsofsherbrooke.ca
- Maram Honey Vinegar | Edmonton | Najm Al-Tameemi | facebook.com/MARAM-honey-and-vinegar-106306180704021
- Mojo Jojo Pickles | Edmonton | Johwanna "Jojo" Alleyne | mojojojopickles.com
- Souptacular | St. Albert | Maureen and Al Obrigewitch | souptacular.com

#### BAKED GOODS, TEA, AND COFFEE

- Arno's Fine French Pastry Inc. | Edmonton | Arnaud Valade | facebook.com/arnosPastry
- The Art of Cake | Edmonton | Gloria Bednarz and Guenter Hess | theartofcake.ca
- Bon Ton Bakery | Edmonton | Gerry and Edgar Semler | bonton.ca
- Boulangerie Bonjour | Edmonton | Yvan and Ritsuko Chartrand | yvanchartrand.com
- Duchess Bake Shop | Edmonton | Garner Beggs, Ewa Jastrzębski, and Jay Downton | duchessbakeshop.com
- Eleanor and Laurent | Edmonton | Abel Shiferaw | eleanorandlaurent.com
- Iconoclast Coffee | Edmonton | Ryan Arcand | iconoclastcoffee.com
- Sugared and Spiced Baked Goods | Edmonton | Amy and Jeff Nachtigall | sugaredandspiced.ca
- Transcend Coffee Roasters | Edmonton | Poul Mark | transcendcoffee.ca

**BEES AND HONEY**

- Good Morning Honey | Stony Plain | Richard and Amber Ozero | goodmorninghoney.com

**CHARCUTERIE AND SAUSAGES**

- Menno's Sausage | Ardrossan | George and Eleanor Janzen | mennossausage.com
- Meuwly's Artisan Food Market | Edmonton | Will Kotowicz, Peter Keith, and Glendon Tan | meuwlys.com
- Otto Food and Drink | Edmonton | (for Steven Furgiuele's sausages) | ottofoodanddrink.com

**CHEESE AND DAIRY**

- For the Love of Cheese Vegan Cheezery | Edmonton | James and Natanya Pearcey | fortheloveofcheese.ca
- Little Bear Gelato | Edmonton | Franck Bouilhol | littlebeargelato.com
- Paddy's International Cheese Market | Edmonton | Fern Janzen | m.facebook.com/Paddys-Cheese
- Pinocchio Ice Cream | Tom Ursino and Family | pinocchioicecream.ca
- Truffula (Vegan Cheese) | Edmonton | Allison Landin | truffula.ca

**CHOCOLATE MAKERS AND CONFECTIONERS**

- Colleen's Chocolates | St. Albert | Colleen Heidecker | colleenschocolates.com
- Jacek Chocolate | Sherwood Park | Jacqueline Jacek | jacekchocolate.com
- Sweet Lollapalooza Fine Chocolates | Edmonton | Brett Roy | sweetlollapalooza.com
- The Violet Chocolate Company | Edmonton | Rebecca Grant | thevioletchocolatecompany.com

**COOKING SCHOOLS AND SPECIALTY FOODS**

- Awn Kitchen | Edmonton | Kaelin Whittaker | awnkitchen.com
- Get Cooking | Edmonton | Kathryn Joel | getcooking.ca
- Pei Pei Chei Ow | Edmonton | Scott Jonathan Iserhoff | peipeicheiow.com

**CRAFT BEER, CIDER, FRUIT WINE, MEAD, AND DISTILLERIES**

- Alley Kat Brewing Co. | Edmonton | Zane Christensen and Cameron French | alleykatbeer.com
- Analog Brewing | Edmonton | Adam Corsout and Bryon Lounier | analogbrewing.ca
- Barr Estate Winery (Fruit Wines) | Sherwood Park | Rick and Amy Barr | barr.ca
- Bent Stick Brewing Co. | Edmonton | Patrick Gaudet, Ben Rix, Cole Boyd, and Lisa Davis | bentstickbrewing.com
- Blind Enthusiasm Brewing | Edmonton | Greg Zeschuk | blindenthusiasm.ca
- Brewsters Brewing Company | Edmonton and Calgary | The Lanigan Family | brewsters.ca
- Campio Brewing Co. | Edmonton | Brett Ireland, Alexander Derksen, and Socrates Korogonas | campiobrewingco.com
- Elk Island Spirits | Sherwood Park | John Stubbington | elkislandspirits.com
- Hansen Distillery | Edmonton | Shayna Hansen and Kris Sustrik | hansendistillery.com
- Irrational Brewing Co. | Edmonton | Nathan Marculis and Wafa Veljee | irrationalbrewing.ca
- Long Roof Brewing Co. | Edmonton | Bent Mollegaard-Laugesen and Cory Gray | longroofbrewing.ca
- Odd Company Brewing | Edmonton | John Toman | oddcompany.ca
- Omen Brewing | Edmonton | The Oswald Family | omenbrewing.com
- Red Cup Distillery | Leduc | Rob de Groot | redcupdistillery.ca
- Rig Hand Craft Distillery | Nisku | Karen Stewart-Marcos and Geoff Stewart | righanddistillery.com
- Sea Change Brewing Co. | Edmonton and Beaumont | Ian McIntosh | seachangebeer.com
- Situation Brewing | Edmonton | Wayne Sheridan | situationbeer.com
- Strathcona Spirits Distillery | Edmonton | Adam Smith | strathconaspirits.ca
- Town Square Brewing Co. | Ellerslie | Megan and Brandon Boutin, Katrina and Tyler McNaughton, and Mellissa & Sterling Nordin | townsquarebrewing.com

#### FORAGERS, FORAGING CLASSES, AND FORAGED FOODS

- From the Wild | Edmonton | Kevin Kossowan | fromthewild.ca/events
- Mo-Na Food | Edmonton | Michael Aventi | monafood.ca
- Untamed Feast | St. Albert | Michelle and Eric Whitehead | untamedfeast.com

#### FRUITS, FUNGI, AND VEGETABLES

- Bokey Blooms (Haskaps) | Morinville | Shauna Bokenfohr and Ross Ehalt | bokeybloomsfarms.ca
- Prairie Gardens and Adventure Farm | Bon Accord | Tam Andersen | prairiegardens.org
- Purple Gem Farms (Saskatoons) | Millet | Eileen Roth | purplegem.ca
- Riverbend Gardens | Edmonton | Aaron and Janelle Herbert | riverbendgardens.ca
- Rosy Farms (Haskaps) | Alcomdale | Andrew Rosychuck | rosyfarms.com
- Sparrow's Nest Organics | Opal | Graham Sparrow | sparroworganics.com
- Sundog Organic Farm | Gibbons | James and Jenny Vriend | sundogorganicfarm.ca

#### GRAINS, SEEDS, AND PULSES

- Gold Forest Grains | Morinville | John and Cindy Schneider | goldforestgrains.com

#### MEAT, POULTRY, AND PORK

- Acme Meat Market | Edmonton | Corey Meyer | acmemeatmarket.ca
- The Butchery by Rge Rd | Edmonton | Blair Lebsack | thebutcheryyeg.ca
- Four Whistle Farm | Millet | Marius De Boer | fourwhistlefarm.ca
- Thundering Ground Bison Ranch | Devon | Larissa Helbig | thunderingground bisonranch.com

#### SUSTAINABLE FISH AND SEAFOOD

- Effing Seafoods | St. Albert | Rob Tryon | effingseafoods.com
- Ocean Odyssey Inland | Edmonton | Pat Batten | oceanodysseyinland.ca

## CENTRAL ALBERTA

#### BAKED GOODS, TEA, AND COFFEE

- Dose Coffee | Red Deer | Rolland Forsland | dosecoffeeco.ca
- Eco Cafe | Pigeon Lake | Tim Wood | ecocafe pigeonlake.com
- Little Bird Baking | Wetaskiwin County | Abby Reimer | instagram.com/littlebirdbakingcamrose
- NRG Coffee Roasters | Ferintosh | Carolee and Jonathan Thiessen | nrgcoffeeco.com

#### BEES AND HONEY

- Nixon Honey | Innisfail | Kevin, Craig, and Bryon Nixon | nixonhoney.ca

#### CHARCUTERIE AND SAUSAGES

- Viva Deli | Red Deer | Vatali and Inessa Kojlo | viva-deli.ca

#### CHEESE AND DAIRY

- Alberta Pike Cheese | Innisfail | Art Snoek | albertapike.ca
- Rock Ridge Dairy | Ponoka | Cherylynn and Patrick Bos | rockridgedairy.com
- Sylvan Star Cheese | Sylvan Lake | Janneke and Jan Schalkwijk | sylvanstarcheesefarm.ca

#### COOKING SCHOOLS AND SPECIALTY FOODS

- The Cooking Room | Red Deer | Selena Hucal | thecookingroom.com

#### CRAFT BEER, CIDER, FRUIT WINE, MEAD, MALTING AND HOPS, AND DISTILLERIES

- Back 40 Distillery | Camrose | Lorne Haugen and Rick Lazaruik | back40distillery.com
- Blindman Brewing | Lacombe | Hans Doef and Kirk Zembal | blindmanbrewing.com
- Delidais Estate Winery (Fruit Wines) | Elnora | The Delidais Family | dnagardens.info

- Fallen Timber Meadery | Water Valley | The Ryan Family | fallentimbermeadery.ca
- Grey Owl Meadery | Alder Flats | Walter, Arleen, and Caleb Schwengler | greyowlmeadery.com
- Hard Hels Hops | Red Deer | Colin and Jaclyn Smith | hardhelshopfarm.com
- Hop To It Hop Farm | Lacombe | Shayne and Jenelle Bjarnason | hoptoitalberta.com
- Olds College Brewery | Olds | Student Creations | oldscollege.ca/shopoc/brewery
- Red Hart Brewing | Red Deer County | Curtis Lawrence-Ross, Kristy Lawrence, Jarod Griesbach, Rachel Griesbach, and Andrew Wieb | redhartbrewing.ca
- Red Shed Malting | Red Deer County | Joe and Daelyn, John and Susie, Joe Hamill | redshedmalting.ca
- Ribstone Creek Brewery | Edgerton | Alvin Gordon, Don Paré, Chris Fraser, Cal Hawkes, and David Beardsell | ribstonecreekbrewery.ca
- Troubled Monk Brewery | Red Deer | Charlie and Graeme Bredo | troubledmonk.com

**FRUITS, FUNGI, AND VEGETABLES**

- Billyco Junction Gardens | Lacombe | Bill and Edie Biel | billycojunction.com
- Blue Mountain Biodynamic Farms | Carstairs | Kris and Tamara Vester | bluemountainbiody namicfarms.com
- Ceres Solutions Ltd. (Cultivated Mushrooms) | Olds and Crossfield | Alex Villeneuve | ceres-ab.com
- Eagle Creek Farms | Bowden | John Mills | eaglecreekfarms.ca
- Fifth Gen Gardens (and Garlic) | Wetaskiwin | Kristin Graves | fifthgengardens.ca
- Grey Arrow Farm | Camrose | Denis and Andrea Forstbauer | greyarrowfarm.ca
- Gull Valley Greenhouses | Blackfalds | Jil and Scott Epple, Levi and Carmen, Carolyn and Phil Tiemstra | gullvalley.ca
- Innisfail Growers Co-operative | Innisfail | innisfailgrowers.com
    - Beck Farms | Shelley and Rod Bradshaw

LEFT TO RIGHT: ELNA AND DOUG EDGAR WITH RANDY AND KERI GRAHAM

    - Edgar Farms | Elna and Doug Edgar | Keri and Randy Graham
    - Hillside Greenhouses | Carmen and Jose Fuentes
    - The Jungle Farm | Leona and Blaine Staples
    - Upper Green Farms | Megan and Hanno Buyks
- Lund's Organic Farm | Innisfail | Gert and Mads Lund | lundsorganic.com
- Pearson's Berry Farm | Bowden | Debbie and Duane Mertin | pearsonsberryfarm.ca
- Reclaim Organics | Pigeon Lake | Ryan Mason | reclaimurbanfarm.com
- Solstice Berry Farm | Crossfield | Marsha and Rick Gelowitz | solsticeberryfarm.com
- Steel Pony Farm | Red Deer County | Mike Kozlowski | steelpony.ca

**GRAINS, SEEDS, AND PULSES**

- Stuka's Flour | Camrose | Jason Stuka | stukasflour.com
- Sunny Boy Foods | Camrose | Patricia and Brad Shapka | sunnyboyfoods.com

**MEAT, POULTRY, AND PORK**

- 609 Farms | Ferintosh | Cherolyn and Nelson Penner | facebook.com/609farms
- Bauer Meats and Farm Basket | Three Hills | Mike and Annette Bauer | facebook.com/profile .php?id=100063566020708
- Big Bend Bison Ranches | Innisfail | Ivan Smith | bigbendmarket.ca

- Big Bend Market | Red Deer | Ray, Natalie, and Dawn Volmer | bigbendmarket.ca
- Brown Eggs and Lamb | Lacombe | Laura Siebenga | facebook.com/browneggsandlamb
- Coen Farm | Ferintosh | Dakota Coen | coenfarm.ca
- Happiness By The Acre | Didsbury | Marcus and Sarah Riedner | happinessbytheacre.ca
- HGB Bison Ranch and Meat Shop | Olds | Heather and George Briggs | hgbbison.com
- Hoven Farms Organic Grass Finished Beef | Eckville | Lorianne and Tim Hoven | hovenfarms.com
- Irvings Farm Fresh | Round Hill | Nicola and Alan Irving | irvingsfarmfresh.com
- Lazuli Farms | Camrose | Kylie and Scott Bartman | lazulifarms.com
- Little Loaves Farm | Sundre | Jerremie and Rita Clyde | littleloavesfarm.com
- Mount Bison and Cattle Company | Caroline | Tyler Mount | mountbison.ca
- Nature's Green Acres | Beaver County | Shannon and Danny Ruzicka | naturesgreenacres.com
- PaSu Farm | Carstairs | Patrick and Susan de Rosemond | pasu.com
- Pine Haven Colony Meat Shop | Wetaskiwin | Tim Hofer | phmeatshop.ca
- Prairie Gold Pastured Meats | Red Deer County | Angela and Blake Hall | prairiegoldmeats.ca
- Redtail Farms | Castor | Dana Blume and Ian Griebel | redtailfarms.ca
- Schielke Farm | | Debbie and Kevin Schielke and Danielle and Jared Doel | schielkefarm.ca
- Sunworks Farm | Armena | Sheila and Ron Hamilton | sunworksfarm.com
- TK Ranch | Spondin and Langdon | Colleen and Dylan Biggs with Jocelyn Biggs and Andre Voortman | tkranch.com
- Whispering Wind Farms | Didsbury | Kelly Worthington and Jon Lendvoy | whisperingwindfarms.com
- YR Bison Ranch | Red Deer | Yvonne and Rod Mills | yrranch.ca

## CALGARY

### ARTISAN PRODUCTS

- Brassica Mustard | Calgary | Eric Giesbrecht | meta4foods.com
- Cian's Mustard | Calgary | Cian, Cameron, Colin, and Colina Clark | ciansmustard.com
- Preserved | Bragg Creek | Vanessa Rundell | preservedyyc.com

### BAKED GOODS, TEA, AND COFFEE

- Crave Cupcakes | Calgary and Edmonton | Jodi Willoughby and Carolyne McIntyre-Jackson | cravecupcakes.ca
- Decadent Brûlée | Calgary | Pam Fortier | decadentbrulee.ca
- The Naked Leaf | Calgary | Jonathan Kane | thenakedleaf.ca
- Ollia Macarons and Tea | Calgary | David and Lyndsay Rousseau | byollia.com
- Phil & Sebastian Coffee Roasters | Calgary | Phil Robertson and Sebastian Sztazyb | philsebastian.com
- Pie Junkie | Calgary | Jo-Anne Caza and Nancy Goemans | piejunkie.ca
- Pretty Sweet | Calgary | Vicki Manness | prettysweetco.com
- Sidewalk Citizen Bakery | Calgary | Michal Lavi and Aviv Fried | sidewalkcitizenbakery.com
- Sugarbakers Cookie Company | Calgary | Michelle and Jennifer De Villenfagne | sugarbakerscookieco.com
- Tea Trader | Calgary | Ted Jones | teatrader.com
- Yum Bakery | Calgary | Deb and David Catling | yum-bakery.com

### BEES AND HONEY

- Apiaries and Bees for Communities (ABC Bees) | Calgary | Eliese Watson | abcbees.ca
- Bear Bait Honey | Calgary | Herman Van Reekum | bearbaithoney.com
- Mob Honey | Calgary | Amber Yano | mobhoney.com

#### CHARCUTERIE AND SAUSAGES

- Empire Provisions | Calgary | Karen Kho and David Sturies | empireprovisions.com
- Illichmann's Sausage Shop Ltd. | Calgary | Dana and Ken Meissinger | illichmannscalgary.com
- Pioneer Butchery and Charcuterie | Calgary | Greg and Allan Dixon, Taylor Gant | pioneeryyc.com
- Spolumbo's | Calgary | Mike Palumbo and Tony Spoletini | spolumbos.com
- VDG Salumi | Calgary | Stuart Kirton and Ivo Andric | vdgsalumi.com

#### CHEESE AND DAIRY

- Flora Fromage (Vegan Cheesery) | Calgary | Janice Buckingham | florafromage.com
- Holy Cow Gelato and Donuts | Calgary | Matt Batey | holycowgelato.com
- Made by Marcus Microcreamery | Calgary and Edmonton | Marcus Purtzki | madebymarcus.ca
- Noto Gelato | Calgary | Stefana Spoletini and Domenic Tudda | notogelato.ca
- Peasant Cheese Shops | Calgary | Crystal McKenzie | peasantcheese.com
- Say Cheese Fromagerie | Calgary | Nancy Brown | saycheesefromagerie.com
- Village Ice Cream | Calgary | Billy Friley | village icecream.com

#### CHOCOLATE MAKERS AND CONFECTIONERS

- The Chocolate Lab | Calgary | Eva Choi and Dallas Southcott | chocolatelab.ca
- cōchu chocolatier | Calgary | Anne Sellmer | cochu.ca
- Dwarf Stars | Calgary | Kathryn Kozody and Gerritt Janssen | dwarfstars.ca
- Goldie Craft Chocolate | Calgary | Amy Horne | goldiechocolate.com
- Master Chocolat | Calgary | Bernard Callebaut | masterchocolat.com
- Volio's Confections | Calgary | Sarah Foy and David Sullivan | voliosconfections.com

#### COOKING SCHOOLS, KNIVES, AND SPECIALTY FOODS

- Barb Sheldon Culinary Nutrition | Calgary | Barb Sheldon | barbsheldon.com
- The Cookbook Co. Cooks | Calgary | Gail Norton | cookbookcooks.com
- Knifewear | Calgary and Edmonton | Kevin Kent | knifewear.com
- Inspirati Fine Linens and Home Essentials | Calgary | Wendy Brownie | inspirati.ca
- The Silk Road Spice Merchant | Calgary and Edmonton | Kelci Hind and Colin Leach | silkroadspices.ca

#### CRAFT BEER, CIDER, FRUIT WINE, AND DISTILLERIES

- Annex Ale Project Brewing and Craft Soda Mfg | Calgary | Andrew Bullied and Erica O'Gorman | annexales.com
- Best of Kin Brewing | Calgary | Ryan and Colin Mortson | bestofkin.ca
- Bow River Brewing | Calgary | Ian Binmore | bowriverbrewing.com
- Cabin Brewing | Calgary | Jonas Hurtig, Darrin Sayers, and Haydon Dewes | cabinbrewing.ca
- Citizen Brewing | Calgary | Ric Cutillo | citizenbrewingcompany.com
- Cold Garden Beverage Co. | Calgary | Blake Belding and Dan Allard | coldgarden.ca
- Common Crown Brewing Co. | Calgary | Damen and Andrew Moreau | commoncrown.ca
- The Dandy Brewing Co. | Calgary | Ben Leon, Derek Waghray, Matt Gaetz, and Dylan Nosal | thedandybrewingcompany.com
- Eighty Eight Brewing | Calgary | Jordan Saracini, Stuart Valentini, Brendan Barnett, and Nick Wallat | eightyeightbrewing.ca
- Last Best Brewing and Distilling | Calgary | Brett Ireland, Alexander Derksen, and Socrates Korogonas | lastbestbrewing.com
- Ol' Beautiful Brewing | Calgary | Chris Carroll and Devon Sidwel | olbeautiful.com

- Sunny Cider | Calgary | Tim and Darlene Kitchen | sunnycider.ca
- Tool Shed Brewing | Calgary | Graham Sherman and Jeff Orr | toolshedbrewing.com
- Trolley 5 Restaurant and Brewery | Calgary | PJ L'Heureux and Ernie Tsu | trolley5.com
- Two Pillars Brewery | Calgary | Jacob May and Boaz Leung | twopillars.ca
- Uncommon Cider | Calgary | Brodie Thomas | uncommoncider.com
- Village Brewery | Calgary | Tim Duffin and Jim Button | villagebrewery.com

#### FORAGERS, FORAGING CLASSES, AND FORAGED FOODS

- Canadian FunGuy | Calgary | Joseph Brennan | canadianfunguy.com

#### FRUITS, FUNGI, AND VEGETABLES

- Deepwater Farms | Paul Shumlich, Kevin Daniels, and Reid Henuset | deepwaterfarms.com
- Dirt Boys Urban Farming | Calgary | Michael Gavin | dirtboys.ca
- Harvest Hub | Calgary | Alina Martin and Sean Fillion | theharvesthub.ca
- Leaf & Lyre Urban Farms | Calgary | Rod Olson | leafandlyre.net
- Micro YYC | Calgary | Vanessa Hanel | microyyc.com
- NuLeaf Farms | Calgary | Ryan and Paul Wright and Dan Clayholt | nuleaffarms.ca
- Verge Permaculture | Calgary | Michelle and Rob Avis | vergepermaculture.ca
- YYC Growers and Distributors | Calgary | Farmer Cooperative | yycgrowers.com

#### MEAT, POULTRY, AND PORK

- Silver Sage Beef | Calgary | Kent Zentner | silversagebeef.com
- Urban Butcher | Calgary | Bob Choquette | urbanbutcher.ca

#### SUSTAINABLE FISH AND SEAFOOD

- Meta4Foods and Oyster Tribe | Calgary | Eric Giesbrecht | meta4foods.com

## ROCKY MOUNTAINS

#### ARTISAN PRODUCTS

- An Edible Life | Canmore | Carole Beaton | anediblelife.ca
- Rocky Mountain Flatbread Co. | Canmore | Michel Leblanc | rockymountainflatbread.ca

#### BAKED GOODS, TEA, AND COFFEE

- Andromeda and Snowdome Coffee | Jasper | Sam and Shelley Koebel | snowdome.coffee
- Banff Tea Company | Banff | Siona Gartshore | banffteaco.com
- Bear's Paw Bakery | Jasper | Kimberley Stark | bearspawbakery.com
- Communitea Cafe | Canmore | Marnie Dansereau | thecommunitea.com
- Eclipse Coffee Roasters | Canmore | Dean Smolicz | eclipsecoffeeroasters.com
- JK Bakery | Canmore | Samantha McConnery | jkbakery.ca
- Jolene's Tea House | Banff | Jolene Brewster and Jess McNally | jolenesteahouse.com
- Le Fournil | Canmore | Pascale Tetrault | fournil.ca
- Stock Food & Drink | Fairmont Banff Springs | Robert Ash | fairmont.com/banff-springs/dining/stock-food-drink
- Wild Flour Bakery | Banff | Peter Poole | wildflourbakery.ca

#### CHEESE AND DAIRY

- Cravings Gelato | Banff | Charlynn Odegard | cravingsgelato.com
- Glowfood Creamery (Vegan) | Banff | Julie Kapuscinski | glowfood.ca

#### CHOCOLATE MAKERS AND CONFECTIONERS

- Le Chocolatier | Canmore | Anna-Engel Lebiadowski | lechocolatier.ca

#### COOKING SCHOOLS AND SPECIALTY FOODS

- Paintbox Lodge and Cooking@TheBox | Canmore | Sara Renner and Thomas Grandi | paintboxlodge.com

#### CRAFT BEER, CIDER, FRUIT WINE, MEAD, AND DISTILLERIES

- Banff Ave Brewing | Banff | Brett Ireland, Alexander Derksen, and Socrates Korogonas | banffavebrewingco.ca
- Canmore Brewing Company | Canmore | Brian Dunn | canmorebrewing.com
- Folding Mountain Brewing | Hinton | Aric Johnson and Jason Griffiths | foldingmountain.com
- Grizzly Paw Brewery | Canmore | Niall Fraser | thegrizzlypaw.com
- Half Hitch Brewing | Cochrane | Kyle and Chris Heier and Britt and Chace Kozloski | halfhitchbrewing.ca
- Jasper Brewing Co. | Jasper | Brett Ireland, Alexander Derksen, and Socrates Korogonas | jasperbrewingco.ca
- Krang Spirits | Cochrane | Susan Ransom and Michael Guenzel | facebook.com/KrangSpirits
- Park Distillery | Banff | Katie Tuff and Mike Mendelman | parkdistillery.com
- Rocky View Brewing Co. | Cochrane | Lyle and Denean Thorson | rockyviewbrewing.com
- Three Bears Restaurant and Brewery | Banff | Stavros Karlos | threebearsbanff.com
- Wild Life Distillery | Canmore | Matt Widmer and Keith Robinson | wildlifedistillery.ca

#### FORAGERS, FORAGING CLASSES, AND FORAGED FOODS

- Mahican Trails Indigenous Experiences (Medicinal Plant Walks) | Banff, Canmore, Sundre | Brenda Holder | mahikan.ca

#### FRUITS, FUNGI, AND VEGETABLES

- Alpine Edible Schoolyards | Canmore | Christian Wright | facebook.com/alpineedible
- Jasper Local Food Society and Jasper Community Garden | Jasper | Janet Cooper | facebook.com/jasperlocalfoodsociety
- Summit Hill Farm | Bottrel | Alberta and Corey Teffler | summithillfarm.ca

#### MEAT, POULTRY, AND PORK

- Big Hill Sheep Farm | Cochrane | Jolene and Howard Airth | bighillsheep.ca
- LJ Ranch | Cochrane | Joy and Lindsay Eklund | ljranch.ca

TRAVIS AND JOY EKLUND AT LJ RANCH, COCHRANE

- Uncle Bernie's All Natural Meats | Banff, Canmore, and Cochrane | The Pagenkopf Family | uncleberniesallnaturalmeats.com
- WineGlass Ranch | Cochrane | Travis and Kara Eklund | wineglassranchalberta.com

#### SUSTAINABLE FISH AND SEAFOOD

- Crystal Rill Trout | Elbow River Valley | Shannon and Jonathan Young | crystalrilltrout.com

## SOUTHERN ALBERTA

#### ARTISAN PRODUCTS

- Alchemist Vinegars | Tippa Distillery | Okotoks | tippadistillery.square.site
- Bustard's Mustard | Pincher Creek | Bradley Bustard | thanksgivingranch.ca/mercantile
- Holy Kraut | Strathmore | Angie Howkins and Tricia Green | holykraut.biz
- Luco's Mustard | Lethbridge | Ben and Robert Luco | lucofarms.com
- Smachno Ukrainian Foods | Altario | Nataliia Mantsybora, Iryna Mazur, and Tetiana Shkolnik | facebook.com/smachno.4ever

#### BAKED GOODS, TEA, AND COFFEE

- Homestead Bakeshop | Fort Macleod | Kim Vanden Brook | homesteadbakeshop.ca
- MadHatter Roastery | Medicine Hat | Josh and Katrina Borrows | mhroastery.com
- Redcliff Bakery | Medicine Hat | Melissa and Joel Graber | redcliffbakery.com
- Red Engine Coffee Roasters and Sonder Coffee Bar | Lethbridge | Jacquie and Paul DeMaere | redenginecoffee.com
- The Westwood | Black Diamond | Erin Kendrick and Theresa Velkova | thewestwood.ca
- Zucchini Blossom Market and Café | Medicine Hat | Kristine Dalzell | zucchiniblossom.com

#### BEES AND HONEY

- Chinook Honey and Chinook Arch Meadery | Okotoks | Cherie and Art Andrews | chinookhoney.com
- Eastern Slopes Honey | Priddis | Bob Robertson and Paul Hoff | easternslopeshoney.com

#### CHARCUTERIE AND SAUSAGES

- Medicine Hat Meat Traders | Cypress County | The Pahl Family | mhmt.ca
- Old Country Sausage Shop | Raymond | Chris Bragg | oldcountrysausages.com
- Soleterra d'Italia | Acme | The Price Family | soleterra.ca

#### CHEESE AND DAIRY

- Bles-Wold Yogurt Products | Coalhurst | The Beyer Family | bles-wold.com
- Bourbon Brothers Craft Ice Cream | Medicine Hat | Kris Nicholas and Brandon de Roaldes | bythebourbonbrothers.com
- Crystal Springs Dairy Company | Coalhurst | The Beyer Family | crystalspringscheese.com
- Fairwinds Farm | Fort Macleod | Anita and Ben Oudshoorn | fairwindsfarm.ca
- Noble Meadows Farm | Nobleford | Carolyn Van Driesten | noblemeadowsfarm.com
- Old West Ranch | Mountain View | James Meservy | mountainview.link/mountain-view-link-home/old-west-ranch-ltd
- Vital Green Farms | Picture Butte | Joe and Caroline Mans | vitalgreen.ca

#### CHOCOLATE MAKERS AND CONFECTIONERS

- Sweetsmith Candy Co. | Strathmore | Dannah Davies | sweetsmithcandyco.com

#### COOKING SCHOOLS AND SPECIALTY FOODS

- Galimax Trading Inc. | Nobleford | Rudy Knitel and Corne Mans | galimaxtrading.com
- Umami Shop | Lethbridge | Patricia Lau and Sven Roeder | umamishop.ca
- Urban Grocer | Lethbridge | Logan Shearer | facebook.com/UrbanGrocer

#### CRAFT BEER, CIDER, FRUIT WINE, MEAD, AND DISTILLERIES

- Balzac Craft Brewing Company | Airdrie | Stewart Ward | balzaccraftbrewing.com
- Chinook Arch Meadery | Okotoks | Cherie and Art Andrews | chinookhoney.com
- Coulee Brew Co. | Lethbridge | Deborah Pallett and Scott Crighton | couleebrew.co
- Eau Claire Distillery | Turner Valley | David Farran | eauclairedistillery.ca
- Fahr Beer | Turner Valley | Jochen Fahr | fahr.ca
- Field Stone Fruit Wines | Strathmore | Elaine and Marvin Gill | fieldstonefruitwines.com
- Hell's Basement Brewery | Medicine Hat | Mike Patriquin and Mike Gripp | hellsbasement.com
- Medicine Hat Brewing | Medicine Hat | Mitch Dalrymple and Warren Vancurren | medicinehatbrewingcompany.ca
- Spirit Hills Honey Winery | Millarville | Hugo, Ilse, Amber, Bjorn, and Fabian Bonjean | spirithillswinery.com
- Theoretically Brewing Co. | Lethbridge | Kris Fischer and Kelti Baird | theorybrew.ca

#### FORAGERS, FORAGING CLASSES, AND FORAGED FOODS

- Full Circle Adventures | Turner Valley | Julie Walker | fullcircleadventures.com
- Tender Living Farm | Black Diamond | Isis Velkova-Andrus | tenderlivingfarm.ca

#### FRUITS, FUNGI, AND VEGETABLES

- Amiable Organics | Nobleford | Joshua Mans | amiableorganics.ca
- Blue Vista Orchards (Haskaps) | Picture Butte | Brendan Grisnich | instagram.com/bluevistaorchards
- Broxburn Vegetables and Café | Lethbridge | Hilda and Paul de Jonge | broxburn-vegetables.com
- Busy Bea's Market Garden | Lethbridge | Trevor Aleman | busybeasmarketgarden.com
- Forage and Farm | Millarville | Cheryl Greisinger | forageandfarm.com
- Johnson Fresh Farms Taber Corn | Barnwell | The Johnson Family | johnsonfreshfarms.com
- Kehoe Lake Farms | Picture Butte | Nelly and Adrian Sinke | klfarms.ca
- Mans Organics | Coaldale | Henk and Rita, Andrew and Denise Mans | mansorganics.ca
- Neubauer Farms | Cypress County | Mark and Nichole Neubauer | neubauerfarms.ca
- New Oxley Garlic Naturally | Claresholm | Jackie Chalmers | facebook.com/newoxleyranche
- Noble Gardens | Nobleford | Brenda and Tim Vriesalaar | noblegardens.ca
- Paradise Hill Farm | Nanton | Karen and Tony Legault | paradisehillfarm.ca
- Phoenix Farms | Monarch | John, Rick, and Joel Mans | phoenixfarms.ca
- Poplar Bluff Organics | Strathmore | Rosemary Wotske and Cam Beard | poplarblufforganics.com
- Prairie Hill Fruits (Haskaps) | Picture Butte | Rex Vandenberg | phfstore.online
- Rafferty Farms—Earthis Ltd. | Okotoks | Nick and Ben Hsu and James Rafferty | earthisltd.ca
- Red Fox Fungi Gourmet Mushrooms and Seasonings | Strathmore | Janine Aube and Brad Wandzura | redfoxfungi.ca
- RedHat Co-operative Ltd. | Redcliff | Red Hat Co-op Members | redhatco-op.com
- The Saskatoon Farm | De Winton | Karen and Paul Hamer | saskatoonfarm.com

#### GRAINS, SEEDS, AND PULSES

- Back 40 Organics | Etzikom | Bernie Ehnes | 403-666-2157
- Grainworks Organic Tillers and Millers | Vulcan | Dwayne and Doreen Smith | grainworks.com

PENNY AND TONY MARSHALL, HIGHWOOD CROSSING FARM, ALDERSYDE

- Highwood Crossing Foods | High River | Penny and Tony Marshall | highwoodcrossing.com
- Van Garderen Ranch | Picture Butte | The Van Garderen Family | vangarderenranch.com

#### MEAT, POULTRY, AND PORK

- Brant Lake Wagyu | Brant Lake | Michelle and Jeff Ball | brantlakewagyu.ca
- Broek Pork Acres | Coalhurst | Joanne and Allan Vanden Broek | broekporkacres.com
- Deerview Meats | Irvine | Chris and Perry Deering | deerviewmeats.com
- Driview Farms | Fort Macleod | Gerritt and Janet Van Hierden | driviewfarms.com
- Eh Farms | Strathmore | Christina and Andy Stender | ehfarms.ca
- Fishburn Ranch | Pincher Creek | Casey and Jaclyn Toews | fishburnranch.com
- Gemstone Beef | Gem | The Doerksen Family | gemstonegrassfedbeef.com
- Glengary Bison | Madden | Gary Sweetnam and Cynthia Austin | glengarybison.com
- The Hartell Homestead | Longview | Nick Shipley | hartellhomestead.com
- Highwood Valley Ranch | High River | Jaimie and Wade Nelson | highwoodvalleyranch.com

- Mitchell Bros. Beef | Pincher Creek | The Mitchell Family | mitchellbrosbeef.com
- Sage Creek Permaculture | Airdrie | Nancy and Chad Hewlett | sagecreekpermaculture.ca
- Spragg's Meat Shop | Rosemary | Bonnie and Gregg Spragg | spraggsmeatshop.com
- Sweetgrass Bison | Foremost | Cody Spencer | sweetgrassbison.ca
- Top Grass Cattle Co. | Drumheller | Calvin Raessler | topgrass.ca
- Trail's End Beef | Nanton | Rachel and Tyler Herbert | trailsendbeef.com
- Whispering Cedars Ranch | Strathmore | Janna and Ryan Greir | whisperingcedarsranch.com
- Winter's Turkeys | Dalemead | Laurel and Darrel Winter | wintersturkeys.ca

TYLER HERBERT AT TRAIL'S END RANCH, PARKLAND

OLD RED BARN AT BROKEN TINE ORCHARD NEAR BEAVERLODGE IN PEACE COUNTRY

# Acknowledgements

Thank you to Taryn Boyd and Tori Elliott of TouchWood Editions for saying yes to this book. And for trusting me to deliver and leaving me to it.

I am grateful to all the team at TouchWood. I love working with you.

Designer Jazmin Welch, you took the raw ingredients and blended them with the alchemy of your talents to this beautiful result. Thanks to in-house editor Kate Kennedy for overseeing this project. Thank you to proofreader Meg Yamamoto for your laser-sharp eyes and brain. Meg, your superpower is to see what my manuscript-weary eyes could no longer see. Thank you to publicist Curtis Samuel for your fun, imaginative, and thoroughly professional ways. And to my substantive and copy editor, Lesley Cameron, I bow to you. Thank you for your clarity, for seeing the overarching, the nitty-gritty details, and everything in between. I learned so much from you and this book wouldn't be half what it is without your sense and sensibility.

And there are so many friends and family to thank.

Thank you, Laura Kowalchuk, for guiding me through Okanagan thrift shops in the summer of 2021 as I started gathering a collection of vintage plates for this project.

Trudy White-Matthews, thanks for scoring me a few finds, and thanks to you and Craig for always believing in and supporting Alberta Food Tours' mission.

Rachel and Tyler Herbert, thanks for the biggest prop of all, Trail's End summer cabin and everything in it! Thanks to you and to Will and Avery for embracing the adventure of hosting our photo shoot in the first full-on blizzard of the 2021–22 winter too. Thanks also for giving me some of your yummy grass-fed beef to help with all the cooking I needed to do for this book.

Thanks to Kent Zentner and Tracey Eftoda of Silver Sage Beef for giving me the beauty of a beast that I needed to make my Cedar-Planked Prime Rib Roast of Alberta Beef (page 159). It tasted as good as it looks.

Tony and Penny Marshall, thanks for allowing me and Nic into your home, for finding the perfect barn wood, for setting up lights on IV poles, for polishing the family heirlooms, and especially for inviting us back after our first invasion of your family home at Highwood Crossing. Thanks also for the gift of a huge bag of your organic flour for all the baking I needed to do for this book.

Terry and Maria Andryo, thanks for inviting me to dig through your treasury of Ukrainian heirloom dishes and hand-stitched linens and borrow whatever

I needed. You are such generous and loving souls. Thanks also for sharing your salsa recipe, Maria.

Cindy and Brad Lazarenko, thanks for your time, talents, props, and food for this project and ALWAYS. Kelly Shepherd and Tim Lazarenko, thanks for volunteering Brad and his kitchen. Suzanne Dennis, thanks for washing dishes and providing loving moral support ALWAYS.

Lisa Neiles, thanks for the stunning cake stand for the sourdough chocolate cake photo. And thanks for being so understanding when I accidentally smashed it all to pieces. Guh!

Donna and Bill Walker, thanks for giving me access to your family vault of linens, china, and silver. And, Donna, thanks for always reading my words, for making me see them more clearly, and for encouraging me to shorten everything.

Yvonne Jobin, thank you for teaching me how to make your bannock. You live by your principle of sharing knowledge and in doing so, you've made it useful to all who will read this book. I am blessed to have experienced you and your late daughter, Amy Willier, as Elders in my life.

Nora Comerford-Seto and Richard Seto, thanks for always offering the use of anything of yours any time, anyhow. Special thanks to Richard for cooking your family recipes with me and for reviewing them with your dear mom, Norma, so they were just right. Richard, you once told me, "If you make a Chinese friend, you have a friend forever." From cooking together on a road trip to Yukon and Alaska, to Stampede Breakfasts for 300, to always including us in Lunar New Year celebrations, and even to picking me up when I fell in my garden and couldn't get up, I know this to be true.

To Mrs. Norma Seto, thank you, kind friend, for lending us dishes from your precious keepsakes from Harry's Café and your collection of family heirlooms. The photos of your family's recipe stand out for the beauty of this presentation. I think Fong would have been very pleased, don't you?

Crystal McKenzie, Michelle Chow, and Adam Liddiard at Peasant Cheese in Kensington, thanks for lending me so many of the shop's cool dishes, bottles, and baskets. I'm so glad we are neighbours.

Wendy Brownie, thanks for all the linens you've lent, given, and inspired me to buy at your Inspirati Fine Linens and Home Essentials over the years, but most of all, thanks for your unfailing support as one business woman to another.

Gail Norton, thanks for lending me some of your beautiful crockery and for always inspiring, mentoring, and believing in me.

Callandra Caufield, thanks for knowing just what I needed for Christmas 2021: more vintage china! Thanks for pitching in on folding and styling burritos and thanks especially for always holding down the fort at Alberta Food Tours and protecting my time so I can write. Shawn and River Caufield, thanks for making our gorgeous green barn board backdrop, you angels.

Thanks to all my Alberta Food Tours family of guides (not already mentioned)—Howard, Simone, Deb, Liane, Elyse, Suzanne, Lisa, Kerry, Barbara, Karen L., Naoto, and Tracy—for your dedication to and passion for Alberta's food culture over the years.

Warren Coles, you are a superb cook. Thank you for your recipe-testing enthusiasm and help cooking the ribs, steaks, hams, and chickens for photo shoots. The fact that you did it all with a smile and assured me it was fun for you kept my energy going. I'm so grateful.

Nicole Liboiron-Coles, where would I be without you? I am blessed for the passion you brought to this project as lead photographer. You've always been a wonderful portrait and nature photographer, and I have loved watching your journey as a stylist and food photographer. I'll jump out of the pan and into the fire with you any time. You are a pro and the very best kind of friend, truly loyal and loving.

Thank you to my sweet friends, photographer Jeremy Fokkens and stylist Sylvia Kong, for your skills and positive attitude in the face of a blizzard for our shoot day at Trail's End. You helped us capture the tone and look of this book.

Thank you, Neil Zeller, for your stunning landscape images of Alberta. You help me show others why I love this place so much and I'm a forever fan of your work.

Thank you to my many cooking mentors and friends in no particular order (and HUGE apologies if I forget anyone): Dee Hobsbawn-Smith, Judy Wood, Rosemary Harbrecht, Pam Fortier, Matthew Altizer, Lou Lou Savoie, Franca and Peter Bellusci, Marianne Spoletini, Theresa Tudda, Penny Marshall, Valerie Andrews, Paul Rogalski, Andrew Hewson, Michael Allemeier, Maxwell Lawrence, Julie Van Rosendaal, and Imran, Khadija and Nasir Mangalji in Calgary; Cindy and Brad Lazarenko and Brad Smoliak in Edmonton; Shelley Adams in Nelson; Aurélie Mahoudeau and Marion Willard in Paris; and Sumeet Nair in New Delhi, Chindi Varadarajulu in Chennai, and Diraj and Suresh in Mamallapuram, India. Most of all, thanks to my beloved friend and second mother, the late Noorbanu Nimji, for so patiently pouring all she knew into me.

Thank you to my besties, Shawnee, Kim, Pauli-Ann, JoJo, Tilly, Anne of the Island, Cin, Weeze, Trout, Di, Babs, Irene, Jen CK, Deidre and my sibs, Laurie (Zig), Keith (Kathryn), Sue (Bruce), and Dean (Barb).

Thanks to my ever-understanding book club: Susan, Trish, Suzanne, Barb, Helen, Joanne, and Jennifer.

To my mother-in-law and father-in-law, Gail and Erik Anderson, thanks for passing down the family heirloom silver right when I needed it. And thanks for being such great cooking and entertaining mentors in my life. I'm grateful for all the fun we've had since I met your son.

Thank you to my husband, Todd, for once again being the world's most high-ranking but underpaid "dishpig." Thank you for the graceful way you make space for my creativity in our lives. And thank you for warming me up when I come to bed chilled to the bone after writing into the wee hours. You and our son, Cole (and his partner, Katie), are the greatest blessing, joy, and taste-testers in my life.

And to my mom, Gerri Robicheau, and my late grandmothers and great-grandmother, Elizabeth Holiday, Doris Robicheau, and Allyne Dyer, respectively: I know how blessed I was to have three generations mentoring me in the kitchen. Your recipe for seeing me flourish was to fill me with equal parts love, care, know-how, and common sense. As I grew up at your sides, you gently kneaded me with the richness of context, tips, and special touches. The result is a general proficiency in cooking and life that once distilled has lifted my spirits for a lifetime.

I hope this book helps others experience all the gifts that come with the life skill of knowing how to source and prepare local food. I hope we as a nation know the joy and prosperity that comes from strong soil, food, and people. Our very lives depend on it.

# Photo Credits

Recipe photography by Nicole Liboiron-Coles, with the following exceptions:

**PAGE 74, 84, 140, 176, 193, 198, 200, 204, 230** (Jeremy Fokkens Photography with styling by Sylvia Kong)

**PAGE 153** (Pauli-Ann Carriere)

Supplementary photography by Karen Anderson, with the following exceptions:

**PAGE 6, 8, 90–91, 124–25, 180–81, 210–11, 308** (Neil Zeller Photography)

**PAGE 13** (Lori Creech Loree)

**PAGE 27, 33** (Dana Pugh)

**PAGE 28–29, 36** (Courtesy of Explore Edmonton)

**PAGE 54** (Tilly Sanchez)

**PAGE 184, 262–63** (Jeremy Fokkens Photography)

**PAGE 245** (Nick Fewings via Unsplash)

**PAGE 342** (Nicole Liboiron-Coles)

**PAGE 356** (Donovan Kitt)

# Index

## D



## E



## F

## G



## H

## N



## O

## Q



## R



## S

## T

NEXT PAGE: HEAD-SMASHED-IN BUFFALO JUMP